Law and the Passions

Engaging with the underlying social context in which emotions are a motivational force, *Law and the Passions* provides a uniquely inclusive commentary on the significance and influence of emotions in the history and continuing development of legal judgment, policy formation, legal practice and legal dogma.

Although the emotionality of the law and the use of emotional tropes in legal discourse has become an established focus in recent scholarship, the extent to which emotion and the passions have informed decision-making, decision-avoidance and legal reasoning – rather than as simply an adjunct – is still a matter for critical analysis. As evidenced in a range of illustrative legal cases, emotions have been instrumental in the evolution of key legal principles and have produced many controversial judgments. Addressing the latent influence of fear, hate, love and compassion, the book explores the mutability of law and its transformative power, especially when faced with fluctuating social mores. The textual nature of law and the impact of literary forms on legal actors are also critically examined to further elucidate the idea of law-making as both rational and emotional, and significantly as an essential activity of the empathic imagination. To this end, it is suggested that critical scholarship on law, the passions and emotions not only advances our understanding of the inner workings of law, it constitutes a fundamental part of our moral reasoning, and has the capacity to articulate the conditions for a more dynamic, adaptable, ethical and effective legal institution.

This interdisciplinary book will be of interest to scholars and students in the fields of law and literature, legal theory, legal philosophy, law and the humanities, legal aesthetics, sociology of law, politics, law and policy, human rights, general jurisprudence and social justice, as well as cultural studies.

Julia J.A. Shaw is Professor of Law at De Montfort University, Leicester, UK. Her interdisciplinary scholarship spans legal theory, law and the humanities, critical and cultural legal studies, and human rights. Recent publications include 'Law and the Literary Imagination: the contribution of literature to modern legal scholarship' in *The Palgrave Handbook of Philosophy and Literature* (2018); 'From Beethoven to Bowie: identity framing, social justice and the sound of law' in *International Journal for the Semiotics of Law* 31(2) 2018; *Jurisprudence* (3rd edition, Pearson 2018) and *Corporate Social Responsibility, Social Justice and the Global Food Supply Chain* (Routledge, 2019).

Law and the Passions

Why Emotion Matters for Justice

Julia J.A. Shaw

Routledge
Taylor & Francis Group
a GlassHouse book

First published 2020
by Routledge
2 Park Square, Milton Park, Abingdon, Oxon OX14 4RN

and by Routledge
605 Third Avenue, New York, NY 10017

First issued in paperback 2021

A GlassHouse book

Routledge is an imprint of the Taylor & Francis Group, an informa business

British Library Cataloguing in Publication Data
A catalogue record for this book is available from the British Library

Library of Congress Cataloging-in-Publication Data
Names: Shaw, Julia J. A., author.
Title: Law and the passions : why emotion matters for justice / Julia Shaw.
Description: Abingdon, Oxon [UK] ; New York, NY : Routledge, 2019. |
Includes bibliographical references.
Identifiers: LCCN 2019016903 (print) | LCCN 2019018263 (ebook) |
ISBN 9780203797709 (ebk) | ISBN 9780415631594 (hbk)
Subjects: LCSH: Law–Psychological aspects. | Law and ethics. |
Emotions (Philosophy) |Compassion–Psychological aspects.
Classification: LCC K346 (ebook) |
LCC K346 .S53 2019 (print) | DDC 340/.19–dc23
LC record available at https://lccn.loc.gov/2019016903

ISBN 13: 978-0-367-78536-9 (pbk)
ISBN 13: 978-0-415-63159-4 (hbk)

Typeset in Galliard
by Taylor & Francis Books

For Piggy

Although future days may amaze,
today
the sun extends her gaze.
And I sit here,
lazy, in the shade
thinking …
I am all things
I am nothing –
without you.

Each day would mean less than
a sparrow's fart;
and so …
I hold your kisses in my little black heart,
which (happily) rhymes with –
Hey! 'let's never part'.

(Just hope I'm forgiven for this rhyme;
it could've been better, but I ran out of time).

Contents

Preface and acknowledgements ix

Introduction 1

1 No slave to reason: The significance of the passions in mapping the legal landscape 4

The impossibility of reason without passion: I feel, therefore I am 7
Robes and lobes: the convergence of law and neuroscience 9
The logos *of law and moral judgment as an emotional* lexis 12
Turtles (and the normativity of law) all the way down 15
Intersubjectivity, law's unconscious and the ethical authority of the human face 18
The life of law as the life of reason and *the passions* 22

2 Law, emotions and aesthetic justice 28

The aesthetic influence on legal sensibilities 29
Narrative creativity as the life of law and the law of life 32
From expressivist aesthetics to expressivist ethics 36
Poetry in (e)motion: expressing the inexpressible 40
Through the looking-glass or the mirror crack'd 45

3 Law as fear 52

Fear and evaluative judgments 55
Fear-mongering and the media: implications for justice 57
Where judges fear to tread: law and the politics of fear 62
Fear, fetish, fantasy and legal framing strategies 69
Legal truths and truisms, moral metaphors and moral panic 75
Reimagining the foundations for justice: overcoming the new politics of fear 81

4 Law as hate 86

Law's symbolic violence: use of linguistic coercion in the constitution of the legal order 88
Law's truth and the Tinkerbell Effect 92
The (in-)visibility of law: 'secret' justice is justice denied 97
Law as hate: killing in the name of the law 103
On ideology and language in the classification of legal subjects: 'them' and 'us' 105
Reimagining the Other as self: the promise of justice fulfilled 111

5 Law as compassion 116

From vengeance to compassion: the two faces of 'justice' 118
Compassionate justice and the ethical significance of vulnerability 123
'Truth waits for eyes unclouded by longing': 'enlarged' (empathic) perception motivates compassionate judgment 127
Compassion and the criminal justice system 133
Compassion without justice is mere sentimentality: justice without compassion is but tyranny 140

6 Law as love 144

Determining the 'right kind of love': love as a moral emotion 146
Love enriches and extends the scope of the lawyer's question 'who is my neighbour?' 152
Law and love: against the entitlement of wealth and the obstruction of justice 158
The heart as law's attorney: there can be no justice without love 167
The imperative of a sentimental education: in recognition of law as an activity of the heart, soul and intellect 171

Bibliography 175
Index 192

Preface and acknowledgements

The relationship between law and society, legal practice and principle, reason and feeling, those 'inside' the law and 'outside' has never been more significant than in our fractured post-9/11 world. This book was written in the course of six years, in the context of the global economic downturn, austerity, the UK's Brexit, increasing prevalence of 'hate crimes', rise of social media and 'fake news'; alongside a series of personal challenges during which I experienced first-hand the retreat from compassion and empathy by a broad range of once-caring public institutions. In an era of growing disenchantment, self-interest and dispassion, it seemed pertinent to investigate what effect the emotions have had, not only on social life but also on 'social institutions' such as law. Throughout my academic career, it has been important to understand the complex connection between law and humanity, and indeed to explore the underlying influence of the humanities on law and in shaping the legal imagination. To be able to extend this area of research to the impact of emotions and the cognitive capacities on the legal institution has been a pleasure – and now here is the most important bit.

In struggling to juggle time-bound academic duties with full-time caring responsibilities it has been necessary to arrange a couple of extended deadlines; so I would first like to thank my lovely and very understanding commissioning editor at Routledge, Colin Perrin. For their insight, sage advice and tireless patience in the reading of interminable drafts of this manuscript, I would also like to express my wholehearted appreciation to Hillary Shaw and Jeffery Shaw. Many people have given their support and encouragement, including William MacNeil, Thomas Giddens, Jeffrie Murphy, Les Moran, David Gurnham, Hilary Sommerlad, Massimo Leone, Anne Wagner, Steven Griggs, Patricia Blanco and Jonathan Davies. I am also eternally grateful to my ex-Lancaster University lecturers Peter Goodrich and Costas Douzinas for inspiring me to pursue an academic career, thereby avoiding the necessity to get a 'real job' or at least a job in the 'real world'. On that note, a final mention goes to my Head of Department Kevin Bampton who, for the purposes of a recent university research review, classified my writing under the heading, 'Law, Culture and *the Meaning of Life*'. Many legal scholars working within law and the humanities might agree that unlocking the answer to this persistent question is the ultimate objective of our fearless, even reckless, forays into the often murky nether reaches of the law of law.

Introduction

All human beings experience life entirely through their thoughts, feelings, impressions and sensory perceptions of the world. As we are constituted according to a set of physiological processes which take place in the mind and body, every thought, feeling and action is essentially a function of these evaluative and motivational influences. Similarly, all cultures develop a distinctive vocabulary of emotions to express a range of feelings about the social world. Those indicative words constitute a primary form of meaning, capable of communicating and sharing (by standing in for, rather than replicating) a range of intuitions, perceptions, sensations and experiences. In this way, emotions – as social constructions and judgments of value – constitute a fundamental part of our moral reasoning that also forms the ethical core of our institutions (Nussbaum 2013). The vocabulary of emotion and consequent discursive consciousness, as evidenced in many historical and modern legal cases, is realised within legal practice and policy as a fully socialised practical consciousness – to the extent that recent scholarship has argued that law in fact produces its own set of emotions (Merleau-Ponty 1962: 180; West 2016: 343). Accordingly, emotions are claimed to have exerted a profound influence on the legal community, not least of all in the evolution and further development of legal judgment, reasoning and policy formation, legal practice and legal scholarship.

Previous research into law and emotion has largely focused on the analysis of either the tension between reason and emotion in law, or on a narrowly conceived role for emotion in a clearly defined bounded area of legal scholarship. Love and attachment, for example, are familiar topics within discussions on family law, and the law of tort seeks to quantify emotional suffering (Huntington 2008). Criminal law has typically addressed the impact of fear, shame and the role of vengeance, forgiveness and remorse, in the aftermath of violence and in relation to conflict resolution (Karstedt *et al* 2011; Murphy 2012). Although the connection between law and emotion is not new, the presumption that emotion (often wrongly conflated with the fickleness of desire) has subversive properties, that the passions are the enemy of reason and have no place in law, is both ancient and persistent (Maroney 2011). Quite possibly the yearning for objective truth about the world is borne out of a fear of uncertainty, which often finds expression in a suspicion of emotion and the subjective. Yet, just as emotions are an inevitable fact of life, the courtroom is an emotional place where judges are exposed to the full spectrum of emotions, many of which are unpleasant.

Since emotions and emotional states are claimed to define and shape our individual and collective humanity, the developmental history of law is understood as centring on the effective harnessing or channelling of particular emotions. From infancy our initial experience of external realities is mediated through the sensibilities, primarily emotion, affect and mood, which in turn enable us to attribute values and categorise our experiences in the social domain, and articulate these through language. As we live in a world of contoured passions and our experience of pleasure and pain is constituted between individuals who stand in a specific relation to each other, it is appropriate that the formation of legal categories and concepts acknowledge the significance of an individual's emotional, intellectual, spiritual and sensory attributes, rather than bracketing these out in the absence of exceptional circumstances. Not only are those who make our laws human subjects, and as such are vulnerable to human feelings, but also our key institutions are constructed on the basis of assumptions about human behaviour and attitudes. Accordingly, 'a good judge … [is] one who is capable of fancy and sympathy, can imagine pain and suffering and understand what it means to be oppressed and excluded' (Ward 2002: 123).

Although there is already an impressive body of research which addresses the influence of a single emotion or how the application of empathic emotions might be useful in specific legal contexts (Goodrich 1996; Bankowski 2001), it is intended to provide a more holistic appraisal of key passions and investigate their persuasive authority in evolving the legal mindset, past and present. To this end, the book begins by examining the history of law as a history of the passions; and, despite all evidence to the contrary, how feeling and emotion have significantly informed the development of legal doctrine, underlying legal principle and the overall character of law. Against the Cartesian dualism of mind and body, in Chapter 1 the work of modern neuroscientists is used to illustrate the impossibility of separating emotions from reason, particularly with reference to making sound moral judgments. Emotions are shown to be not merely expressions of arbitrary subjective inclination; they can realise authentic objective standards which have the ability to provide both rational justification for behaviour, and can themselves be rationally justified. Consequently, not only is emotion an integral part of the human psyche, but a reduction in, or absence of, emotion has also been proven to 'constitute a significant source of irrational behaviour' (Damasio 1996: 53).

Chapter 2 discusses how the cultivation of an empathic literary imagination is essential for the promotion of both a rational and emotional sense of justice. Speaking at a conference in 2009, former Vice-President of the UK Supreme Court, Lord Hope of Craighead, stated: 'In our tradition writing judgments is an art, not a science' (2014: 78). Even though 'law and affect' may have, to some extent, superseded 'law and literature' (Olson 2016: 336), it is maintained that the passions are arguably stimulated and elaborated most effectively through the rich rhetoric of literature, art and aesthetics. This may explain why judges often utilise references to literature, popular culture and poetry to introduce empathy and creative imagination into their judgments, and in so doing offset the deadening effect of dry legal jargon. Various affective influences which permeate law as text and performance are explored, suggesting it is possible to meaningfully distinguish between a range of emotions and even between different instances of the same emotion by showing how these play out similarly in literature, real life and in the courtroom. The remaining chapters on fear, hate, compassion and love comprise an interdisciplinary exploration of the complex interaction between emotion, social organisation and law by applying a variety of diverse modern controversies, case law examples and writings from a range of leading ancient and modern thinkers from Aristotle to Žižek. A wide range of disciplines, representing *inter alia* the social sciences, politics, psychology, arts and the humanities, are used to shed light on the disregarded or often hidden collection of emotions that currently pervade the legal system.

The emotions and emotionality are demonstrated to exert a profound influence on the legal community in terms of the evolution and further development of legal judgment, reasoning and policy formation, legal practice and legal scholarship. However, there are clearly vast differences between types of emotion, their degree of adaptivity or transformativity, their potential for disruption, and their effect on reasoning, especially legal reasoning. This means it is imperative to understand the impact of emotional states on law-making, and to distinguish the characteristics of positive, and positively directed, emotions from those emotional states that give rise to, for example, fear and suspicion. Fear is often a major directing force, as revealed in case law judgments and in hastily constructed statute, but this motivation is largely unacknowledged or concealed. It tends to manifest itself as anger, which is described by Maroney as 'the quintessentially judicial emotion' (2012: 1207–1208). Perhaps the only way forward to avoid laws and rulings made via negative reactions, and non-beneficent emotions, is to embrace the idea of emotional judgment, and channel those passions into laws which have greater legitimacy and resonance for those individuals (the non-lawyer majority in society) with whom the law seeks to connect and represent. After all, the history of law is also a history of mutability, with the proven ability to transform itself and adapt to reflect changing social mores and morality. In which case, the legal culture is eminently capable of producing judges and law-makers who openly acknowledge the impact of emotions on law-making, and who may eventually acquire a passion for law's passions – finally understanding why emotions matter for justice.

1 No slave to reason

The significance of the passions in mapping the legal landscape

since feeling is first
who pays any attention
to the syntax of things
will never wholly kiss you;
... and kisses are a better fate
than wisdom

lady i swear by all flowers. Don't cry
the best gesture of my brain is less than
your eyelids' flutter which says
... life's not a paragraph
and death i think is no parenthesis

e.e. cummings (1926)

The passions are at the heart of law, just as they comprise an integral part of human life. They are not simply reducible to expressions of arbitrary subjective inclination, rather the emotions are shared equally by all humans and connect us closely to an external value system which is capable of creating its own 'organic unity' (Nozick 1990: 88, 90). The critical development of legal authorities comprises an evaluative process in which emotion and desire are key motivational forces, and those values which create and sustain the legal system are said to form the starting point of morality and the core of all moral considerations (de Sousa 1987: 307). Whilst formal (legal) and informal (ethical) obligations encompass a broad set of intellectual concepts and theoretical perspectives which mediate social relations, without emotion there is no shared humanity and no inclusivity, only instrumentality. As influential phenomena, Marx credited emotions with promoting understanding and marshalling the energy of mobilised groups and, in his later writing, Durkheim firmly implicated emotions and collective sentiments in the development of social cohesion through moral community.

Although there is some consensus that non-rational emotions such as compassion, love, empathy-driven goodwill and sympathy have the ability to motivate people to treat each other well, there is reluctance within the legal community to formally map their potential content or admit to the authority of moral maxims as socio-political norms.

This dispassion for law's passions has been attributed to, for example, a simplistic view of emotions as blind causes for action and so free of principled judgment, a legalistic conception of moral rationality associated with Kantian ethics, and a correspondingly simplified view of moral language as either prescriptive or expressive (Williams 1973). Both Kantian deontology and utilitarianism presuppose a top-down, reason-based approach to moral judgment. The chief impasse for lawyers, however, has been the persistent belief that emotions interfere with rational thinking, and since reason and emotion are perceived as cleanly separable, the law rightly admits and privileges only the former. Accordingly, the separation of reason from emotion is a fundamental tenet of Western jurisprudence and remains deeply ingrained in the legal imagination. Notably, Judge Holmes advised:

> If you want to know the law and nothing else you must look at it as a bad man who cares only for the material consequences which such knowledge enables him to predict .... When studying law, one should wash [moral] notions like duty ... with cynical acid (Holmes 1897: 457–478).

Hobbes declared a 'good judge' must 'in judgment divest himself of all fear, anger, hatred, love and compassion', and in a similar vein Aristotle famously stated 'the law is reason, free from passion' (Hobbes 2005: 210; Aristotle 1996: III.16, 1287a32). Yet, in describing the characteristics of moral virtue, Aristotle acknowledged the essential connection between the passions and action, suggesting that:

> fear and appetite and anger and pity and in general pleasure and pain may be felt both too much or too little, and in both cases not well; but to feel them at the right times, with reference to the right objects, towards the right people, with the right motive, and in the right way, is what is both intermediate and best, and this is characteristic of virtue (1998: 38).

In *Nicomachean Ethics*, Aristotle invests the basic human traits of emotions and feeling with considerable moral significance. Recognising their tendency to influence our actions and choices, he associates virtue with the idea of properly directed emotions, which are aligned with the moral imperatives of 'right motives', 'right objects' and good timing. It is, therefore, not through the imposition of determinate rules or interferences from past principles alone that we are motivated to treat others well, but by moral education which encourages inculcation of the virtues so as to be able to recognise the right action, situation and individual(s), and fully embrace the idea of an ethical life.

Moral judgments are inevitably based on a reaction, feeling or inclination towards or away from a particular object, and not on a discursively established view or formal judgment. For example, it is argued that to judge something as wrong is to harbour a feeling of disapprobation towards it. That is not to say such a decision is devoid of rational influence, as emotions reflect established beliefs and principles, and so it is difficult to understand the double standard operated by the law in its treatment of emotion. While simultaneously promoting only a narrow definition of rationality, the legal tradition has co-opted, for its own use, a set of 'right' feelings, emotions and values. This is particularly evident in criminal law, where decision-makers must determine levels of culpability based on their evaluation of the emotional reactions of others; for instance, in the case of hate crimes and award of damages for psychological injuries such as post-traumatic stress disorder. Historically, the influence of emotions on law-making is evident from the practices of Ecclesiastical law, Canon law and the Chancery Court, specifically the early Court of Conscience, in which the principles of equity as justice and fairness were developed. There are many such examples, varying from the *res gestae* exception to the hearsay rule in American law to the English tort law claim for the negligent infliction of emotional distress. Many such legal provisions assume a role for the passions and, accordingly, transmute emotional suffering and distress into monetary terms with the award of substantial damages – yet in most other areas of law, emotions have no role to play in legal judgment.

In spite of the continuing resistance of mainstream law, there is a steadily growing and diverse body of research which investigates the function and influence of specific emotions in regulation, particularly by criminologists and socio-legal theorists (Karstedt et al 2011; Murphy 2012; Sander & Scherer 2009; Sellers 2017). The twenty-first century has also witnessed the representation of emotions as highly functional and adaptive phenomena, having essential evolutionary significance in individual as well as in social and cultural terms (Vandekerckhove et al 2008). Telling the story of humanity to produce a collective social reality requires accessing the world of social relations and, significantly, acknowledging the intrinsic emotional nature of humans and the impulsive attachment of particular sensorial meaning to their own activities and intentions. Emotions emerge from and at least partially constitute all individual choices and actions, and cannot be easily disregarded or set aside. They play a part in facilitating the possibility of the fullest and most meaningful interaction with others in the world, which is important because 'man can find justification of his own existence only in the existence of other men' (de Beauvoir 2000: 17).

Emotionality underpins the judicial endeavour, and yet the prevalence of the myth of 'judicial dispassion' is a 'cultural script of unusual longevity and potency', as judges continue to deny the influence of emotion in the courtroom (Maroney 2011: 643). Research into law and emotion is often treated with ambivalence and is still viewed as an anomalous academic pastime by the mainstream legal academy. There appears to be a failure to grasp the pragmatic potential of a rigorous interdisciplinary analysis of the emotions which can assist in normative thinking about the law, in terms of either its amelioration or its role in determining the affective lives of its subjects (Abrams & Keren 2010: 1998, 2034). The challenge for modern legal scholarship therefore is to enable the legal community to recognise its affinities with the passions, the constructive influence of emotions on judgment and in shaping legal culture and law's rich rhetoric, and then consciously admit the best possibilities into the legal lexicon.

The impossibility of reason without passion: I feel, therefore I am

Various assumptions concerning what it means to be a Cartesian *res cogitans* depend on a strict separation of cognition, or reason, from emotion. This is not to say that emotions are unimportant; rather that they are routinely considered to impede rational thinking and therefore have no part in constructing the rational human being. Emotions have commonly been understood as a type of excess; unfocused, unconscious and dangerous, in need of restraint and suppression. There has been a great deal of disagreement about the nature, scope and utility of the passions, and especially with regard to their origination; for example, do they originate from the convictions of the mind, the impulses of the heart or the desires of the soul? Whether emotions are considered to be experienced only individually, as hopelessly subjective, or as performing a social function determines the degree of censure and acceptance conferred on their expression by judges. Modern models of judgment and decision-making could be described as Platonic in the sense that they endorse the continuing antagonism between reason and emotion embodied in the analogy of Plato's two horses, forever pulling in opposite directions.

The mechanistic Cartesian concept of a disembodied mind has cast a long shadow in Western society. In Descartes' *Meditations on First Philosophy* (1641) his *cogito ergo sum* inaugurates a tradition that promotes mind divided from body, mind privileged over body, reason over emotion, and the passions are introduced as *confusi status mentis* or bodily-based confused states of mind. Emotions are, therefore, considered to be passively and directly caused in the soul by bodily processes alone. This idea is qualified in Descartes' later treatise, *Passions of the Soul* (1649), where he focuses on bodily passions, suggesting that the senses are stimulated to an initial reaction, by either an internal state (no food and water) or an external situation (presence of food and water), causing a bodily response which then triggers an emotion. Experiences are either good, bad (like being chased by a bear) or significant, and relate to our sensory-driven primeval responses without necessarily disclosing the details; providing further justification for his dualistic construction of mind and body.

Passions, for Descartes, are 'perceptions or sensations or excitations [emotions] of the soul which are referred to it in particular and which are caused, maintained, and strengthened by some movement of the spirits' (1989: 11: 349). They 'dispose the soul to will the things nature tells us are useful and to persist in this volition', but otherwise originate from merely reflexive and 'unintelligent' bodily mechanisms (1989: 11: 372). Although the passions are perceived to be adaptive mechanisms, Descartes does not acknowledge any cognitive mediation which would suggest an evaluation of the object or circumstances, or indeed vitalistic concepts such as an Aristotelian 'sensitive soul'; the possession of which facilitates the capacity and will to desire, as conceptually distinct from mere perception (1989: 11: 202). The consideration of the passions as purely mental dispositions, that bind perception to action, focuses on their physical manifestation and impedes any attempt to understand them as holistic and irreducibly social. By supposing the rational self to have only an inner relationship with the mind and an outer relationship with the body, the individual may even be conceived instrumentally; as belonging to nature and therefore an appropriate object of control. In his later writing Descartes distinguishes between 'primitive' body-first passions and intellectual passions, derived from volition (for example, love of God, and pleasure or sadness consequent on being moved by literature), which do not come from the body as sensory stimulation but rather fall outside of his idea of 'passions of the soul'; however most scholars have glossed over this aspect of his writing as it less fully developed.

Modern law-makers are not expected to contemplate the metaphysical issue of dualism, the idea of an interacting yet divisible mind and body; nevertheless law has a deep-rooted history of dualistic thinking. For example, the alignment of women with the body, especially the reproductive capacities, and men with culture and the mind has resulted in a degraded subjectivity for women. Recent work by legal feminists has sought to challenge and develop alternatives to the idea that law and the body exist in separate spheres by illustrating the many ways in which 'material bodies are regulated and written on by the law, are generative of law and connected throughout material social networks' (Davies 2018: 50). Historically, the so-called higher cognitive capacities were not only typically associated with men, but also with the mind, in contrast to emotions or feelings which were more commonly associated with the body. In Ernst Kantorowicz's fictionalised account of *The King's Two Bodies*, influenced by medieval and early modern political theology, the King is described as a 'twinned being' a *persona gemina*; being possessed of both a temporal nature 'subject to Passions and Death as other Men are' and a perpetual nature, 'a body politic and the members thereof are his subjects' (1957: 7–9). Following 'the demise *demissio regis, vel coronae* [suggesting a transfer of property, not death] of the King ... the Body politic is transferred and conveyed over from the Body Natural now dead, or now removed from Dignity royal, to another Body natural' (Kantorowicz 1957: 13). Based on *Duchy of Lancaster* ([1561] 1 Plowden 212, 75 ER 325) and *Willion v Berkley* ([1561] 1 Plowden 223, 75 ER 339), outlined in Edmund Plowden's sixteenth-century law reports, the papal doctrine of Christ's two bodies was co-opted by the judiciary to curb the power of the monarch. Later English jurists (who fashioned themselves as 'Priests of Justice') overcame the difficulty of disentangling the fallible corporeal (body and emotions) from the irreprehensible non-corporeal King by, in 1688, extending the Crown in its political capacity to government ministers; giving them immunity and conferring privileges, rights and powers under the royal prerogative. By the reign of George III (1760–1820) much of the monarchical power had been ceded to Parliament and, consequently, his alleged porphyria-induced bouts of 'madness' validated the disrespectful systematic mistreatment and violation by medical professionals of the once-sacred kingly body. The idea that law emanates only from the sovereign, or sovereignty, while the emotions originate from an unfathomable, intimate and potentially dangerous place was further driven by the influence of Enlightenment rationalism. Reason was thereafter commonly taken to imply the accurate assessment of things in determining what constitutes right action, against the unruly passions which move us to action of their own accord.

English law has laid claim to a basis in the ideal of reason and many key legal doctrines are similarly founded; key examples being that of the 'reasonable man' and the requirement of 'reasonable suspicion' in the case of a lawful arrest. Rationality, which originates from reason, has even been described as 'the touchstone of legal responsibility and culpability' (Morse 2004: 266). Although beleaguered by the *passiones animae* or animal passions, Aquinas identified humans as essentially rational beings, having the unique capacity of moral agency with reason posited as the source of truth, virtue and morality. The distinctive rationality of humankind has been largely undisputed from the time of the Ancient Greeks. Of the threefold division of the soul, Plato considered reason (*logistikon*) to be the 'divine element of the soul': unlike the appetitive (*epithumêtikon*) and spirited (*thumoeides*) elements, the rational part of the human soul was considered to rank the highest due to its ability to construct complex intellectual processes and moral judgments. Plato offers the example of a thirsty man who is able to overcome the desire to quench his thirst by reflecting on the consequences of drinking; urging the control of appetites such as 'loves and hungers and thirsts' which emanate from where one 'feels the fluttering of any other desire' (1991: 439).

While Plato dismissed emotions as irrational reactions of the lower psychosomatic levels of the soul, since two-thirds of the human soul was determined to be emotion-driven, his devotion to an idealised conception of reason seems overly slavish and unwarranted. Some 23 centuries later, existentialist philosopher Jean-Paul Sartre characterised emotions as 'magical transformations', and free choices which have purposefulness and intentionality, as opposed to being simple deterministic processes. He further claimed they have the capacity to inform our understanding and influence the formation of individual judgment (Sartre 1989: 58–59). Similarly, recent advances in neuroscience suggest that emotional and cognitive stimuli differentially engage the brain's default mode network (DMN) supporting, for example, inductive reasoning, future-oriented thought and meaning-making in general (Immordino-Yang 2016). The emotional drives, our desires, inclinations and intuitions, impose on our individual psyche and are further inured by social interaction. After all, what inspired the drafters of universal human rights declarations, or framers of constitutions to give life to words such as *liberté, égalité, fraternité*, goes beyond the bare application of rule-based rationality. It could also be argued that the negative emotion of fear – of revolution, riots, crime and instability – precipitated the extension of voting rights in the Catholic Emancipation Act of 1829 and the great Reform Act of 1832, even though both measures were significant in helping to achieve parliamentary democracy. So although rationality is traditionally presented as a restraining, compelling and legitimating authority, the passions can be argued to define our relationships with others in the world.

Robes and lobes: the convergence of law and neuroscience

The intersection of neuroscience and law is a recent phenomenon, to the extent that 'neuro-law' is a rapidly developing interdisciplinary sub-field of legal inquiry.

One reason for this growing interest in the brain is that affective neuroscience has much to offer in explaining the integrated processes connecting emotion and judgment within a social setting; and since Descartes emphasised the bodily aspect of emotions, it is possible to argue that his hypothesis anticipated modern neurological theories. Mounting a defence of an emotion-driven 'core consciousness' in order to discover how it is possible to imagine the unimaginable (an emotion-driven rationality), neurologist Antonio Damasio studied patients with impairment to those parts of the brain that direct emotions and discovered they could not make even the simplest of choices. Elliot (a given pseudonym), a patient whose prefrontal cortex (the thinking and decision-making area) and limbic brain area (associated with emotion) were surgically severed to relieve seizures, was unable to function rationally afterwards – even though his intellect was undamaged. He was able to process factual information but could not attribute any meaning. Without an emotional nudge one way or the other, the patient would get stuck in a loop whilst attempting to deliberate 'rationally' over a trifling decision. For Damasio, this case study underpins his *Somatic Marker Hypothesis* and illustrates the importance of abstract thought processes in calculating possible future outcomes; but even more significant is the finding that in order to decide between alternatives requires our choices to be assigned a value. The value derives from our association of each option with an emotional condition, leading to the conclusion that whilst 'emotions and feelings can cause havoc in the processes of reasoning … the absence of emotion and feeling is no less damaging, no less capable of compromising rationality' (Damasio 1996: xiv). This research suggests that our subjective interpretations, intuitions and emotions are intrinsic to rational behaviour, also fundamental in assuring conformity to social norms; although this is not a study of the social brain according to any understanding of what it means to be social.

The influence of emotions on the human psyche is immense, creating a bridge between rational and non-rational processes, also cortical and sub-cortical structures; weaving a magic thread between brain, body and soul. Importantly, emotion and feeling are described as providing a 'frame of reference', and have 'privileged status' as they 'come first in development and retain a primacy that subtly pervades our mental life … feelings have a say on how the rest of the brain and cognition go about their business' (Damasio 1996: 158–160). Damasio's scientifically constructed 'feeling brain' has important implications for the role of emotion in the construction of consciousness and culture and is 'a key to the formulation of principles and policies capable of reducing human distress and enhancing human flourishing' (2003: 8). Against the ratification of a united and stable self, proposed by Cartesian dualism, this study offers convincing evidence that emotion is a deeply ingrained part of human cognition; it also suggests the sheer impossibility of our capacity to reason *without* emotion.

Damasio further suggests that all living organisms are born with the ability to survive and solve the problems of human life (such as locating sources of energy, fighting physical illness), yet 'automated solutions' are inadequate to dealing with the complexities of our physical and social environment because conflict easily arises due to competition for necessary resources (2003: 166). Elliot understands rationally what a range of 'right' decisions may be within theoretical situations but is unable to care enough about his own welfare or that of others to make satisfactory judgments. Taking a distinctly unKantian turn, Damasio deduces that regulating our lives according to emotion and feeling constitutes an 'embryo of ethical behaviour' especially when we demonstrate a '*concern* for the desires and feelings of others, expressed as social conventions and rules of ethical behaviour' (2003: 162, 166). As well as determining one's own well-being and survival, emotions are able to stimulate a mutual obligation of care and responsibility, which renders them fundamentally moral. The body, mind and all interactions with the physical and social environment supply the mostly unconscious foundations for our understanding of what is real, which extends to what is moral and meaningful. So then, we are able to form judgments and assess situations by virtue of emotions, by dint of being emotional creatures.

Whilst ostensibly regarding the use of emotional input as subjective and subversive, the legal community connect with society through the language of emotions such as anger, pity and even negative emotions such as outrage, which inform the cultivation of their idea of justice (Solomon 1990: 34). Criminal cases, which are typically wrongs against individuals, are described in the USA as crimes against 'the People' or 'the State' and retribution in the form of criminal sentences from community orders to capital punishment may be construed therefore as revenge by state proxy. It could be argued that the corollary of the offender's shame (inflicted through the visually oriented nature of community service, chain gangs and distinctive prison attire) is the judiciary's collective feeling of disgust. A well-known appeal to the rhetoric of disgust and moral contagion was made by English judge and jurist Lord Devlin in response to the 1957 *Report of the Departmental Committee on Homosexual Offences and Prostitution* (Cmnd 247), more famously known as the Wolfenden Report, which proposed to decriminalise homosexuality between consenting adults. He believed that the 'deeply felt disgust and indignation toward homosexual behaviour' evinced by 'the man on the Clapham omnibus' signified widespread intolerance which should be endorsed as this would be universally echoed in the disgust of the jury (Devlin 1965: 17, 90). In another case relating to sexual preference, this time concerning the content of a film, Louis Malle's *The Lovers* starring Jeanne Moreau, the judge struggled to articulate the border between erotic art and obscenity in relation to finding a definition of 'hard core pornography'. In *Jacobellis v Ohio* [1964] 378 U.S. 184, 197, attempting to classify what sort of material constituted precisely 'what is obscene', Supreme Court Judge Justice Potter Steward resorted to relying on his 'gut' instinct, giving a purely emotional response: 'I shall not today attempt further to define the kinds of material I understand to be embraced … But I know [pornography] when I see it, and the motion picture involved in this case is not that.' While much of our reasoning, reflecting and ruminating occurs consciously as we ponder various plans and strategies, emotions do most of their work behind the scenes. As Damasio elucidates, the physical body acts as a theatre for both the intellect and emotions (1996: 155). Whether by implication or articulated in more explicit terms, emotion is a formative tool of the judiciary and provides the basis for many key legal concepts and principles.

The *logos* of law and moral judgment as an emotional *lexis*

In common with Freud, Damasio conceptualises the mental machinery as a complex psychophysical 'sympathetic ganglion' that mediates between the stimuli and demands (drives) arising from the internal milieu of the body and the practical constrictions of external social reality; the context wherein those impulses might or might not be satisfied. Mental processes and particularly those relating to cognition, such as procedural memory and sentiment, are located by Freud in the unconscious. Within the psychoanalytic Freudian and Lacanian tradition, the variety of social forms which connect individuals such as language, literature, history and culture are also responsible for grounding the empty space of meaning, the unconscious; 'all thought by its very nature occurs according to unconscious means' (Lacan 1992: 11). Freud's crude spatial metaphor of a house casts the unconscious as the entrance hall and the conscious as the drawing room which is policed by a doorkeeper, vigilant as to who is admitted (1979: 242–254). Signifying a repressed unconscious, the unfamiliar or unwelcome visitor is denied an audience and their intentions remain unexpressed. It is just possible to glimpse from beneath the drawing room door the shadows which constrain the fragmented whispers of the unspoken. Only a thought, an idea, an intuition which can be presenced, grounded in language and preferably located in a form of discourse, is admissible and can entertain the possibility of being constitutive.

Whilst language and society are mutually dependent – in that we must assemble an identity for ourselves which is recognisable by others from within an infinite labyrinth of signifiers comprising the pre-existing structures of language – discourse alone is unable to convey completely anything which is 'intuitive, material or lived'. There is a lack or incompleteness which constitutes, for Lacan, an 'impossibility' which refers to that which cannot be conveyed, the indescribable excess. Attempts to represent and constrain, within any formal discourse, this excess-beyond-words have a tendency to result in obscuring or diminishing what is real. These so-called 'phantasms cannot bear' and in any case are not best served by the mere 'revelation of speech', being situated outside of the normative social order and its representative discourses. Instead, they occupy the void space which is the locus for unlimited improvisation and the construction of sense and meaning (Lacan 1992: 80).

The elemental phantasmic, the empty space which has exceeded and eluded the possibility of discourse, can be characterised as *inter alia* fantasy, desire and feeling; accessible and understood through divergent and less formal modes of expression. Accompanied by memory, fantasy is capable of imagining another world, one which is opposed to reality and can envisage a better life by employing the language of the passions. Marcuse draws on Freud when he emphasises the liberating 'beautiful moment' of fantastical pleasure and its need for gratification, 'which arrests the incessant dynamic and disorder, the constant need to do all that has to be done in order to continue living' by refusing to 'accept as final the limitations imposed upon freedom and happiness by the reality principle' (Marcuse 1966: 149). In common with the Freudian unconscious and together with language, this emotional excess (or beyond) corresponds to an ideal of language as truth which is constitutive of the *whole* human subject. So then, the cognitive unconscious incorporates an 'emotional unconscious' which encompasses both the 'somatic demands upon the mind' as well as expressing unconscious emotional recall and fantasy (Freud 1964: 148). The unconscious and conscious, dream and reality, experience and intuition are mediated by the passions, which in turn are filtered through the lens of history and culture where they are able to assume a social dimension. In this way reason and the senses are reconciled, creating a sensuous order.

The passions give form to a dynamic social field of the imagined and abandoned, the forbidden and permitted, also to that which is silenced and sanctioned; they have capacity to affect or modify judgment without confusion or otherwise creating difficulty. Without emotion, the communicative possibilities of language and consequently identity are constrained, and it could be argued that the act of judgment or formulating an opinion is bound together with both the passions and the art of rhetoric. For Aristotle rhetoric is 'an ability, in each [particular] case, to see the available means of persuasion', and in his distinctive rhetorical and ethical philosophy of the passions, he appears to have anticipated the emergence of many contemporary theories (1991: 36). *Rhetoric* offers a systematic account of how the passions are the property of rational mental activity and rhetoric, by which the contours of our linguistic world of understanding and pre-cognition are commonly determined. Emotions (*pathe*) are described as 'those things through which, by undergoing change, people come to differ in their judgments, and which are accompanied by pain and pleasure, for example, anger, pity, fear, and other such things and their opposites' (Aristotle 1991: 121). The source of the passions – the oppositional virtues (moral excellence) and vices (moral deficiency) of the 'non-rational soul' – are understood to form the basis for all human motivation and, importantly, condition our ability to critically assess the world. Emotional reaction results from intelligent behaviour based in human cognition; it is referred to as irrational because it does not follow from the strict rules of formal logic.

Linked to both the cognitive and the concrete, rhetoric based on emotion can offer an alternative mode of perception and consciousness. Aristotle explains their social character, material grounding and logical grounds by reference to his rhetorical *protaseis* or the premises of opposed emotions. Unlike Descartes and Damasio, Aristotle does not prioritise between primary and secondary emotions; rather he maintains that emotional causation is linked to a series of factors, such as social status and enabling conditions which have more in common with the inequitable distribution and exchange of social goods. He offers the example of anger to illustrate the importance of understanding all the components responsible for an emotional display: 'what is their *state of mind* when people are angry and against *whom* are they usually angry, and for what sort of *reasons*' (1991: 121). Just as it is possible to become angry due to an imagined insult or injury, Aristotle entertains the possibility of anger as a reasoned, even moral, emotional articulation; in that an individual becomes angered often when confronted with an unwarranted slur or injustice against oneself or one's own. So *pathos* or argumentation based on emotional entreaty can be an important element of legal rhetoric, by supplementing or reinforcing an argument otherwise based purely on *logos* or reasoned discourse. What is clear from the Aristotelian thesis is that the involvement of emotions and affective states does not nullify or vitiate fair punishment and retribution provisions; rather the identification of affective drives may enable us to distinguish between the right and wrong type of motivation and even facilitate the formation of moral judgments.

In Nietzschean philosophy, the real world is not intrinsically rational; it is incomplete, chaotic and based on historical contingencies and so the rational structures imposed by reason are themselves irrational. In this case, where one size does not fit all, the passions take precedence over reason. Although Nietzsche wrote at great length about the damaging effects produced by *ressentiment*, characteristic of the 'slave moralities', he was broadly in agreement with Aristotle in not distinguishing between negative and positive passions. He reasoned that 'all passions have a phase when they are merely disastrous, when they drag down their victim with the weight of stupidity – and a later, very much later phase when they wed the spirit, when they "spiritualise" themselves' (Nietzsche 1954: 487). Once the passions are sublimated, transformed by the 'spirit' of reason towards a moral purpose, it would be possible to make a 'right' choice according to one's own, for example, emotionally, spiritually and creatively determined criteria. The influence of the cultural context, social environment and its prevailing ideologies were also acknowledged as determinative factors in deciding on a right course of action; however this would still be subject to a proper orientation towards both reason and the passions. Nietzsche did not support the privileging of reason above the emotions, referring to the 'misunderstanding of passion and reason, as if the latter were an independent entity and not rather a system of relations between various passions and desires; and as if every passion did not possess its quantum of reason' (1968: 387). What he perceives as the frailty of humans in *Human, All Too Human* also impacts on the ability to reason in isolation from the influence of the passions and, by extension, aesthetic stimuli, which inform any inquiry into moral responsibility (Nietzsche 1996). The idea of developing a hierarchy of passions (as either good or bad) or other transcendent measure of moral judgment was not supported in Nietzsche's moral system; 'all moral injunctions are concessions to a society of savages' (Musil 1996: 835). He believed this militated against 'human flourishing' and the requirements of the creative disposition, especially in relation to genius; stating that, through their work, Beethoven, Schopenhauer, Stendhal and Goethe all experienced themselves as the origin of value (Nietzsche 1996: 375). Humans must be free to express themselves and create their own values because what Nietzsche referred to as the 'will to power' surpassed traditional boundaries of morality as it always defeated any attempt at subjective classification.

Accordingly, in *The Will to Power*, the world as we interpret it is presented as essentially no more than a work of art, which we have fashioned through the will to power (Nietzsche 1968).

For Nietzsche, the conflicting Apollonian reason and the Dionysian passions were both necessary creative energies; however the emphasis on the former relegated the source of our myths, intuitions, passions and creativity to a lesser supporting role (1967: 8). For this reason he advocated an appeal to aesthetics as imperative in order to make sense of things, considering great art to be a unifying force as well as the essential expression of emotion. The intrinsic connection between aesthetic judgment and moral judgment was articulated as:

> That which we feel instinctively opposed to us aesthetically is, according to the longest experience of mankind, felt to be harmful, dangerous, and worthy of suspicion: the sudden utterance of the aesthetic instinct, (e.g. in the case of loathing or disgust) implies an act of judgment. To this extent beauty lies within the general category of the biological values, useful, beneficent, life-enhancing (Nietzsche 1968: 804).

From this perspective, the artistic representation is a type of becoming that is inseparable from the social traditions and cultural practices that allow for this art to be recognised as the type of art that it *is*. At the same time, the experience of art as judgment (as ugly or beautiful) lies beyond conceptual thinking and is not attributable to any predetermined conceptual identification. The inner processes of 'thinking' and 'willing' are complex; they are connected to emotional affects, and for Nietzsche this is an important distinction which militates against dualistic means–end rationalism.

Turtles (and the normativity of law) all the way down

In the European pre-Copernican astronomy of the Middle Ages, it was fashionable to perceive the universe as a gigantic clockwork mechanism, a *machina mundi*, invented and wound by God. Although the role of the Deity was diminished in later thought, the mechanistic (and therefore predictable) nature of the universe persisted in the cosmology of Newton and Cartesian logic. Once the idea of progress in society is disconnected from the arguably fallacious idea of *a priori* foundations and the search for universal meaning and timeless truth, it is possible to understand that what we can know at any juncture is merely interpretation – contingent on historical perspective. Physicist Stephen Hawking begins *A Brief History of Time* with an anecdote where a renowned scientist of the stature of Thomas Huxley or Bertrand Russell once gave a public lecture on astronomy, describing the earth's orbit around the sun and, in turn, the sun's orbit around the centre of a constellation of stars called the galaxy. At the end of the lecture, from the back of the hall, a little old lady got up and said 'What you have told us is rubbish. The world is really a flat plate supported on the back of a giant tortoise.' Asked disdainfully by the scientist what the tortoise might be standing on, the old lady replied 'you're a very clever young man, but it's turtles all the way down' (Hawking 1995: 1). A version of this metaphor was used by Justice Scalia in *Rapanos v United States* [2006] 547 US 715, 754 to disparage what he referred to as his colleague's unsubstantiated logic. In agreement with the apocryphal 'old lady', Nietzsche coined the term perspectivism to describe how the world is 'knowledgeable' only in as much as what we know results from how we interpret what constitutes knowledge as both subject and object.

The social and physical worlds may be real and although we can reach an understanding of meaningful things about them, we cannot possess knowledge about them in an absolute sense. Only by using adjectives such as contextual and interpretable, belonging to the hermeneutic tradition, is it possible to define both (1) the method by which we come to know and (2) the content that we learn. The objective world is not merely a compilation of brute facts (which, in any case, cannot of themselves determine an appropriate response); it is also directed by human will, just as the subject is 'not something given'. Only one thing in life is certain and that is the variable estimation of the limits of power and reason as each person constitutes a thinking, willing and feeling subject, and so:

> It is our needs that interpret the world; our drives and their For and Against. Every drive is a kind of lust to rule; each one has its perspective that it would like to compel all the other drives to accept as a norm (Nietzsche 1968: 267).

The possibility of 'countless meanings', the infinite regress of interpretation, would suggest the impossibility of an absolute truth or any epistemological or ethical absolute and, significantly, would call into question the foundational authority of law based on reason without the passions. Aside from any concession designed to privilege the moral passions, the idea of humanity with all emotional states bracketed out would also be impossible.

The entire progression of enlightened traditions nevertheless pays tribute to the archetypal significance of a set of key moral traits, most of which are based on an elitist and secularised account of rationality along with a censorship, or at least a weakened acknowledgement, of the passions. Sharing the same etymological roots, the words territory, text and terror all indicate 'the spatial quality of law' which restricts itself to a privileged and bounded territory of text and culture (Goodrich 2006: 33). Those on the outside of law – either by choice or misfortune – are aliens and strangers and cast as the enemy to whom no tolerance, love or generosity can be extended. Those on the inside may be treated with equal circumspection if they exhibit too much curiosity regarding law at the limits or a propensity for recognising the auto-referentiality of the subject, as in defending the possibility of outlaw justice. That is not to say, literal outlaws of the criminal, burglar or thief variety; rather there is a fear of, for example, a 'fundamental *founding* violence … violence [that is] able to present itself as having a right to right and to law' (Derrida 1992: 13, 14). Just as the lawful authority of the sovereign body politic in Kantorowicz's account transcends the unlawful authority of the transgressive body natural, legitimacy belongs to that which is legitimate and not to any right which seeks to justify itself in advance of its existence by contesting the current legal order. The role of the judge is essentially that of a memory-keeper, who recollects 'conceptual, theoretical or normative apparatus surrounding justice' in order to signify and sustain law's own self-legitimating mythical foundation (Derrida 1992: 19–20). As enchanting as originality, creativity and the work of the imagination may be for the allegorical thinker aspiring to conceive inventive associations between diverse objects, they are viewed as a subversive influence when it comes to defending and enforcing law's 'wise restraints that make men free' – an endangerment to the recurrent game of 'snap' (matching a specific act with a particular legal rule or ruling and *vice versa*) comprising the scaffolding of law, which would be reduced to nothing. Similarly, in the nineteenth century a judge who made a habit of 'looking into the heart of things' was said to be a constant hindrance to the natural course of the legal process and 'presents the most unworthy and revolting spectacle that can exist for anyone imbued with feeling for the holiness of the law' (Schelling 1978: 196).

Laws are often regarded 'in their most general signification, [as] the necessary relations arising from the nature of things'; yet for Montesquieu in his eponymous treatise, 'the spirit of the laws' is not found within law itself; rather it 'consists in the various relations which the laws may bear to different objects' (1977: 105). In a constant movement between recalling the past, responding to the present and anticipating the future, law as text and culture is developed through layers of strategic choices grounded in memory, experience, language, reason and emotion. At each moment, instruments of socialisation such as religion, science, economics and law have all been devised by means of human rational deliberations in order to create order out of chaos, improve our individual chances and collective well-being, and promote human flourishing. Although the pronouncement and justification of legal judgments is traditionally normative all the way down, bearing in mind their social function our law-makers and legal interpreters have a duty to discover what the law *is* (rather than merely stating the law) beyond and in excess of traditional legal forms. Since law 'speaks in the mode of repetition; it is dogma and so speaks in the manner of dream, through symbols, allegories, metaphors and other species of irony and dissimulation' (Goodrich 1996: 143). What is on the other side of the law, beyond the limits of statute and precedent, must also be addressed in order to reformulate legal practice as social practice, which recognises not only a set of external social relations but also those which are already inherent within the subject. In this endeavour, a lawyer is always at best more than simply a lawyer, just as the law is never nothing but the law, because:

> the words of the law contain more than they say. The texts are not just words. They have *anima*, spirit and that is to be preferred and to be followed. The words are in Lacanian terms enigmas, things half said, references to erudition and history, plurality and invention, congeries and collections that could not and cannot be reduced to definitions, black letters, mere rules (Goodrich 2011: 270–271).

The law described here is not a prosaic law of common sense; rather, it constitutes a common law of the senses. Accordingly, the judiciary has a responsibility to discover, if at all possible, a sound basis for any consistent theory about legal rights, taking into account established law and principle alongside non-legal influences, which can explain and justify all applicable prior legislation and inform future judicial decisions in a particular circumstance.

Intersubjectivity, law's unconscious and the ethical authority of the human face

Many of our most fundamental characteristics, such as the capacity for language and the conceptual framework through which we understand the world, are handed down and further developed through our interactions with others. Since the social context in a literal sense constitutes us, it follows that social institutions such as the legal institution (which rely on an understanding of individual actions and motivations) need to nurture a fuller appreciation of the social dynamisms and quotidian intersubjective exchanges that unite people and order their experiences. This would require recognising that law is not only the product of a variety of institutional relationships but is also an intersubjective reality. Intersubjectivity frames the individual more closely in relation to others rather than against others by becoming alert to the selfhood, emotions and experience of others; as a consequence of both our own experience of being and our interrelationships with others, including even those we have never met. For eighteenth-century philosopher David Hume, it is a thoroughly moral phenomenon through which it is possible to establish ethical principles (1967: 537). An intersubjective approach requires the relinquishment or loosening of restrictions, boundaries and 'foreclosures' imposed by existing structures of power, in order to accept the possibility of alternative representations and the previously 'un-thought' as a means of relating to the other (Butler 2000: 153). The cultivation of intersubjectivity in legal judgment is arguably essential to overcome the muted and self-censored silence of 'law's unconscious', its unwritten and 'excess' beyond the spoken word or text.

In rendering a largely privileged body of legal knowledge absolute in the theatre of law, it has been necessary to sacrifice the now 'forgotten texts of institutionally unremembered subjects', and to negate 'the proximities, relationships and other bodily qualities that [legal] science must incorporate yet simultaneously exclude in the name of the distance or objectivity of the law (Goodrich 1996: 122). This speechless embodiment masks the suppression of alternative legal contexts, voices, emotions and impulses, along with any history of resistance to law's indeterminacy, injustices and infidelity to its own principles. Yet, a number of examples have demonstrated at least a partial revival of the juridical unconscious in its expression of humanity against the traditional processes of legal consciousness, which condition the standing of the individual in relation to the law, without violating its own premises. In the famous case of *West Virginia State Board of Education v Barnette* [1943] 319 US 624 which reversed *Minersville School District v Gobitis* [1940] 310 US 586, the judiciary adopted an uncharacteristically hermeneutic methodology which resulted in a bold rejection of the normative 'insider' hierarchy, in favour of extending the category of striking a blow for outsider jurisprudence. The case concerned the rights of Jehovah's Witnesses to refuse compliance with a decision of the Supreme Court demanding a compulsory flag salute from all students, and was defended on the grounds that to coerce participation in patriotic rituals was unconstitutional (against the First and Fourteenth Amendment provisions, also the rule of law). Freedom of speech, enshrined in the Bill of Rights, was equated with the free exercise of religious belief, and it was decided that there was an entitlement to resist a dubious view of the law on the grounds of individual conscience and, in any event, patriotism may be encouraged in other ways without recourse to either force or punishment. This was a landmark civil liberties judgment in which the court decided against *stare decisis* and rejected the precedent *Gobitis* decision, mounting a challenge to the so-called democratically made policy decisions of the government and legislature. The judges here were not simply rebelliously originating new law; rather, for Dworkin, they were engaging in an intersubjective process of discovering what the law is in order to converge on an appropriate response. Also the outcome in *Barnette* corresponds to his 'protestant' theory that an interpreter is at liberty to advocate his own evaluation of the law against competing explanations, even when the latter views are widely held or exert influence:

> A citizen's allegiance is to the law, not to any particular person's view of what the law is, and he does not behave unfairly so long as he proceeds on his own considered and reasonable view of what the law requires … [if] it is arguable that the Supreme Court has made a mistake, a man is within his social rights in refusing to accept that decision as conclusive (Dworkin 1978: 214).

The corollary of this line of reasoning is that individuals, either in the form of senior members of the judiciary or as lay people, are vicariously liable for laws of exclusion – those rules which oppose the ideals of noble values such as generosity, hospitality and compassion – so we all bear joint responsibility for the consequences of not speaking out in defence of, what might be described as, core moral values. This brings to mind the famous poetic statement (of which there are multiple versions) attributed to German Lutheran pastor Martin Niemöller, which is displayed on a wall of the Hall of Witness in the US Holocaust Memorial Museum in Washington, DC:

> First [the Nazis] came for the Communists, and I said nothing – because I was not a Communist. Then they came for the Socialists, and I did not speak out – because I was not a Socialist. Then they came for the Trade Unionists, and I did not speak out – because I was not a Trade Unionist. Then they came for the Jews, and I did not speak out – because I was not a Jew.

This famous reproach of the German intellectuals, for their apathy and cowardice in the face of a divide and rule regime of oppression, concludes 'then they came for me, and there was no one left to speak for me' (Gerlach 2000: 47). The boundaries created to categorise, organise and control citizens are ultimately artificial and arbitrary. Waldo Tobler explained in his 'First Law of Geography' that although near things are more related than distant things, 'everything is related to everything else' and, by extension, in a physical and metaphysical sense, everyone is connected to everyone else (1970: 236). A similar articulation on the closely interwoven nature of all life forms was presented by Victorian poet Francis Thompson in his 1897 'The Mistress of Vision':

> All things by immortal power,
> Near or far,
> Hiddenly
> To each other linked are,
> That thou canst not stir a flower
> Without the troubling of a star.

Lord Justice Brown maintained in *R (Khadir) v Secretary of State for the Home Department* [2006] 1 AC 207 at para 34, it is not enough to cower behind legal rules and look the claimants in the eye whilst endorsing, along with the judge, a harsh judgment simply because it has been sanctioned by Parliament. Also for Lord Denning MR, in *R v Metropolitan Police Commissioner, ex parte Blackburn (No. 2)* [1968] 2 All E.R. 319 at para 320 (CA), 'silence is not an option when things are ill done'. To militate against the effects of a cold and abstract conception of justice, public justice (founded on often arbitrary legal rules) must be reconciled with the private justice as the exercise of empathy and imagination in the everyday collective and non-rational realm of social relations (Lister 2011: 208). If deliberative judgments are conceived intersubjectively this would address the lack of proximity of otherwise disparate and previously excluded individuals, bringing into focus the face and gaze of the Other to whom justice is due (Levinas 1989: 211–226). The body of law would then become directly connected to, and reflective of, the needs of real people rather than abstract concepts and principles derived from the judicial reasoning and the arguments of lawyers. In his 1986 essay on 'Uniqueness', Levinas explains that justice is conditioned by the uniqueness and incomparability of the Other, and that 'the moment of justice' is characterised by a love that overwhelms and mitigates the intrinsic violence of public justice, namely a 'sociality of love' that recalls and commands our humanity. He elaborates:

> Justice requires and establishes the state. There is, to be sure, the indispensable reduction of human uniqueness to the particularity of an individual of a human genus, to the condition of the citizen. A derivation. But still its imperative motivation is inscribed in the very right of the other man, unique and incomparable. [...] But justice itself cannot make us forget the origin of the right or the uniqueness of the other, henceforth covered over by the particularity and generality of the human. It cannot abandon that uniqueness to political history, which is engaged in the determinism of power, reasons of state, totalitarian temptations and complacencies. [Justice] awaits the voices

> that will recall, to the judgments of the judges and statesmen, the human face dissimulated beneath the identities of citizens (Levinas 1998: 168).

Just as all faces are unique, all faces are equally vulnerable to insult and injury as the face is the part of the body which is, in most cases, exposed. The face is even described as inviting an act of violence, while simultaneously 'the face is what forbids us to kill … or at least it is that whose *meaning* consists in saying "thou shalt not kill"' (Levinas 1985: 86, 87). It follows, therefore, that the presence of the face constitutes a summons; it is an ethical authority without force, a command that does not make murder impossible but nonetheless forbids it. Only in the extreme vulnerability of the face are we are reminded of, what Levinas refers to as, the ethical inviolability of the Other (1969: 209).

Notwithstanding the diversity of human beings as a species, at the same time Levinas finds a utopian commonality and unity in the 'nakedness', or vulnerability, and lived proximity in which we find ourselves *qua* human beings in a society. The experiences of seemingly different groups (for example the underprivileged and 'white working class', and racial and ethnic minorities) often share common characteristics such as poverty, prejudice, negative stereotyping; and all culturally disadvantaged groups typically suffer from neglect or oppression by indifferent elites. Yet frequently such 'outsider' groups tend to engage in internecine battles which work against their mutual best interests. For Levinas violent confrontation arises when one does not look at the Other directly, face to face; which is when the Other is understood as pure opposition. The most authentic way of reacting to the shared sense of powerlessness, therefore, is by rediscovering our oneness with those who are suffering.

Through the exercise of empathic imagination in the intersubjective construction of objective realities relating to nature and social community, it is possible to make the essential connection between the experiences of oneself and others, joining both together as equal participants in a given community and in wider society. In *Ethics*, Spinoza argues that human emotions or affects are more than simply internally experienced expressions of arbitrary subjective inclination; rather, they are stimulated in the mind in response to an external cause and produced by the impact of other bodies on our own (2002: III 58, 59). By sharing the experience of pain, we gain entry to a world of compassion and discovery in relation to a wider set of limits and possibilities. In any case, all human beings (past, present and future) are ultimately responsible for, and linked to, the societies they have constituted – which includes both physical structures and social structures. Such social systems of organisation and governance, through their law-making function, are able to maintain existing power relationships by eliciting the adoption of particular attitudes or by requiring the performance of specific duties as a condition of membership of that society, and in order for people to secure access to a system of resources and rewards.

Bridging the contradistinction between law and justice, a more inclusive and participatory system of legal and political rights would naturally extend the generalised perception of reciprocity by increasing an awareness of the peculiar sensibilities of marginalised communities, namely, those individuals whose identity or status habitually locates them outside the typical legal framework. To realise the potential of such a methodologically innovative approach – which utilises the communicative and intersubjective nature of the emotions – requires decision-makers and lawgivers to embrace an enriched vocabulary, language, versatility and openness against the current uncontested dependence on pre-existing and taken-for-granted systems of meaning. Nurturing the requisite moral sense and empathy requires moral courage. It would also herald an end to the privileging of reason over the emotions in decision-making, acknowledging that emotions comprise the contours of a dynamic social field evident in what is imagined and overlooked, what is commended and rebuked, and what is sanctioned and silenced.

The life of law as the life of reason *and* the passions

In his dialogue *Phaedrus*, Plato described emotion and reason as two winged horses pulling a chariot in opposite directions while the charioteer struggles to control and reign in these disparate steeds (1997: ss. 246a–254e). The charioteer represents the intellect or reason, while the two galloping horses portray the appetites or unruly impulses (dark horse) and moral or 'noble' passions (white horse). The challenge is to guide the soul to enlightenment – the attainment of wisdom, truth, courage, beauty, goodness and justice – by making both natural inclinations work as a team, as allies in pursuit of 'the ridge of heaven' where they can stand and 'gaze at what is outside heaven' (1997: s. 247). In part this is because for Plato it is undesirable to construe reason too narrowly, as 'the greatest goods come to men through madness', or via the non-rational impulses as a 'divine madness' (1997: s. 244). On the conflict in the mind between reason and the passions, Hume went further than this and famously noted that 'reason is and ought only to be the slave of the passions and can never pretend to any other office than to serve and obey them' (1967: 416). Against the Kantian opinion of ethical judgments which are only possible on the basis of pure *a priori* reasoning, for Hume reason is unable to control the passions, fully comprehend them or enter into ethical judgments because they are the raw materials of reason. Moral distinctions cannot, therefore, be derived from reason alone; rather, they arise from sentiment, feelings of approval and disapproval experienced by an individual towards a particular character trait or action. Similarly, seventeenth-century scientist, philosopher and mathematician Blaise Pascal, a contemporary of Descartes, proclaimed 'the heart has its reasons, which reason does not know', and it is upon the emotions that reason must establish itself and thereby create the foundation for all its discourse:

> We know the truth not only through our reason but also through our heart. It is through the latter that we know first principles, and reason, which has nothing to do with it, tries in vain to refute them. The sceptics have no other objection than that, and they work at it to no purpose. We know that we are not dreaming, but, however unable we may be to prove it rationally, our inability proves nothing but the weakness of our reason, and not the

> uncertainty of all our knowledge, as they maintain. For knowledge of first principles, like space, time, motion, number, is as solid as any derived through reason, and it is on such knowledge coming from the heart and the instincts, that reason has to depend and base all its argument (Pascal 1995: 28, Fragment 110).

The suggestion that emotions are thought-dependent, and have their own logic rather than being merely capricious, is illustrated in our response to an act of violence or brutality. The first reaction is a feeling of injustice which, in turn, gives rise to an unfavourable judgment on the act. Our response to the vulnerability of another is what connects us to them, by directing our imagination, emotions and intuitions towards a feeling for justice and injustice. This aligns with the sentiments of Edwardian novelist, screenwriter and playwright Arnold Bennett: 'There can be no knowledge without emotion. We may be aware of a truth, yet until we have felt its force, it is not ours. To the cognition of the brain must be added the experience of the soul' (1932: 23). As Fyodor Dostoevsky explained at great length in *Notes from Underground*, 'suffering is the sole origin of consciousness'; it also alerts our senses to the one in need and signifies an ethical order which equates with sympathy, goodness and moral truth (1960: 31). Similarly for Simone Weil, it is only by extending compassion, love, respect or consideration for another person that justice is even possible (2005: 93). For that reason, bare legal rules and concepts will always have a limited reach in addressing the fullest extent of human suffering, because common humanity rather than common law is the primary, if not sole, basis of justice. The inability of practical reason alone to engender ethical responsibility and moral motivation means the passions, as sensations, impressions, intuitions and emotions, are necessary in order to reach out and connect with the wider world of human experience.

In supporting the thesis that the impulse to act arises from the passions, Hume famously claimed that 'reason alone can never be a motive to any action of the will' and 'can never oppose passion in the direction of the will'; therefore, the rational application of legal rules and routine justifications does not, of itself, explain judicial decisions (2007: 413). Accordingly, legal realists believe that the law, being a human invention, is subject to the same idiosyncrasies, prejudices and imperfections that affect every other sphere of human behaviour and activity. As stated in the famous and oft-quoted aphorism of Oliver Wendell Holmes, Jr., 'The life of the law has not been logic, it has been experience' (1923: 1). Another leading American legal realist and fellow member of the US judiciary, Jerome Frank, famously claimed that it was possible to predict the outcome of a hearing by ascertaining 'what the judge ate for breakfast'. This very point was addressed in a 2011 study undertaken by the Ben-Gurion University of the Negev, and published in the *Proceedings of the National Academy of Sciences*. The researchers looked at 1,112 judicial rulings made by 8 Israeli parole board judges over a 10-month period. Each judge heard between 14 and 35 cases in a day and took mid-morning and mid-afternoon meal breaks. Overall, prisoners saw a 65% success rate if their cases were heard early in the workday or immediately after a judge had eaten, but the number of requests granted dropped to nearly zero just before a break period and at the end of the day. It was found that a hungry, tired judge was much less likely to grant a defendant's request for parole than one who has just eaten or taken a meal break (Danziger *et al* 2011: 6889–6892). Although many find it preferable to imagine a decision is founded on rational thinking, pre-existing written texts and legal rules, non-rational factors play a significant yet rarely acknowledged role in judicial decision-making. Clearly, as the study suggests, justice is best served following a pleasant and hearty meal.

As a social institution, the oral and written tradition of law operates in a sensory environment where other communicative forms and feelings continually augment, adapt, reinforce and often purposefully challenge each other. Sociologist and communications theorist Marshall McLuhan insisted that the imaginative, emotional and sensory impulses are fundamental to all manner of performance and text-based expression because we humans inhabit a sphere of sensations (2001: 240, 241). He makes a profound distinction between a percept (emotion) which is social, participatory and infused with feeling, and a concept (reason) which is detached and explains, rather than participates in, the world. For McLuhan, 'concepts are wonderful buffers for preventing people from confronting any form of percept although in fact, we perceive [something] whether we conceive it or not. The percept is what does the work in changing our experience and our organs of perception' (1999: 83). In his 1759 *The Theory of Moral Sentiments* Adam Smith placed 'sentiments' or the affection of the heart, sympathetic perception and emotional reaction at the centre of moral judgment. He claimed that it is in the nature of individuals to adopt and adhere to a specific emotion-laden procedure for making moral judgments and this practice was natural for any lawgiver; it was even considered to be the fundamental starting point for formulating ethical principles pertaining to justice, equality, impartiality and rights (Smith 2002: 22–25). He also took the view that legal judgment similarly finds its ultimate foundation in emotions and sentiments. To situate institutions such as slavery and destitution within a discourse of mercy, for example, comprises a form of sentimental jurisprudence which prioritises the synthesis of morality and compassion with social reality, but more importantly requires the ability to visualise, without self-interest, the circumstances in which the oppressed find themselves (Shaw 2017: 83). From this premise, Smith determined that judgments relating to right and wrong, just and unjust are as much a property of feeling as of intellectual understanding or reason.

As discussed earlier, recent cognitive neuroscience research claims that impassioned reasoning is preferable to cool reasoning, since a more harmonious integration between reason and the passions in making an appraisal or judgment is advantageous, if not unavoidable, in most circumstances. Their findings have shown that emotional processing constitutes an inherent part of rationality itself by facilitating quick, effective and accurate decision-making. Quoted in the first epigraph of *Self Comes to Mind: Constructing the Conscious Brain*, the poet Fernando Pessoa, who wrote under several aliases in different styles, described his soul to be 'like a hidden orchestra; I do not know which instruments grind and play away inside of me, fiddle strings and harps, timbales and drums. I can only recognize myself as a symphony' (Damasio 2010). The complex and symphonic-like nature of the brain engaged in producing the conscious mind was discovered by neuroscientists in a clinical study of patients with brain lesions. In spite of their capacity to reason being unaffected, they were incapable of making good decisions because their emotions were impaired. From this premise, Damasio proposes that:

> reason may not be as pure as most of us think it is or wish it were, emotions and feelings may not be intruders in the bastion of reason at all: they may be enmeshed in its networks for worse *and* for better (1996: xii).

Whilst most forms of knowledge are acquired by means of the rational capacities such as perception and cognition, values (in particular, moral values) are based principally in emotion and affect, and are most evident in the pre-reflective and intuitive emotional experience unique to humans (Scheler 1979). Emotion is, therefore, a profound and essential part of human cognition, fundamental to processes such as memory, language, problem-solving and planning. The cognitive dimension is significant, therefore, as it makes ethical thought possible:

> Emotion and cognition, to the extent they are separable, act in concert to shape our perceptions and reactions. But more than that, much of the scholarship [on the role of emotion in the law] posits that it is not only impossible but also *undesirable* to factor emotion out of the reasoning process: by this account, emotion leads to truer perception and, ultimately, to better (more accurate, more moral, more just) decisions (Bandes 1996: 368).

Similarly, as moral philosophers such as Martha Nussbaum have pointed out, although admittedly there are significant differences between the role of emotion and reason in law, this does not mean they should be strictly demarcated or emotion bracketed out of the reasoning process. Rather, the presence of emotions cannot be easily dismissed as they are an inevitable consequence of the legal reasoning process, even though the historic sets of emotional variables which underscore legal reasoning have become so ingrained in the law that their contingent nature and effects are often invisible. As Benjamin Cardozo pointed out in his seminal work *The Nature of the Judicial Process*:

> the forces of which judges avowedly avail to shape the form and content of their judgments … [including] the complex of instincts and emotions and habits and convictions … are seldom fully in consciousness. They lie so near the surface, however, that their existence and influence are not likely to be disclaimed (1921: 167).

Since, however, the privileging of emotionless rational judgment has ostensibly subjugated the emotions as the 'slave of reason', the challenge for modern legal scholars of law and the passions is to expose the emotional content in legal judgment and legal discourse, and rehabilitate the forgotten or disregarded emotions. To return to Plato's Chariot Allegory, the dark horse is a force that has both good and bad aspects, and its use depends largely on the mastery of the charioteer. In order to train and utilise the power latent in the forces of their soul, a judge must understand the peculiar nature of his own horses and how to harness their strengths and temper their weaknesses.

The development of a truly holistic overview of how emotional phenomena infuse and influence legal judgment, and significantly impact on a broader conception of justice, depends on an interdisciplinary approach which embraces shared values and goals. This requires not only understanding the origins of key contemporary legal innovations but also necessitates engaging with other disciplines, for example with particular branches of philosophy, psychology, anthropology, history, social sciences, neuroscience, behavioural biology, literature, and the arts and humanities. For example, from the viewpoint of moral and political philosopher Adam Smith expressed in *The Theory of Moral Sentiments*, we can consider the passions in terms of the capacity we share equally as human beings, to be able to place ourselves in another person's position and imagine what it would feel like to be standing in their shoes. This is a view shared by his contemporary, David Hume, who similarly held that the imagination is fundamental to the production of even the *idea* of someone else's feelings. Social scientists have reflected on empathy as a foundation for cognitive development, which not only promotes general perspective taking but also may result in better prosocial responses than rationality alone, while psychologists have demonstrated that empathy is a prerequisite for the development of emotions and, in turn, the notion of self. Accordingly, emotions cannot be simply reduced to an instinctual response to another person's suffering; rather, they can be understood more generally as a more multi-faceted 'emotional intelligence' which has been mooted to be the main hallmark of social intelligence.

There has been a tendency to overlook the value of emotional intelligence as an epistemological tool, rather classifying cognition as the worthy advocate of objective truth and emotion as a capricious and unruly primeval jungle which must be restrained by reason. Aside from the misconception that reason and emotional sense are in opposition and incompatible, recent research has confirmed that emotions are not simply internal states; they have the capacity to act as dynamic processes, which are developed according to societal and formal institutional environments, because of being circumscribed by culture and embodying shared and settled belief structures. This means the passions can provide a means of strategically theorising aspects of legal culture which are otherwise overlooked or supressed, and even act as an indicator of insufficiencies within mainstream legal discourse. It is then possible, through the application of positive emotions, to realise authentic and practical objective standards which have the ability to provide rational justification for actions and which, in turn, can themselves be rationally justified.

The next chapter discusses how empathic imagination is essential for the promotion of both a rational and emotional sense of justice, and is arguably stimulated and elaborated through the rich rhetoric of literature, art and aesthetics.

The legal profession is alleged to 'have always recognised literature as one of its chief sources of nourishment' and a 'good lawyer' is described as being also a 'good reader, good play goer, good concert goer, and a good patron of the arts' (Smith 1977: 3). In Sir Walter Scott's 1815 novel *Guy Mannering*, one of the main characters, Paulus Pleydell Esq. (described as a 'good scholar, an excellent lawyer and a worthy man'), shows an acquaintance his extensive home library filled with books, while insisting that 'a lawyer without history or literature is a mechanic, a mere working mason; if he possesses some knowledge of these, he may venture to call himself an architect' (Scott 1954: xxxvii). It is also suggested that the influence of literary works on the legal imagination, their potential to extend the human capacity for understanding and further develop the faculty of critical judgment, posits literature as a form of ethical codicil to law. In this way a lawyer is always at best more than a lawyer, just as the law is never simply the law. While their interpretive strategies and focus differ, proponents of both the 'law in literature' and the 'law as literature' movements agree that the study of literary forms and application of the legal imagination in adjudication is likely to produce better lawyers. This is because the acts of imagination and projection involved in exploring literary works and aesthetic forms encourage the lawyer as reader to both think and feel, to shed the protective layers of cautious reasoning that obstructs empathy in the real world, and ideally experience a sense of shared humanity which is arguably necessary for good legal judgment.

2 Law, emotions and aesthetic justice

Without Art, Nature can ne'er be perfect;
and without Nature, Art can claim no being.

Ben Jonson (1906: 127)

This chapter explores the normative and analytical significance of aesthetics – its ability to redirect the sensibilities and empathic imagination – in the formation of legal concepts and principles, without which law would lose most of its persuasive force. The legal aesthetic is not merely present in the literary devices of judges or in the architecture of the court or the trial; it permeates all legal practice and judgment. Robin West points out that because 'legal theory is narrative, it is also art', and so the aesthetic dimension remains an essential component, the raw material, of human experience and essential to meaning-making (1985: 209, 210). It represents free play of the imagination and assists in our understanding of the world through our senses, as alternately beautiful and grotesque, alluring and repellent. The communicative power of this sensory information allows for richer intellectual and emotional engagement with objects and concepts as they really are, according to their sensible essence. We are made more conscious of a multiplicity of dissident perspectives and sensuous content from which to inform our individual life choices and, importantly, influence our capacity for moral judgment. This proposition can be understood in semiotic terms, on the basis that we respond to images and experiences which resonate with an individual or shared history of particular cultural traditions and practices. Our sensate relation to these symbols and metaphors constitutes a productive force which, in relation to the legal community, can be understood as underpinning the formation of legal principle and judgment.

A feeling as an emotion is engaged in practice by being expressed in the spoken or written word; this constitutes an affective, meaningful and intellectual unity, which in turn becomes an object for reflection. Although aesthetic expression is often subjective and considered to be beyond the remit of formal concepts or universal standards, it can be understood as representing a form of interaction between individuals and the precognitive world of established meaning. The persuasive influence of those aesthetic forms which rely on narrative and imagery – such as poetry, the visual arts and of course literature – is at least partially due to their cultural embeddedness. The legal culture is itself, simultaneously, a co-producer and a by-product of such cultural forms; it uses poetic and aesthetical tools to create an illusion by which the audience will see only what the 'producer' wants them to see (Sherwin 1992: 9, 10). This leads to the conclusion that the power of the legal institution to incite, induce, seduce or coerce its subjects is possible because social relations are always charged with emotion and expressed by means of an appropriate aesthetic medium. Law self-consciously assimilates the world into itself, and its various emotion-laden aesthetic expressions, mythologies, fantasies and mystical discourses facilitate the construction of both social values and legal dogma.

The aesthetic influence on legal sensibilities

Law claims to have a logical structure assisted by an architectonic set of normative commitments which purport to maximise efficiency. Meaning and order are imposed by means of supporting authoritative categories and concepts which are founded on a privileged set of values, embedded within an overarching grand narrative. This collection of historical antiquities, ambiguities, contradictions and misnomers we first experience as sensation. A range of persuasive images and allusions compels from us an instant physical reaction (such as joy, hope, relief, fear or disgust) only later augmented by reason, logic and the search for truth and meaning. All life is constructed from such instinctual aesthetic reactions, since our experience of the world is mediated by aesthetic forms and intuitions which constitute a semiotic relation indicating the origin of, and basis for, organised thought and expression. In this way the aesthetic form, as all manner of literary endeavour and narrative expression, enables us to decide which laws deserve our observance and those we would refuse or defy. It allows for the dissection of the implications and consequences of dominant cultural forms and importantly has the ability to engage with and stimulate the innate creativity of the human intellect and spirit.

Literary texts are dynamic dramatic devices; their value is in the manner of presenting a story or acting out a conversation, and they are not reducible to a specific purpose. Also, as an expressive medium, literature shares many similarities with law; not least of all the reinforcement of traditions, dispelling of myths and the construction of identity – which are elemental features of both the social and legal world. The substitution of obvious fact for legal fictions, for example, has enabled law to evolve through the invention of new principles and precepts, despite critics such as Jeremy Bentham warning that they constitute a 'wilful falsehood', 'delusion' and 'subterfuge' (1977: 509). Both law and aesthetics have an essential relation to the sensate world, and require a movement from the objective to the subjective, from observation to intuition and from fact to feeling (Shaw 2012: 73, 74; Shaw 2014; Olson 2016).

Throughout history aesthetic formulations, in a variety of subtly coded guises, have been used as a medium for raising significant social concerns relating to the effects and implications of law on individuals and societies. The legal tradition and the liberal arts share language as their working medium, and both utilise language as a means of organising and evaluating the randomness of human experience, choosing their words deliberately in order to evoke the right images and insinuations. Moreover they are both products of intellectual resourcefulness and imagination. Constructing a legal argument can be compared with writing a story, inasmuch as the lawyer must organise the material facts, time frame and characters (client, witnesses, legal opponent, judge, jurors) along with considering the wider setting or context in terms of relevant statute and legal precedent, and then construct the whole into a coherent narrative. Not unlike the novelist, working through their 'evidence', the legal advocate imagines at least a partial resolution following a carefully constructed trajectory towards an anticipated conclusion; the 'philosopher, lawyer, poet – all three do their real work in the conversations they establish with their reader, or among their readers' (White 1999: 20).

In the case of a jury trial, *how* a case is presented is often more decisive than *what* is presented in terms of influencing the court by, for example, clever rhetorical flourishes and emotive articulations. An appeal can also be made to the sensibilities of jurors by framing the case on trial in the context of colourful and captivating stories they already know. When juries are confronted by conflicting testimony, piecemeal reconstruction of the crime scene and disjointed presentation of evidence by many witnesses and experts, along with a perplexing collection of subplots, familiar stories are useful in helping to organise such large amounts of information into a coherent narrative. As Richard Sherwin points out:

> To effectively persuade another requires gaining control over reality. The reality that counts most in this context is the one that people carry around in their heads: the popular images, stock stories and character types, the familiar plot lines and recurring scenarios (Sherwin 1995: 893).

It is evident that by moving deftly from fact to feeling by means of a judicious choice and arrangement of words, it is possible to elicit similar emotions in both the legal and literary audience of spectators – for example, revulsion, sadness, compassion or simply amusement. An expertly constructed narrative can elicit the necessary empathic connection with a hitherto unfamiliar situation and sentiment, enabling the identification with the suffering of another. So then, the emotionally articulate legal advocate may be the starting point for giving law a human face; however, only a general commitment by individual judges, Members of Parliament and government to acknowledging the value of the emotional sensibilities can ultimately influence the promulgation of more humane decisions and laws.

In *Poetic Justice: The Literary Imagination and Public Life*, Nussbaum critiques the deficiencies of moral philosophy and suggests that literature, above all else, can activate a habitual inclination towards employing the 'imaginative sympathies'. She further claims that poetry in particular has the unique ability to articulate the idea of injustice, and act as the central conduit through which we are first able to appreciate both justice and injustice. For example, some women and most men 'cannot imagine what women suffer from sexual harassment ... and won't have a vivid sense of that offence as a serious social infringement that the law should remedy' (Nussbaum 1995: 91). Percy Bysshe Shelley similarly observed that poetry 'strengthens and purifies the affections, enlarges the imagination, [and] adds spirit to sense' (1977: 97). Depending upon the degree of emotion and the complexity of the language and ideas, poetry has such a profound and potent effect on us that our brains appear to be wired to recognise and appreciate the rhymes and rhythms used by poets to elicit an empathic response. As well as rousing the emotions and 'elevating our souls', recent neuroscience research has found that by contemplating poetic imagery and the multiple layers of meaning in poetry, specific areas of the brain are activated, including some of the same areas that are used to interpret everyday reality (O'Sullivan et al 2015: 146). Poetry and literature in general forces the reader to use their own imaginative resources to release the affective capacity of language and create their own space of meaning. According to Martin Heidegger, in 'The Origin of the Work of Art', it is a form of language that offers potential for 'projective saying' and the revealing of truths, by bringing to the fore articulations which are ordinarily hidden (2002: 44–47). In line with this tradition of thought, literature has distinctive properties which stimulate subjective self-realisation, and the capacity to act on and shape the world. Literature is, therefore, more than a just a catalyst for meaning; it is, in and of itself, transformative.

There is a rich variety of historical and modern examples of evocative and transformative literary narratives: Charles Dickens' *Hard Times* (2003) offers an insight into the dehumanising grind of life in Coketown, where the point of education is depersonalisation; to impoverish the imagination, quell dissent and provide a constant supply of soulless functionaries to the local factory. As a commentary on the corruption of state actors and institutions, whose chief purpose is frequently to perpetuate the rise of their own power, it alerts the sensibilities to the plight of a subjugated people living without hope of deliverance. Harper Lee's *To Kill a Mockingbird* (2010) and E.M. Forster's *Maurice* (2005) similarly offer a privileged insight into the experiences of those who have had to endure the consequences of racial and sexual bigotry. Manuel Puig's *Kiss of the Spiderwoman* (1984) and Jeanette Winterson's *Oranges Are Not the Only Fruit* (1995) exemplify how popular literature is able to evoke the lived experiences of scorned subjects, and bring these to life in a variety of social and political contexts. In chapter five of *Northanger Abbey*, Jane Austen's heroine is asked what she is reading. She follows her reply '*only* a novel' with:

> it is only some work in which the greatest powers of the mind are displayed, in which the most thorough knowledge of human nature, the happiest delineation of its varieties, the liveliest effusions of wit and humour are conveyed to the world in the best chosen language (1994: 21).

Scholars of law and literature have *inter alia* championed the novel as a rich source of material which often exposes the harshness of legal doctrine, allowing us to imagine a situation in advance and work out its consequences. Aside from the constitutive language which is of semantic importance, the physical properties of the story suggest a multi-level complexity – variously, *theme* (love, hate or revenge), *style* (tragedy, comedy), *genre* (romance, horror) and *plot* – all of which construct what they narrate. Importantly, the foregrounding provides a mere backcloth to the real work of the imagination, without which the possibility of actualising some great 'truth' becomes impossible.

There are many instances of the expressive art forms exemplifying law as oppressive and unjust; and the narrative form, shared by both law and literature, has the capacity to attune the sensibilities to recognise injustice. In the words of William James: 'In listening to poetry, drama, or heroic narrative, we are often surprised at the cutaneous shiver which like a sudden wave flows over us, and at the heart-swelling and the lachrymal effusion that unexpectedly catch us at intervals' (1950: 457).

Likewise, when our judges and law-makers can allow their story-fuelled imaginative sympathies to supplement the tyranny of unmitigated rational judgment, this can be an important developmental stage in resolving to tackle law's transgressions and assist in determining the future history of law as a history of justice. Although there are limitations in terms of, for example, excess sentimentality, distortions, rearrangements or illusory 'truths', which will be addressed later in the chapter, the idea that a more evolved faculty of judgment is possible because of a positive engagement with the literary form is compelling.

Narrative creativity as the life of law and the law of life

Every person is a storyteller and lives each day 'surrounded by his own stories and those of other people, he sees everything that happens to him in terms of these stories and he tries to live his life as if he were recounting it' (Sartre 1964: 56). Much like the actor who brings the author's script to life, a lawyer also performs the law; in legal practice, recounting and reimagining the experience of their client in the courtroom and in scholarship, retelling the stories of discrimination representative of outsider law. Although one performance is an imaginatively dramatised narrative construction of experience in the form of a story and the other elaborates on fixed legal concepts and formulas, both exhibit analytical and theoretical skill, and each requires an imaginative representation and relies on persuasive flourishes of clever rhetoric. This is not a modern phenomenon; historically, storytelling was the primary method of promulgating law from one generation to the next, and was purported to be the primary skill of classical Greek lawyers – who were widely regarded as excellent orators. They often used mythical *exempla* in their speech, not merely for decoration but because of their aptitude for telling a story with moral import to a diverse audience.

As a cloistered profession, the legitimisation of legal authority was premised on the sacral myth of perfect speech. Quintilian, in his AD 95 *Institutio oratoria*, juxtaposed the art of law with the art of persuasion, deducing sophistry to be a necessary prerequisite to legal science and, similarly, 'rhetoric precedes justice' (1976: II.17.25–26). Aided by the employment of figurative language and tropes as a natural extension to any literal meaning, Quintilian espoused the view that skilful oration uniquely enables the connection between idea and image, after which the next consideration is the intended audience of participants – 'know your listener' (1976: IV.2.121). Citing the words of Cicero on the 'ideal orator', taken from the third book of *de Oratore*, he advised:

> As regards the composition of continuous speech, as soon as we have acquired the smoothness of structure and rhythm ... we must proceed to lend brilliance to our style by frequent embellishments both of thought and words. For great effect may be produced by dwelling on a single point, and by setting forth our facts in such a striking manner that they seem to be placed before the eyes as vividly as if they were taking place in our actual presence. This is especially effective in stating a case or for the purpose of illuminating and amplifying the facts in course of statement, with a view to making our audience regard the point which we amplify as being as important as speech can make it (Quintilian 1976: IX.1.26–28).

Even today, the performance of literature can be compared to the performance of law in that each seeks to recreate and resonate with lived experience; both assume an uncontested hierarchy of social relations; and each aspires to a form of transcendence.

Narrative forms and their expression are constitutive of the individual and at the heart of the legal imagination; they can be used to serve all purposes, from obscuring an underlying structure of oppression or to nurture a real sense of unity and common purpose. The term 'narrate' originates from the Latin *narrare*, itself derived from the Indo-European *gnarus*, meaning 'to know'. In its fullest form the 'narrator' can also be described as a collector and curator of information who must discover the most effective way to communicate this knowledge. The concepts of narrative and narrator suggest, therefore, authorial intent or an implied consciousness, which may privilege certain elements or ideas and encourage a particular reading or interpretation. A common metonymic maxim, the pen is mightier than the sword or, similarly, 'words are more powerful than munitions' (Camus 1986: 55), infers the power of the overtones or associations produced in the listener, beyond the confines of the text. This is a significant consideration since legal conventions and categories are formulated on the premise of a hierarchy of authoritative texts, and these have been used to frame and organise law's rhetoric, adjudicate competing narratives of reality and structure a culture of argument. As a dominant discourse, law comprises an unassailable symbolic moral legality, inasmuch as it purports to represent the ideological centre of values and beliefs associated with a just legal order.

Structurally, law's textual truths are presented in the communicative form of a grand or master narrative. Whether in court or within the walls of Parliament, its narrative transactions take the shape of a story – having a discernible beginning, a middle and an end. The end, as the successful passing of an Act or the *ratio decidendi* (the rationale for the court's decision in a case), is evidenced to resonate more meaningfully with the beginning or initial premise; for example, in the headnote summary of the relevant facts, issues and specific points of law in a case. For Sartre in *Nausea* (2007) and Frank Kermode in *The Sense of an Ending* (2000), the telling of a story is only possible at the end, as full conceptual grasp of a particular era, event or circumstance can happen only after it has run its course. Much like Hegel's mythical Owl of Minerva, a bird of superior vision and memory which 'spreads its wings only with the falling of dusk', the wise owl only flies at twilight in order to survey the world after it has been formed (1967, preface). This would be acceptable if the developmental logic of the deliberative and formative stages were given equal weighting. The conflicted middle or interiority – comprising competing perspectives, argument and alternative truths or interpretations – is however, customarily forgotten or perceived in fragmented form, as the *obiter dicta* ('by the way') or *Hansard* deliberations suggest, as yet, indeterminable potential. Only the expurgated denouement can offer an enlightened reconsideration and generous elucidation of the initial premise. It is the end of the tale which casts a long shadow by reimagining the whole into the story of the champion; conforming to prevailing prejudices, and corresponding with an existing legal precedent. The ending transforms all that has gone before. This resultant canonical narrative imposes form on time and events, all of which exerts a persuasive influence on shared concepts such as history, and ultimately reality.

Aside from what is created using the arts of skilful orators, individual reality is not merely given; it exists only *after* being perceived. It is only in retrospect and by a process of recollection that events or actions can be recognised as irrelevant, significant or contingent. The reality or truth of lived experience is, therefore, accessible only by means of directing our own individual creative consciousness towards various conduits, which may enable the construction of identity from a range of diverse equivalences and differences; for example, by exploring the debris of the discarded formative middle, the *in medias res.* In this way it is then possible to gradually comprehend the underlying assumptions, incremental evolution and narrative accrual of the new legislative stance. Furthermore, the tacit adoption of a redemptive narrative style and an insistence on ritualistic normative language too often extinguishes the power and, perhaps more importantly, the desire to excite and disrupt. It is only by iconoclastically transgressing dull legal formulas, categories and concepts that taken-for-granted moral assumptions can be challenged by those within and outside the legal tradition; thus obliging law to evolve beyond the condition of stasis and an over-reliance on rigid general rules and the principle of certainty.

The narrativity of law constitutes an omnipresent force and, from a constructivist perspective, we assemble our world and understand our lives in the form and context of narrative: while physics and art could be described as informative mediums, no other communicative form is capable of encapsulating the idea and sense of lived time and space (Ricoeur 1984). Our (his-)stories may originate in the actual 'lived world of experience'; yet, as autobiographers, we are compelled to selectively edit our experiences in a constant cycle of reimaging and reinterpretation. In the process of stating and restating our connection to the world of reality, the physical world of objects, as metaphysical beings we are also susceptible to the vagaries of our imagination. Consequently critics have claimed personal narrative to be an unreliable source of record because stories do not take place in the real world; rather, they are constructed in the head of the author. In other words, stories are successfully compiled only by those who know how to assemble and narrate them; referred to, by Henry James in his preface to *The Ambassadors*, as 'the hero and historian endowed with the romantic privilege of the first person' (2009: 14).

Although subject to a variety of cultural and linguistic influences and commonly beyond independent authentication, self-narrative is verifiable by means of interactive ratiocination. Accordingly, a culture is able to transmit itself through narrative construction if it can claim a multiplicity of connections with other individuals and events indicated within the development of the story and the characters. In this way one's own narrative identity is always supplemented by the distinctive voices of others against the backdrop of a collective memory, to form a broader, systematic and conceptual exposition of recall. Under the common law, it is the responsibility of the judge to connect meaning to experience within the margins of the law, and this requires the privileging of one personal narrative above another. Both lawyers and judges must choose from amongst the raw data of human experience a story which represents a narrative of truth in legal terms, and then determine how this account might attach to others in a hierarchy of narratives of truth. In the courtroom, bound together in a personal and mutual archive of attested capabilities and vulnerabilities, meaning is only accessible at a reference point external to and beyond the individual.

The expressive universe of language, whilst maintaining an essential connection to the physical world, is essentially a symbolic space where anything and everything is possible by naming and ordering. In phenomenological terms, the natural or pre-scientific 'life-world' is 'the intuitive surrounding world of life, pre-given for all in common' within which the structures of thought and action are contemplated but not pre-packaged, labelled and classified; because 'the life-world is neither an object nor a conceptual framework that could be replaced by another. It is the ultimate pre-given horizon of *all* perceptible objects and practical goals' (Husserl 1980: 142, 43). Neither 'real' nor idealistic (being beyond ordinary idealism and realism, and beyond the very distinction between them), it does not belong to any specific school of thought, yet is considered to be the point of departure for all theoretical investigation (1980: 121). The life-world comprises a uniquely human experience and activity, shaped by both history and language. As the product of past embedded cultural traditions that exercise their power over the present and future, it is through the development of contemporary praxes towards which individuals direct and organise their lives. For instance, for Alain Supiot, by integrating the uniquely human, infinite, intellectual and sensate universe with the finite physical existence, law performs an anthropological function by creating the *homo juridicus* – a rational being united by the fusion of the biological and symbolic dimension (2007: xi). At this juncture, logic and intuition work together to produce a mythic unity between person, culture and legal text. From this perspective legal justice has the capacity to metamorphose into creative justice via the imaginative combination of the many varied and contradictory positions that a lawyer can assume within the diversity of contrasting legal discourses.

From expressivist aesthetics to expressivist ethics

The study of literature can encompass many forms of aesthetic expression, including poetry, performance art and music. Even the non-elite media, such as television and the Hip-hop genre, have the capacity to encapsulate the rich heritage of a particular moment in a society's evolution and expose the roots of a range of cultural predispositions and prejudices. Song and verse have been credited for uniting people, often from disparate social and cultural backgrounds, and literary representations of the inclusive and exclusive effects of law on society have aroused strong sentiments and even galvanised resistance. By having wider accessibility and appeal to a diverse audience, the poem and poetic song lyrics have acted as tools of liberation for otherwise muted voices of dissent, those remonstrating against injustice and the consequences of social ills such as discrimination, war and poverty. Bob Dylan is often touted as the foremost catalyst for social reform in 1960s' America. Widely identified with the American civil rights movement, he articulated their concerns using lyrical expression and was, in this way, able to reach a new generation of popular music enthusiasts who were at the same time eager for social reform. Although renowned for his anthemic musical compositions, Dylan was a master of rhyme, imagery and pithy epithets which integrated social, political, philosophical and literary references – in this he belonged to the tradition of great American poets.

In the lacerating song 'Idiot Wind' (1975), the lyric 'Idiot wind, blowing like a circle around my skull, from the Grand Coulee Dam to the Capitol' – referring to the allegorical relationship between the human head and the US Head of State – was described by the celebrated American 'Beat Generation' poet Allen Ginsberg as an 'amazing rhyme' juxtaposing the mood of 'raw fury' in his admission of personal (romantic) foolishness and in relation to the wider political object. In an imperfect but perfectly apposite lyric, Dylan deftly captures the frustration and despair of the activist weary from listening to 'hot air' or the impotent deliberations characteristic of the reactionary American socio-political system of that period. Wind is a common metaphor in Dylan's work. In 'Blowin' in the Wind' (1963) Dylan evoked the menace of growing racial tension in sixties America, signalling the need to recognise social injustice: 'how many times can a man turn his head, pretending he just doesn't see?' Moreover, he uses his words to provoke the political will for change, intimating the solution is out there but, as yet, elusive: 'the answer my friend, is blowin' in the wind'. Whilst he claimed the song was not an intrinsically political statement, the open structure of Dylan's stream-of-consciousness narrative style helped to bring into sharp focus the truth and reality of racially motivated aggression more powerfully than previous attempts by various civil rights campaign groups.

Music, past and present, as composition, improvisation and performance exerts a profound influence on the human psyche, will and emotions, leading Plato to describe it as 'a more potent instrument than any other, because rhythm and harmony find their way into the secret places of the soul' (1991: 88). Music contains this transformative possibility because it idealises not only the individual but also the wider social world they inhabit. It has the ability to influence the construction of self-identity by creating and maintaining a mixture of particular feelings, with varying degrees of conscious awareness, which affect the way in which social actors produce themselves (Shaw 2018: 307). As socio-musicologist Simon Frith explains, 'music constructs our sense of identity through the direct experiences it offers to the body, time and sociability; experiences which enable us to place ourselves in imaginative cultural narratives' (1996: 124). Consequently, music not only reflects and articulates social identities but also plays a formative role in the construction, negotiation and transformation of socio-cultural and legal identities.

> An epoch of primitive ignorance, of inarticulacy, brute gesture, a state of nature depicted as a universal state of war, comes to sociality only through poetry or eloquence, rhythmic speech which subordinates grammar to music, to euphony and harmony or beauty of sounds (Goodrich 1990:160).

Rousseau, in his posthumous 1781 'Essay on the Origin of Languages', noted that 'feelings speak before reason' and emphasised the importance of the language of melody and literature, so 'in place of arguments [this evocative language] would have aphorisms, it would persuade without convincing, and would represent without reasoning' (1966: 15). Edmund Burke, although a fierce critic of Rousseau's sentimental view of human nature, similarly advised in his 1790 *Reflections*, 'our passions instruct our reasons' (2001: 331). Persuasive imagery, poetry, skilful prose and music comprise alternative texts and strategies which compel our recognition of injustice; and in this way we are enlightened and socialised by the creative endeavour of storytellers and poets.

History has witnessed various attempts to articulate a doctrine of aesthetics. The early Victorians were particularly keen to relate art to truth via a sanitised notion of 'natural' beauty, along with the imposition of strong religious overtones. This is evident in the work of John Constable, John Ruskin, Dante Gabriel Rossetti and Matthew Arnold. The novels of Elizabeth Gaskell and George Eliot represented a shifting trend towards realism in aesthetics – the relationship of art and literature to other modes of discourse, for example science and religion – as later ideological advancements of the newly mechanised and increasingly materialistic era led to widespread anxieties relating to the modification or collapse of existing social structures. The aestheticians of the ensuing *fin de siècle* period were of the 'art for art's sake' creed who, whilst acknowledging the importance of aesthetics in life, sought to free art from any didactic moral or social claims. The foremost member of this movement, Oscar Wilde, suggested in his 1889 satirical social critique *The Decay of Lying* that 'life imitates art far more than art imitates life'

(2010: 18). Even nature is said to imitate art, in that the only effects she can show us are those we have already seen expressed through poetry or in paintings – in other words we move closer to reality, to understanding its essential properties when represented through the creative powers of the imagination. If, as Wilde insists, aesthetic forms 'refashion, invent, imagine and dream life', this creative capacity offers the possibility of being able to appreciate and empathise with the experiences of others; people of whom we have no first-hand knowledge and whose lives are far removed from our own.

Although the liberation of aesthetics from a responsibility to moralise was a constant feature of his writing, much of Wilde's poetry and prose fiction comprised moralising allegories; with the intention of mobilising the masses into pressing for social reform by appealing to the literary imagination, against the tyranny of facts and form (2001). Law's truth and truisms are said to be based on certainty and accuracy; it professes its objective detachment in mimetically reproducing objects as they are. Wilde doubts the veracity of such claims due to the impossibility of possessing such a 'truth' from mere reality, which in its utility to us imposes an intentional fallacy – being premised on an obvious, arbitrary, if not a closed or settled, meaning. He refers to the 'feigned ardours and unreal rhetoric' of members of the Bar, and further warns against the 'careless habits of accuracy' developed from 'a morbid and unhealthy faculty of truth-telling' beloved of the well-informed; asserting that only 'Lying, the telling of beautiful untrue things, is the proper aim of Art' (2010: 7–8, 37). For Wilde, since truth does not exist, in its place and in the place of political and legal truths is a form of honesty in being downright dishonest. The inversion of truth and lies is rationalised in the sense that it is only by lying, or rather through the regenerative capacities of the imagination, that social reality can be made accessible.

Given that art is both 'surface and symbol', the microcosmic focusing lens of the artist is uniquely capable of illuminating the human condition by stripping away the superfluous and redundant (Wilde 1997: 3). For Nietzsche, a person's existence is not premised on a need to know as we can manage with only partial knowledge; rather, art is the most distinctive *gestalt* of the 'will to power' – it is about disclosing and bringing forth. The transcendent quality of art lends itself to higher order thinking, in facilitating novel and richer possibilities of understanding: 'the man of science calculates the numbers of the laws of nature; the man of art gazes at them – in the one case, conformity to law; in the other, beauty' (Nietzsche 1979: 53). As Wilde warns 'if something cannot be done to check or at least to modify our monstrous worship of facts, art will become sterile, and beauty will pass away from the land' (2010: 8).

Of greater value than narratives of truth (being fixed and therefore impoverished), art is the will to create and so constitutes the means of life, since:

> we live only by means of illusions … owing to the superficiality of our intellect we indeed live in an ongoing illusion, i.e., at every instant we need art in order to live. Our eyes detain us at the forms (Nietzsche 1980, VII: 435, 435).

From this premise, individuals have instinctively pre-arranged the world into a set of forms by means of which it possible to understand the world. Each form reflects on to the senses, the image of an original idea. In turn the unconscious artistic influence creates the forms which enable the mirroring of each image on the eye and in our thoughts, just as it determines the ever-present possibility of new forms of representation. This proposition is no more eccentric than the phenomena of time and space; both are interdependent, circular, metaphorical forms through which we are able to organise the world, yet they attain full meaning only within the context of our individual and collective consciousness. We experience the world spatially and temporally; each property is also a condition of our existence. Similarly, the myriad impressions and illusions borne out of appearances, mediated through the free play of aesthetic interpretative forms, comprise beautiful untruths which are taken to be truths. Perhaps then, as Nietzsche suggests, only in the instant of the object's rebirth through the mode of representation and signification does its essential truth, its authentic presence, become apparent.

As a social and aesthetic phenomenon, law cannot maintain a separate discourse and rely solely on internal definitions and coherence; the corollary of the narrativity of law is its dependence on a range of other expressive disciplines. This may explain why members of the judiciary often refer to literature, popular culture and poetry, thereby introducing empathy and creativity into their judgments in order to offset the deadening effect of dry legal jargon. For example, in *Pawel Bachanek v Regional Court in Warsaw* [2013] EWHC 258 (Admin), Poland wished to extradite the appellant for breaching the conditions of a suspended 14-year prison term, imposed for the minor offence of burglary of pigeon lofts when he was aged 17. The court compared the circumstances of the case to the plight of the hero in Victor Hugo's famous novel *Les Misérables* (1982), who was pursued in his respectable middle age for having stolen a loaf of bread many years earlier.

Aesthetic expression is not presented as a separate entity, additional or peripheral to law; neither does it assume a privileged position in relation to law – rather, both are intertwined to the extent that neither can be fully appreciated without taking into account the possibility of the other. According to Goodrich:

> The [legal] text circulates as an image, a symbol, a painted word, and the power of its effect is largely resident in that aesthetic quality rather than in its supposed rational content, for few ever read the law [and] none ever read all of it (1996: 97; 2015: 8).

Law, like art, idealises the world and in doing so produces a cornucopia of images which demand classification. According to the unconscious activity of internal necessity, some features are purposefully reinforced, others ignored or eliminated. This ordering process is understood as fundamental to developing the moral and rational capacities and has been stated as having three main components – namely, memory, imagination and analogical reasoning – corresponding respectively to history, poetry and philosophy (Bacon 2001: 86). Of these three, it is suggested that poetry – in its most potent form – can uniquely explain the social world, and has the ability to signify a panoply of impressions relating to complex ideas such as morality and justice, which in turn enable the 'synthesising and communicating [of] reality' (Day Lewis 1834).

Poetry in (e)motion: expressing the inexpressible

Normative disciplines define their territory according to simple categories which establish absolute principles purporting to offer a single truth as to what is just and unjust, right and wrong, good and bad. As the legal tradition seeks to structure reality primarily through the medium of language, the application of allegorical terminology, imagery and metaphor is fundamental to the founding of legal principles and concepts, which are embedded in a diverse interplay of meanings. A variety of linguistic and extrasemantic devices, such as synecdoche, symmetry, rhythm and sound shapes, serve a referential function with which to penetrate our collective consciousness. The metaphoric practices of lawyers, for example, depend upon the apparatus, style and cadences of the poetic form and, inscribed within a formal legal structure, each metaphor exemplifies a particular meaning. It exists, however, not in its relationship of one individual idea to another, but rather as one system of thought and symbols to another interrelated system – as a resource for understanding one domain of experience in terms of another. As each metaphor draws out and accentuates certain actual similarities to the source and devalues others, the nature and degree of legal protection or punishment attributed to any action depends on the chosen metaphor.

The core assumptions derived from the implementation of such socio-linguistic mechanisms transform the nature of legal analysis. This is illustrated in the application to the Internet, by the courts, of property and tort metaphors ('entering', 'visiting', 'intrusion') in developing the modern doctrine of cyber-trespass, despite the fact that when a website address is entered into the browser, information is sent to a server which is conveyed via a set protocol to the user's computer without the browser visiting any other place. These metaphors have strict legal force in spite of the false assumption of a correlative relationship between the real and virtual worlds, which is negated by reality. Such language games originate in a variety of social institutions, cultural practices and historical developments. They comprise a complex hierarchy of serially ordered actions, indicating intricate design and developmental stages, and so require more than the mere arbitrary adoption of simple grammatical devices. Performing a key symbolic function, the linguistic habits and rules underpinning the interpretative evolution of the common law – which govern our perception of time and space, history and memory – may be understood as sharing a common foundation with another emblematic form, the poetic. Although law would banish the idea of poetry in its performance of truth, legitimacy and justice, the legal enterprise is claimed to be characterised by the study of systems of inscription, of the forms of memory and of their social enactment, their staging or reproduction, and also poetry (Goodrich 1990: 111–148).

Signifying the recognition of 'alterity' and the concept of difference, the ethical value of any socio-linguistic discourse 'may be gauged in proportion to the poetry that it presupposes' (Kristeva 1980: 25). To the extent that law articulates social cohesion, it relies *inter alia* on the sensibilities of community, and images of identity, morality and integrity that poetry is able to inspire. The global economic turmoil of the 1930s witnessed a resurgence of interest in verse as a political medium, typified by the poems of Auden, Spencer, Isherwood and Day Lewis. In 1934 Cecil Day Lewis produced his acclaimed *A Hope for Poetry*, declaring:

> [the poet] is come into a world of law and logic and he must try to speak its tongue ... The means by which the poet explores reality and the image ... is also the poet's way of reducing the real world to manageable proportions and of revealing its patterns ... Our world may be in a state of chaos but it is the business of the poetic reasons to create order out of chaos (1936: 16, 112).

Day Lewis and his contemporaries were profoundly aware of the political and psychological effects of the Great Depression on a ravaged society, and of the need to rediscover the stabilising core of human connectedness which they accomplished through the poetic medium. The poetic form has, however, been variously accused of elitism, inaccessibility and, more significantly, of aestheticising the brutal realities of power, constituting a lyrical complicity with the agents of human suffering. A masking of the darkness, pain and terror associated for example with a monstrous act not only defies any principle of aesthetic integrity but can also distance us from the consequences of such atrocities. Baudelaire famously asserted: 'The intoxication of art is more apt than any other to veil the horrors of the eternal abyss' (1964: 269–273).

In his 1949 essay 'Cultural Criticism and Society', Adorno conflated the lyrical dramatisation of events with a diminishment of acts of torture and genocide perpetrated in Auschwitz: 'To write poetry after Auschwitz is barbaric' (1983: 17–34). In the immediate aftermath of the Holocaust, Adorno suggested that any attempt at rhetorical reflexivity could only reproduce and, in the act of recognition, implicitly condone such acts of barbarism. The impossibility of poetry as free representation of individual autonomy, when the Shoah had liquidated the very concept of human agency, was the basis for his theoretical inquiry into the moral status of art in the context of a cultural aporia. However Adorno was not abandoning the use of poetry or promoting aesthetic silence; rather, he sought to draw attention to the tension between ethics and aesthetics inherent in an act of artistic creation that reproduces the cultural values of the same society that was responsible for the Holocaust. In his 1966 *Negative Dialectics* he even insists that art must bear witness and give full recognition to suffering – 'the need to lend a voice to suffering is a condition for all truth' – only bearing in mind the inherent limitations and dangers of allowing lyric form to the unspeakable (1973: 17–18). In any case poetry, by definition, tends to be about something that cannot be addressed directly but only alluded to; so that (to misquote Hans Christian Andersen) 'when words fail poetry speaks'.

This might explain why many judgments contain literary citations of the work of novelists, essayists, poets and philosophers: For example, from Robert Frost's poem 'Mending Wall', used by US Supreme Court Judge Scalia to illustrate his application of a variation on the idea of separation of powers in *Plaut v Spendthrift Farm Inc* (1995) 514 U.S. 211, to Lord Justice Wall quoting from Philip Larkin's 'This Be The Verse' in a postscript to his judgment in *R (A Child)* [2009] EWCA Civ 358. Although law and poetry may appear to occupy opposite realms of human experience, the capacity of poets and the moral duty incumbent on lawyers to give voice to that which is otherwise indescribable, repressed or forbidden cannot be understated. Transcendent and inherent to the idea of law as singularly rule-bound, the notional connectivity of human beings can communicate a moral order, within which it is possible to recognise and act on a shared understanding of injustice, and conceive the ethical basis for rejecting an inhumane law or outcome.

Law has often been described as an artistic enterprise not least in its efforts to identify and categorise those aesthetic attributes customarily connected with, for example, authority and reason. Although rhapsodical and ornate expression are less important to making an impressive legal address, the tools of the dramatic arts such as structure and apt use of metaphor are invaluable in moving from an actual fact or function to the representation of an ideal truth. Manderson argues that the discourse of law is fundamentally governed by rhetoric, metaphor, form, images and symbols, and expressed through form and structure and style and ritual (2000: 52, 191). Even in judicial practice, metaphors are used to structure new categories of thought; their relational properties help create and maintain law's truth and reality, constituting a *poesis* of law and justice. As a rhetorical device the poetic form of construction assumes not only semantic and pragmatic significance but also, in resisting arbitrariness, it offers the capacity to relate each signifier to the signified. Because full meaning can be situated within the articulation due to a particular phonological, semiological, grammatical or lexical structure, this enables the poem to reach a wider range of other signifiers beyond the usual prescribed theories of meaning within a legal context. As an adjunct, even alternative, to scientific inquiry Aristotle prized poetry as 'more philosophical and more studiously serious than history ... because poesy dealeth with the universal consideration [whereas] history [deals] with the particular'; similarly for Wordsworth, 'its object is truth, not individual and local, but general, and operative; not standing upon eternal testimony, but carried alive into the heart by passion' (Cooper 1913; xvi).

In 'A Defence of Poetry', Shelley esteemed the vitally figural nature of poetic language for its capacity to 'strip the veil of familiarity from the world, and lay bare the naked and sleeping beauty which is the spirit of its forms' (1977: 505). In this way an expression of the imagination may transform the familiar world into a multi-dimensional 'chaos'. The skilled poet has the potential to solve a mystery or unmask some essential truth, layer by layer, without the imposition of meaning. This is possible because of the unique ability of 'all sentient beings ... to produce not melody alone, but harmony, by an internal adjustment of sounds or motions thus excited to the impressions which excite them' (1977: 480). Devoid of intentionality and, ideally, pure of motive, the poet may hope to elicit an impassioned response only through the relational properties of each revelation to the observer. Believing them to be possessed of some exemplary moral influence, Shelley dubbed poets the 'unacknowledged legislators of the world' (1977: 221). This does not mean poetry performs an obvious social function or that poets wish to be recognised as actual public legislators, as this would conflict with the autonomy of the poetic imagination. It is their lack of personal ambition, their impartiality and dissociation from both the mundane and from the influence of any totalising regime, which renders them morally pure or at least pure of a self-interested motive. Too often subject to an anodyne interpretation, as if the 'unacknowledged interior decorators of the world', for Shelley poets are revolutionists, subversive and fearless – willing to challenge the unlawful use of force and authority by imagining the forms and feelings which might shape the social order against any prevailing political power or agenda (Rich 2007: 7). Although no ideal expressive structure has been conceded, it is evident that art, especially the poem, has the singular capacity to reveal, for the purposes of critique, that which is absent, invisible and often forbidden, and so hidden from view. Aside from its imitative function, in some cases the artistic medium provides the only way to expose to public gaze the secrets buried deep within the underbelly of the social order.

Early philosophers often equated great literature with human endeavour. Plato determined the aesthetic form as sharing the character of a living organism, to which Aristotle added that each literary genre, such as an oration or tragedy, attaches to a specific determinant principle or function compatible with, and appropriate to, the effect produced on the spectator. 'Imaginative literature' – of which poetry was posited as the clearest mimic of human activity – was divided into tragedy, comedy and the epic, of which tragedy was cast as the noblest of the species. The correlation between form and function suggested the type of influence realised within the observer; for example, a tragedy would ideally arouse the emotions of pity and fear. In this manner, for Aristotle the genre as a stimulant to action is connected in the same way as the body and soul functions in Christianity – as inner and outer relational facets of the same object. A perfect symmetry is sought in the representational form and the object of its desire, namely the audience of prospective enlightened and motivated observers. Equilibrium is realised when the hyper-reflectional mirror image and the imitated world of appearances and experience transcend an inauthentic mundane juxtaposition and, rather, present a unified sublimity which comprises a transcendent reality. At that moment the poem provides significantly more than a mere imitation of society and its values; perhaps actualising the only possible means of access to this abounding and luxuriant collection of possibilities, 'poetry lifts the veil from the hidden beauty of the world, and makes familiar objects be as if they were not familiar' (Shelley 1977: 487).

The poetic articulation belongs to a common tradition from which meaning is attainable *a priori* to evidence, precedent, space and time. Although suspicious of the dismissive attitude towards reason, Plato perceived in poetry a divine quality, as a medium through which meaning was 'transmitted by the gods', as poets are but 'interpreters of the gods' (1972: 534e). He further insisted that:

> All good epic poets recite all their fine poems not by skill but because they are inspired and possessed, and the lyric poets do likewise. Just as corybants dance when they are not in their right minds, so too lyric poets compose their fine lyrics when they are not in their right minds. Rather when they enter upon their harmonies and rhythms, they revel like bacchants and are possessed, and are not in their right minds (Plato 1972: 533e–534a).

By the phrase 'not in their right minds' Plato is likening the creative endeavour of poets to that of 'prophets and soothsayers' in that they did not accomplish their compositions through bare ability, but rather through a combination of instinct, imagination and inspiration – a form of divine madness. Inspired communicative forms like poetry perform a symbolic and semiotic function by serving as instruments of signification (Kristeva 1984: 23, 24), with the symbolic representing the full range of societal conventions, categories, codes and rules, and the semiotic occupying the space of the imagination or unconscious. The dialectic between these twin non-rational modalities then determines the type of rational discourse with which to engage, producing a mixed discourse which is neither logic nor corybantic insanity. For Plato and Aristotle the vivid expression of the poem emulates human activity and gives it full force; neither magical nor enigmatic, rather it is knowable and understandable.

The highest form of mimetic relationship simply allows for the substitution of an Idea as a feeling, in place of an object. The poet seeks to reproduce in rhythmical and figural language what they have imagined, in order that this representation can be perceived and comprehended by the senses. Cicero, referring to Phidias, explains:

> Neither did this artist, when he carved the image of Jupiter or Minerva, set before him any one human figure as a pattern which he was to copy; but having a more perfect idea of beauty fixed in his mind, this he steadily contemplated, and to the imitation of this all his skill and labour were directed (Reynolds 1997: 45).

The mode of evaluation becomes how well the image corresponds to the reality or idea of the objective world it purports to represent; it may, for example, comprise either a transcendent authenticity or a mundane beautification of the meaning exposed.

Although art and poetry have been said to 'turn all things to loveliness', that is not to say the mirror always presents an idealised image: It 'adds beauty to that which is most deformed, it marries exultation and horror, grief and pleasure, eternity and change; it subdues to union under its light yoke all irreconcilable things' (Shelley 1977: 505). This is no ordinary beauty or deformity, as that which is 'most deformed' may be the consequence of a particular fashion which conceals, even despises, nature. The modern so-called beauty industry, for example, relies on inducing people to subject themselves willingly to varying degrees of physical masking and mutilation which could be more aptly described as the rituals of deformity. The poet or artist must distinguish between the caprices of the changeling and the eternal invariable idea of the beautiful as a form of truth and authenticity. In any case, as the poet seeks to engage not the eye but the mind's eye, aesthetic and intellectual integrity is an essential prerequisite. Even though the poetic imagination in its purest form is disinterested in a definitive end or closure, it is a seductive art form and therefore a potential source of corruption. That the poem can function as either a mirror or a shield imposes a moral obligation to a foundational 'principle of integrity' which acknowledges the role of reason, and accordingly tempers the free play of the poetic imagination which acts upon thoughts to produce other thoughts (Shelley 1977: 480). Unlike the transitory and variable nature of empirical truth, the highest level of human knowledge is said to reside within the realm of Ideas and universal principles and can only be attained by human reason (Lodge 1953). On the part of the poet, this requires an *a priori* engagement with the faculty of critical judgment, and for the reader it poses an interpretative predicament which can be resolved by the rational application of the passions.

The sensuous nature of the poem means it is particularly adept at exposing the contours of the social world, according to the senses and sentiments of individuals who stand in a particular relation to each other. It is this capacity for feeling which enables us to understand and importantly empathise with the stranger and that which makes us moral and renders us human (Shaw 2008: 224). In *Poetic Justice* Nussbaum argues that judicial decisions informed by the literary imagination are likely to be more thorough and insightful than judgments reached by other means; adding 'storytelling and literary imagining are not opposed to rational argument, and can provide essential ingredients in a rational argument' (1995: xiii). The poem constitutes a meeting place where it is possible to encounter the unfamiliar and that which is otherwise. In an act of revealing and disclosure, the poet captivates and enchants his audience by creating a spectacle with the intention of eliciting an imaginative identification which produces an emotional effect. It is that very rhapsodic and sensuous nature of the poem which has, via the application of the narrative imagination, the capacity to arouse the senses and render visible and comprehensible that which was previously hidden. The oral and written tradition of law operates in a sensory environment where other communicative forms continually augment, adapt, reinforce and often purposefully challenge each other. A causal link already exists, therefore, between the laws of poetry and the poetry of laws.

Through the looking-glass or the mirror crack'd

In Tennyson's famous 1842 poem *The Lady of Shalott*, the eponymous heroine is forbidden by curse from gazing upon Camelot, and makes use of a mirror to reflect the everyday comings and goings whilst busy weaving. One day she spies the handsome knight Sir Lancelot and is compelled to turn and look. In that same instant her fate is sealed: 'Out flew the web and floated wide, the mirror crack'd from side to side; "The curse is come upon me" cried the Lady of Shalott' (1999: 31). Similarly, the common law tradition negates the search for meaning outside the confines of its hermetically sealed inner sanctum and insists on valorising its own image of law's truth as the only authentic version. There is little possibility of alternative representations or interdisciplinarity, or room for the necessary contemplation which would allow either. Rather:

> [Law is] variously depicted as true philosophy (*vera philosophia*), as knowledge of things divine and human (*rerum divinarum humanarum-que scientia*), or simply as written reason (*ratio scripta*), the textual cor-pora of law embodied not only truth but majesty or the aura of divine, and so in secular or non-professional terms, unknowable sources. [... It] is always attached to a body, to a territory, or in common law terms the *leges terrae* are tied to a thesaurus, to a system of texts or writs, to the bodies of its subjects but also to the duality of the natural body and the *corpus mysticum* of the sovereign itself (Goodrich 2004: 142, 149).

To ensure the longevity of the conviction that the authenticity of law is preserved within a strict sovereign body of rules, modern legal education is still largely ordered according to the inculcation of a single narrative of truth. This highly subjective, interpretive representation of the world often has little in common with the realities law seeks to describe and mediate. The transformation of all human activity, including historical events, *ex nihilo* provides too much opportunity for lawgivers to create their own rules and principles or at least amend, apply or misapply on a whim. In a famous dissenting judgment, Lord Atkins claimed he was aware of only one authority which might justify an unsound method of construction and the departure from common sense, and that was Humpty Dumpty, a character from *Alice's Adventures in Wonderland and Through the Looking Glass* (Carroll 2003: 169).

> 'When I use a word', Humpty Dumpty said, in a rather scornful tone, 'it means just what I choose it to mean, neither more nor less'. 'The question is' said Alice, 'whether you can make words mean so many different things.' 'The question is,' said Humpty Dumpty, 'which is to be the master, that's all' (*Liversidge v Anderson* (1942) AC 206).

Just as the courts make liberal use of legal fictions, such fluid propositions allow law to effect factual and institutional changes with minimal disruption. Consequently legal education has been described as producing the same diminishing effect as litigation, likened to 'a machine which you go into as a pig and come out of as a sausage' (Bierce 1911). In English legal practice, large law firms divide client cases between various individuals according to their specialisation, so that few lawyers are able to see the bigger picture. A trainee may spend months researching one topic – for example, damages for use in a single case – or have to sift through and organise many documents acquired in the course of discovery. Compelled to generate billable hours, there is no time to ponder their client's case using multiple sources offering a variety of perspectives.

The legal culture comprises an artificial unity of shadow citizens whose members, through a regenerative process, are central to the recollection and reproduction of the shared legal consciousness. Since one of the primary functions of the legal community is to replicate itself, it constantly seeks to justify and legitimate the continuation of its own practices and traditions exhibiting interest only with its own self-image. When Alice stumbled through the looking-glass in Lewis Carroll's eponymous novel, she entered a world which is governed according to the arbitrary demands of the Red Queen without any mandate other than her rightful authority. There is no rule of law and no guiding moral principle; only everything has changed and is different in the manner of 'bad is good and good is bad'. Although no explanation or rationale is provided, Alice's every move is subject to the strict rules of an allegorical chess game which imposes an obligation to adapt. As the Red Queen explains, 'it takes all the running *you* can do, to keep in the same place. If you want to get somewhere else, you must run at least twice as fast as that!' (Carroll 2003: 152). In this chessboard world, there is no outside, only elliptical signs which create rules that exist only for themselves. If the rules were transgressed and the players were to disappear, there would be no game and consequently the rules maintain this interior world of appearances.

Legal rules create and sustain law's own game based on networks of symbolic social relations, which determine what Heidegger refers to as a 'circle of understanding'; this belongs to a structure of meaning, necessarily grounded in a 'fore-structure', which understands in advance that which must be interpreted (1990: 194). Where law has subjugated the circle of understanding to a dominant ideology and refused to work out the fore-structures – or 'the things themselves', namely their ontological significance and wider application – this results in a 'vicious circle' and fails to contribute to understanding (1990: 195). The legal tradition maintains an outlandish world of novel concepts such as form and procedure, rules and decisions, command and obedience, in which familiar words are given arbitrary new meanings which, in turn, signal unfamiliar categories of thought. As a set of causally ordered particulars, whole branches of law emerge as inflexible, unresponsive and inappropriate; this undermines the notion of impartiality and risks the imposition of arbitrary justice. Any 'potentiality-for-being' is lost as law's self-certainty contains no truth since it merely exists for itself, having never experienced pure abstraction – the negation of its objective self by emerging out of itself and achieving a different kind of enlightenment consequent upon a widening out of old horizons and adding to these other horizons (1990: 232). The faithfulness of the mirror world, by means of which the legal culture constructs the world in relation to itself, is always specious.

In the concluding pages of *The Consumer Society: Myths and Structures* (1998), Baudrillard refers to a 1930s' expressionist film of the German School, *The Student of Prague*, in which an impoverished student makes a Faustian bargain to relinquish part of himself, his reflection, for money. The film dramatises a form of contemporary alienation and suggests that although we may continue to exist, there is a loss of unconscious meaning in the lost mirror image. A significant part of us escapes from us in this process (our essence or soul), and we are incapable of escaping the missing part, since it is forever present in its aching absence. Thus, the transparency of our relation to the world is expressed by our unimpaired – and unmediated – relation to the image in the mirror, and symbolically this indicates reciprocity between the world and oneself. When this connection is broken or weakened, if the image is missing, it signifies the world is becoming opaque and we have no perspective on our identity; as if we are at once estranged from ourselves. Baudrillard explains:

> there is no longer any soul, no shadow, no double, and no image in the specular sense. There is no longer any contradiction within being, or any problematic of being and appearance [as] the individual no longer produces his own reflection, but is absorbed in the contemplation of multiple signs/objects, is absorbed into the order of signifiers of social status, etc. He is not reflected in that order, but absorbed and abolished (1998: 191, 192).

This final irreversibility has imploded any distinction between reality and the imaginary, being and appearance, knowledge and belief. As Bauman states in *Postmodern Ethics*, 'all things stand ultimately for nothing but themselves – there is no division between things that mean and things that are meant' (1993: 36). The artificial world of simulation functions on the basis that 'signs are exchanged against each other rather than against the real … *on condition* that they are no longer exchanged against the real' (Baudrillard 1993: 7). The communication of laws and inculcation of lawyers relies on the privileging of arbitrary written and vocalised symbols, to ensure that fundamental bounded concepts can be understood and transmitted by means of a wider culture of perpetual supporting referents, signs and signifiers.

The application of any unauthorised symbolism or imagery in legal expression is perceived as a potential flaw in law's otherwise formalist nature. Confined to a set of narrowly defined parameters in the pursuit of certainty and optimal standards, any prior intellectual horizons or aesthetic values are constrained; the only authentic image is that of law's own reflection in its legal codes and followers. Although the modern lawyer is required to behave more like a businessman than a man of letters, disinclined to 'neglect the concoction of a pudding for the sake of a poem, or the sauce for a sonnet', this was not always the case (Preston 2004: 13). Plato is credited with having recommended music as a moral law:

> [Music] gives a soul to the universe, wings to the mind, flight to the imagination, a charm to sadness, gaiety and life to everything. It is the essence of order, and leads to all that is good, just and beautiful, of which it is the invisible, but nevertheless dazzling, passionate, and eternal form (cited in Avebury 1908: 173).

He also warns in *The Republic, Book IV* that 'musical innovation is full of danger to the state' (Plato 1991: 98). In the Ancient Greek world and medieval era however, an appreciation of a wide range of aesthetic forms was considered pedagogically essential for the enrichment of intellectual and moral life and a necessary prerequisite for public office. Lawyers were expected to be well-versed in the classics and were chosen as much for their mastery of oratorical skill as their knowledge of legal practice. They were expected to have the ability to inspire and excite their audience. Just as literary jurisprudence introduces students to the musings of William Shakespeare, W.H. Auden, Cecil Day Lewis, Jonathan Swift and Friedrich Nietzsche, early legal minds would have been tutored in a wide range of subjects found within the liberal arts tradition:

> the useful compendium of morality which the multitude supposes to be that of Cato, and let him pass from the *Eclogue of Theodulus* to the eclogues of the *Bucolics* [of Virgil] … . Then let him read satirists and historians, so that he may learn about the vices to avoid in the age of minority, and let him look for the noble deeds of those [who ought] to be imitated. From the joyful *Thebaid* [of Statius] let him pass to the divine *Aeneid*, nor let him neglect the poet [Lucan] whom Cordoba brought forth … . Let him reserve the moral sayings of Juvenal in the secrecy of his breast, and study hard how to avoid the shamefastness of nature. Let him read Horace's *Satires* and *Epistles* and *Art of Poetry* and *Odes* with the book of *Epodes.* Let him hear Ovid's *Elegies* and *Metamorphoses*, but especially let him be familiar with the little book [by Ovid] of *The Remedy of Love* (Orme 2006: 97).

Early legal scholars were equipped to provide insightful commentary, expected to engage in philosophical debate and make judgments in a world in which the arts and sciences did not exist in isolation.

Just as the use of exaggeration, imaginative interpretation, rearrangement and embellishment constitute the proper domain of aesthetics, these same aptitudes form the primary toolkit of the legal advocate, which further suggests a symbiotic relation between law and art. Since medieval times, however, the blackletter tradition has endeavoured to claim knowledge of what can only be understood as an illusory order of causes and motivations, found in the empty spaces of a limited legal imagination. Major principles are premised on barely explicated ideas such as honour, duty and public interest, and such normative terms are used to define and regulate all social life. The critical and socio-legal traditions have offered an alternative perspective which has gained some popularity amongst academics; however since this modern era is marked by a compulsion to measure, quantify and prove, there is a growing tendency to belittle the utilities of intuition and imagination. Modern culture is marked by a distinct 'lack of aesthetic appreciation, a dulling of emotional affect, and an apparent inability to understand symbolic and conventional meaning' (Manderson 2000: 27). Yet law, moral values and aesthetics are mutually constitutive and our lawgivers have a duty to resist blind conformity and to be critically engaged, just as we, as citizens, must do the same. The implications for liberty and justice are profound and rejection of the unreflective mindset demands, instead, deliberating with both reason and passion, and comprehending the production of law as dependent upon dialogue which is exemplified in text, music and art.

The legal tradition engages in games of representation and, much like art, claims to go to the root of things and do justice in constructing reality. Both demand selective abstraction from the totality of given raw materials in order to make subtle adjustments and originate an idealised image; to this extent social realism is another term for the absolute aestheticisation of everything. Aesthetics are then already a part of, if not inside, the law and not only as a means for intellectual comparison; rather, art is said to be the 'mathematical result of the emotional desire for beauty' and is already an innate expression of human consciousness (Wilde 2007: 41). The work of aesthetic representation, whether in the form of a painting, verse, heraldic banner or an Act of Parliament, is claimed by Goodrich to be more than what it appears to be; rather as an act of creation and authorship it infers 'another presence', signifying for instance the moral authority of God, or reason, or the legislative force of law.

> Because the image … belonged to the emotive body of a natural or unwritten tradition of law, to a secret knowledge of the heart, it could threaten or hold the invisible body, the emotional body, the affective subject or soul of those subject to the law (Goodrich, 1990: 261, 262).

Western law is, then, an effective influence on its subjects because of the interplay of icons, images and signs on the collective imagination. In his *Critique of Practical Reason*, Immanuel Kant famously linked aesthetic consciousness – the sensuous awesomeness of the 'starry skies above me' – with the imperative to cultivate a sound moral predisposition, appealing to 'the moral law within' (1956: 169).

Artfully presented rhetorical configurations have the capacity not only to arouse the senses, but can also stimulate the emotions and actualise or represent that which can otherwise only be accessed abstractly. Intrinsic to the rational moral agent is, therefore, an understanding of the value of emotional data in both writing and interpreting the narratives of law as 'the trajectories plotted upon material reality by our imagination' (Cover 1983: 5). In this way, each emotional and aesthetic encounter of justice and injustice is able to inform the progression of society as a series of sequential interconnecting stories recounted individually and collectively. At an institutional level, meaning is attributed to those stories which claim to tell the truth in legal terms. As shared public narratives they represent lived fictions and order various segments of human existence, which enable individuals to make sense of the world. They also provide the basis from which it is possible to navigate the 'endless dialectic between despair, thought and action; between emotion, philosophy and politics, [which] is what opens temporality and creates history'; and, significantly, creates the conditions from which law, and the misuse of power, can be held to account (Douzinas & Gearey 2005: 138).

The following chapters will address the influence and wider implications of a range of complex and definitional emotional states on the historical and modern formation of legal judgment, legal principles, the legal subject and legal scholarship. A particular focus will be on the directional impact of key passions in formulating legal doctrine and the ideals of justice.

3 Law as fear

'Twas brillig, and the slithy toves
Did gyre and gimble in the wabe:
All mimsy were the borogoves,
And the mome raths outgrabe.

'Beware the Jabberwock, my son!
The jaws that bite, the claws that catch!
Beware the Jubjub bird, and shun
The frumious Bandersnatch!'

Lewis Carroll (1871)

From childhood myths of monsters lurking under the bed, the menacing Jabberwock and creepy killer clowns in dark alleyways, fear is a common experience to which everyone is susceptible. Many fears are universal; some fears are contagious and lead to moral panics and, according to political philosopher Judith Shklar, 'To be alive is to be afraid' (1998: 11). Certain fears are rational and worthy of further examination; for example it is natural to fear what we do not know, what we do not understand, and what we do not like – as such unknowns threaten to collapse our world of meaning and the key values which underpin various fundamental certainties and realities which attach to that world. We may feel afraid not only when an actual threat is encountered but also when something is perceived as threatening or dangerous. Associated with heightened arousal, negative or aversive subjective experience, it is the mainspring and chief psychological component of terror. Also, in some instances fear weakens people, renders them powerless and produces regressive behaviour in otherwise responsible adults. This can lead to an unwarranted dependence on parental substitutes, such as governments or corporations which purport to offer protection from monsters and malefactors.

Bruno Latour in *We Have Never Been Modern* famously declared the defining characteristic of modernity to be the production of many frightful 'monsters, hybrids and uncertainties'. These present-day monsters are said to comprise an agglomeration of networks of mediation, which blend together 'knowledge, interest, justice and power … heaven and earth, the global stage and the local scene, the human and the non-human' (Latour 1993: 3, 6). Such quasi-objects are not reducible to one order of knowledge as they inevitably combine the natural and social worlds. It is also significant that they represent an historical movement away from the traditional industrial or 'organic' society, towards a new world typified by polymorphous networks of information and webs of power. While hybridity is a distinguishing feature of the modern socio-cultural environment, a fear of the proliferation of these quasi-objects – which is to some extent justified within the context of recent and largely unrestrained, yet transformative, scientific and technological advancements – has spiralled out of control, and tends to dominate the toxic narrative of everyday life. Alternatively, in *Simians, Cyborgs and Women: The Reinvention of Nature*, Donna Haraway outlined the importance of connecting disparate topics such as technology, feminism and social democracy, in order to better understand the fullest consequences of their impact and influence on future developments. In any case, the various tensions between organisms and machines are already embodied within technoculture because 'technology is not neutral. We are inside of what we make, and it is inside of us. We are living in a world of connections, and it matters which ones get made and unmade' (Haraway 1991: 149). Although these 'monstrous' hybrid discourses are presented as a 'rhetoric of alterity' that may even promote alternative conceptions of otherness, identity and difference, the typical response has been to eschew informed public debate, and rather to introduce various forms of cultural and intellectual closure.

Against the spectres of, for example, global warming, terrorism, economic Armageddon, resource depletion, artificial superintelligence and nanotechnology, nuclear war, the imminent prospect of autonomous weapons, bioengineered pandemics and antibiotic-resistant infections, to name but a few bogeymen, people have become fearful. In the shadow of such anticipated terrifying catastrophic and apocalyptic events, without hesitation they have been willing to relinquish their most intimately held and sacred rights in order to feel safe. This is in spite of the inappropriateness of this new raft of legislation and notwithstanding our safety, rights and freedoms already being guaranteed and enshrined within settled constitutional principles, such as the rule of law and international treaties – for example, the Universal Declaration of Human Rights (1948), International Covenant on Civil and Political Rights (1966), International Covenant on Economic, Social and Cultural Rights (1966), and the Convention against Torture and Other Cruel, Inhuman or Degrading Treatment or Punishment (1984). These and other similar provisions still provide at least a minimum standard of security and protection in their sanction-supported pledges to respect our standing as distinct and autonomous individuals. Yet a series of oppressive policies and draconian laws have been drafted and imposed in response to the intensification of a largely media-orchestrated climate of fear. This includes the recently passed Investigatory Powers Act (IPA) 2016, otherwise known as the 'Snooper's Charter'.

The right to communicate privately and, more significantly, securely has been surrendered against the backdrop of fears over 'national security threats' posed by serious and organised crime and radical Islamist terrorist attacks. Although threats by terrorist organisations are not unique phenomena there is a danger that, particularly at times when the political focus is on increasing the repression of organised crime and terrorism, the new measures are too often not only less effective than existing legislation, but may also be unfair. The IPA 2016, for instance, was enacted in the wake of the Snowden revelations and forms part of a move to increase public and private powers vis-à-vis surveillance and monitoring without the need for 'reasonable suspicion', and to further facilitate the bulk collection of personal communications data and decrypt the Internet. Accordingly, the Act inevitably means greater web insecurity for millions of innocent users, as it substantially undermines the strength of cryptography across the entire cyber market. It also represents the forfeit of what has traditionally been considered to be an inalienable human right, and was passed in spite of a large number of petitions questioning the reasonableness and proportionality of the legal response to the scale, scope and incidence of such threats; and despite a lack of evidence that the transformation of the UK into 'Fortress Britain' would automatically thwart further attacks. In fact, many of those culpable for terrorist acts and other serious offences are already known to intelligence personnel, thereby casting further doubt on the need for extreme digital surveillance powers. To misappropriate Benjamin Franklin's famous declaration in his 1755 letter to the governor of Pennsylvania, 'those who would give up essential liberty, to purchase a little temporary safety (especially when safety is not guaranteed by the recent raft of Orwellian legal provisions) deserve neither liberty nor safety'.

Fear is the antithesis of reassurance, faith and contentment, which are all purported to be legitimate aims of 'law as justice' according to the ancient moral, legal and political philosophy of Aquinas and Aristotle. In practice, however, the characteristic and originating violence of law and the customary evocation of fear have served to empower and enable law's effectiveness in minimising dissent and motivating consent. According to Derrida, in his famous consideration of Walter Benjamin's essay 'Critique of Violence', it is impossible to distinguish between the force of law as a legitimate power and the supposedly 'primary violence' responsible for establishing this authority which 'could not have been authorised by any anterior legitimacy', and therefore can only be in force from force itself. Accordingly, the coming to power of a ruling authority, whatever the nature of the force that brings it into being, must be a movement that is in itself 'neither legal nor illegal – or neither just nor unjust' (Derrida 1992: 6). From this perspective, the meaning of law is violent, as well as the legality that presumes legitimacy. As an integral part of the 'mystical foundation of the authority of law', the twin competencies of fear and force are therefore woven into the fabric of incentive, punishment and ideological devices so that even when not directly implemented, fear 'shape[s] the materiality of the social body upon which domination is brought to bear' (Poulantzas 2000: 81).

In our brave new hypermediated world of instant information, the manufacture of a politics of fear, characterised by media sensationalism and a culture of disinformation, means it is no longer necessary to apply force to encourage compliance with government edicts, to quell dissent or to instil obedience. People consume a daily diet of scare stories, from the collapse of governments to poor urban planning, to the spread of infectious diseases, to infrastructure failures, cyberattacks and potential environmental disasters as a result of climate change. In light of the current trend for catastrophic imagining which is with increasing frequency used to justify unwarranted intrusions on civil liberties and basic human rights, this chapter will explore the impact of the cultivation of a climate of fear on law and policy-making – both in relation to the formation of legal judgment and with respect to the influence on policy-makers who have in recent times been driven to rhetorical excess.

Fear and evaluative judgments

Emotions are described as 'judgments about important things'; they have purpose and intention which tend to relate to people, things or circumstances; and by 'appraising an external object as salient for our own well-being, we acknowledge our own neediness and incompleteness before parts of the world that we do not fully control' (Nussbaum 2001: 19). Among the complex forces that shape human behaviour, Martha Nussbaum also considers emotions to be forms of thought, or 'judgments of value', which express profound and often hidden assumptions about how to interpret reality, and how to determine to what extent particular features of reality matter. Judgments which relate to matters of justice, causality, right and wrong are often instigated by discrete forms of emotional experience which tend to have immediate impact, and are embodied and impelling. However, there is a world of difference between positive emotions such as compassion and love which trigger more associative, creative and expansive patterns of thought and negative emotions such as fear or anger which tend to have a narrowing effect, reducing attention and alertness to an actual threat. Although fear is an appropriate and accurate judgment in the case of someone who faces an impending threat to someone they cherish or something they value, such as their reputation, it is often understood as one of the coarser, negative, drive-motivated emotions along with pugnacity, wrath and ferocity. Fear frequently falls into the category of anticipatory rather than actual emotions, which means it has a tendency to amplify and overestimate the expectation of danger and, in turn, lead to the selective and unreliable perception and assessment of threat.

Since fear is a response aroused by some of the same objects that produce ferocity, in *The Principles of Psychology* William James observes, 'the progress from brute to man is characterised by nothing so much as by the decrease in frequency of proper occasions for fear' (1950: 416). While this is a seemingly simple proposition, and in spite of the evolution in human nature in response to a relatively safer environment, fear is still a feature of modern life; and there remains radical disagreement as to its origins, definition and scope, and in regard to whether it is a force for good or evil. Distinguishing between the *object* and *cause* of fear is also fundamentally important, as the object of an emotion is frequently distinct from its cause. Wittgenstein uses the example of an injured child whose present adult fear of fire results from past experience of being burnt: 'the *belief* that fire will burn me is of the same kind that it will burn me' (2009: 473, emphasis added). The experience of being burnt is stored along with the emotions, physical sensations and beliefs that were felt at the time. These memories are revisited and revitalised when something occurs in the present that is similar in some way to the original event; however, the body/mind has difficulty in distinguishing between the source of the past and present reactions. Such responses also apply to future-facing emotions such as longing or dread, where the object of the emotion belongs to something merely anticipated rather than experienced in the present. To claim that a yet-to-happen or never-to-happen event can function as a cause for fear is, therefore, problematic.

For Wittgenstein, 'a face which inspires fear or delight (the object of fear or delight) is not on that account its cause, but – one might say – its target' because the objects of emotions are amenable to reasons, justification and motive (2009: 476). The distinction rests on (1) the *objective attributes* of the world that have meaning and significance for individuals by providing reasons for and against a particular course of action; and (2) the *causal basis* which comprises our personal experience of those objective features. Even though causes are usually recognised as explanatory while reasons are justificatory, the causal basis often supports at least some of the meaning and values ascertained by reason. This is illustrated by the conviction that 'fire will burn me', in which fear is equated with belief and understood to be an intentional state. However, when fear discloses nothing about the object, only its purported power to frighten, it confounds and defeats inquiry.

In *Powers of Horror: An Essay on Abjection* Julia Kristeva talks about the fear-paroxysm or phobia as being 'precisely [the] avoidance of choice, it tries as long as possible to maintain the subject far from a decision', or far from the very idea that the object of fear could be a matter for decision (1982: 42). Possessed by something akin to a state of somatic delusion, the creeping paralysis of fear robs the individual of autonomous reasoning, as the possibility of alternative perspectives relating to the object of fear is obliterated by the experience. Although it varies so much from one person to another – and 'healthy' fear has an obvious protective function – it is clear that many of fear's manifestations must be considered 'unhealthy' and pathological rather than useful. For instance, when using the 'availability heuristic' there is a tendency to overestimate the probability of incidents we know examples of, while at the same time underestimating events which are hard to recall. The fear impulse may then lead to a hasty and irrational decision, founded on erroneous inferences drawn from innocuous events imagined to be evidence. Being familiar with recent reports of plane crashes and having the ability to recall some of these incidences with ease can, for example, justify a fear of flying in spite of a lack of supporting statistical evidence. Similarly, after the release of the movie *Jaws* in 1975 many people suffered from vicarious traumatisation and were reluctant to swim in the ocean. Although shark attacks are relatively rare, the vivid imagery and media attention surrounding the movie resulted in a distorting interplay between anxiety, fear and an overestimation of probable harm.

Fear-mongering and the media: implications for justice

For William James, recalcitrant emotions such as fear have no initial motivational or cognitive content; rather, this is subsequently acquired through learning. In his seminal paper 'What is an Emotion?' James reasoned that human emotion follows a series of events, beginning with physiological arousal which is connected to the sympathetic and parasympathetic nervous system which, in turn, instigates and then activates the corresponding emotion. He used the illustration of running from a bear to explain that our fear stems from the action of running away from the bear, not because the bear is the source of our fear (James 1884: 189–190). Our instinctive bodily responses are triggered by non-cognitive, but nevertheless conscious, perceptual states. Since there is commonly a discrepancy between the fear people experience in relation to a specific risk and their cognitive evaluation of the threat posed by that risk, fear-driven risk appraisals are likely to lead to decision-making which is inimical to personal or societal well-being. Accordingly, although fear may serve a useful purpose in the case of prompting action to avoid being chased by a bear, it becomes problematic when motivating the individual to act in a way that conflicts with the rational pursuit of a set of goals and may lead to irrational actions.

While emotion generally enables a person to form an attitude about risk that expresses their values, negative emotions such as fear have the ability to permeate, and distort, both personal and popular beliefs about risk. Since individual responses are shaped by shared cultural and social contexts, what people read and see further impacts on their capacity for reasoned decision-making, which may be compromised. For example, the media-fuelled alternating undercurrents of myopia and hysteria underpinning various modern narratives of fear – such as imminent environmental degradation, over-population, nuclear apocalypse and financial calamity – animate popular risk perceptions. Although endless news reports, infotainment broadcasts with accompanying images sourced from global news agencies, increase the individual's socio-cognitive repertoire, as Baudrillard claimed in *The Gulf War Did Not Take Place*, a 'hypermediated representation' enables the creative reconstruction of an event so that it is neither real nor unreal. Consequently, via the distorting media lens, 'the closer we supposedly approach the real or the truth, the further we draw away from them both, since neither one nor the other exists' (Baudrillard 1995: 49). Communication of the reported incident or event takes place in a new virtual space fashioned by digital technology which has reshaped and controlled what has been delivered; and inside this new 'cultural matrix', information is reconstructed as spectacle, at which point the real collapses into the hyperreal realm of signs, the signified and signifiers.

The daily onslaught of pre-digested, fast information, frequently delivered by media 'personalities' and 'celebrities', is held by Marshall McLuhan to increase the sense of disjunction from one's own grounded 'life world', within which significance and meaning is determined by our own lived experiences (Shaw 2015: 254). Even if there is some element of truth buried deep beneath the continuous flow of hyperbolic fear-mongering, the endless barrage of 'fake news' or misinformation, constant exposure and recirculation via social media may ultimately impede the decisions people might make concerning their own well-being and the welfare of others. These fear-induced rash decisions may be out of character, irrational or illogical because:

> When things come at you very fast, naturally you lose touch with yourself. Anybody moving into a new world loses identity … So loss of identity is something that happens in rapid change. But everybody at the speed of light tends to become a nobody. This is what's called the masked man. The masked man has no identity. He is so deeply involved in other people [the anonymous collective of 'the public'] that he doesn't have any personal identity (McLuhan 1996: 33, 34).

Digital media not only reflects social opinion; it also has a hyper-intensifying effect on whatever object, subject or realities it mediates or represents, and is capable of leading a person to lose perspective and even their sense of self. It also has the ability to construct social attitudes and eradicate, or at least diminish, an individual's sense of personal responsibility. Søren Kierkegaard describes this phenomenon as 'levelling', which comprises a neutralising of the uniqueness of individual reflection via a mundane restructuring of society into a series of shared common denominators (Kierkegaard 1962: 51). A modern example is the Twitter microblogging forum, one of the most popular communication conduits and favoured by both the US President and the Pope, which uses hashtags to index keywords, issues and topics. It gives publicity to the widest range of activities, from people sharing updates of what they ate for breakfast, to enumerating petty slights and everyday perceived and actual injustices – and, in the case of the #MeToo movement, undermining the principles of criminal justice and the rule of law by encouraging an alternative justice system, namely, 'trial by lynch mob' or vigilante justice.

If people are to call for justice and for important changes in the law, public debate and peaceful protest are essential features of an open democracy. The use of microblogging services, where users create online communities via social media, to share information, ideas and other content, has to a large extent replaced the traditional form of physically embodied demonstration. In 2019 when people become angry, frustrated or fearful they post a tweet with a link to a video, image or a retweeted message, and often this is accompanied by an emoticon or, more recently, an emoji. Given the rapidity of communication transfers in the Twittersphere, very soon the original cause of consternation has been forgotten and a fresh outrage provokes yet another tweet or Facebook post. René Descartes' original philosophical proposition *cogito, ergo sum* has become in modern life *cogito, ergo pipiatum*, 'I think, therefore I tweet', or perhaps more correctly, especially given the meagre 280-character limit per tweet, 'I don't think, therefore I tweet.' It is alarming, however, to consider that one of the most common ways of receiving breaking news is via Twitter on a mobile device, given the decline of print media and radio and television broadcasts. A majority opinion tends to be formed early on and any dissenting views are often subject to a tirade of personal insults and accusations, while real threats which merit public censure and discussion such as poverty and homelessness are buried beneath the groundswell of reactionary hysteria. More concerning is the fact that this most prevalent means of communication is not subject to the usual guarantees of journalistic integrity or an appropriate legal framework; and, even worse, alternative perspectives can be subject to 'shadow-banning', a practice where social media companies limit the visibility of a particular user's content. It might be argued that this is nothing more than a form of covert corporate censorship.

In an era of dangerous communication where the blunt instrument of 280-character tweets all but beg to be misinterpreted, the online culture of denunciation means Twitter users frequently form their own consensus as to who is guilty, and who needs to be eradicated. The now ubiquitous hashtags, along with a variety of slogans and symbols which accompany such condemnations, while also generated by Twitter members, are often produced by mass marketeers who are employed by intelligence agencies and state departments. Such signifiers are routinely used to help manipulate public perceptions, and even influence the outcome of general elections and destabilise democratically elected governments. The specific words and phrases which are categorised and aggregated into corpus-based searchable lexicons that users can selectively explore and incorporate into their own messages can quickly define a political debate and function as a particularly effective form of propaganda by spreading misinformation and facilitating smear campaigns. Yet it is evident that most people passively assume the 'public opinions' constructed by the information media – as the constant 'silent, mathematical, and abstract occupation which shuns upheavals' – prevent or at least discourage the modern individual from engaging in authentic thought, forming their own judgments and taking action (Kierkegaard 1962: 54). For Kierkegaard, this is characteristic of 'a sensible, reflecting age, devoid of passion, flaring up in superficial, short-lived enthusiasm and prudentially relaxing in indolence': whereas a passionate era 'accelerates, raises up, and overthrows, elevates and debases', a reflective apathetic age does the opposite – it stifles and impedes (1978: 68). Perhaps the appeal of such ready-made, easy to digest and phantom-like public opinion resides not so much in their content as in the fact that they appear to belong to everyone as part of a legitimate, yet in reality illusory, community.

In the early days of social media, mobilised networking has been useful and effective in organising protests, marches and uprisings, such as the 'Arab Spring' Tunisian and Egyptian revolutions of 2010–2011. More recent political movements created via social media have, however, tended to be chaotic and unpredictable. Fundamental concerns have also emerged in more recent times over the invasion of privacy, mass surveillance and monitoring, and ownership and control of the digital infrastructure, in particular, the corporatisation of social media. The disembodiment that once allowed anonymous communication is no longer possible, at least not on commercialised social networks. Facebook, as a developing market model, represents a specific distortion of the original open culture of sharing and connecting as its version of openness is dependent on centralisation and ownership of the user's information (such as documenting location information, contact networks, calendars and messages) for commercial purposes. The core algorithmic thinking behind such platforms prioritises efficiency as it continually searches for patterns based on implicit assumptions about the world, as well as mapping natural human behaviour and tendencies in relation to what we might click on.

As the new arbiters of human decision-making, these algorithms reflect our proclivities, such as what may enrage or outrage us, our desires or what we love and what will frighten us. The engineering and computer science mindset has little tolerance for the fetishisation of words and images, for the mystique of art, for moral complexity or emotional expression. Privacy is equally dispensable, as the algorithm at the heart of a recent Facebook breach involving the data-analytics and messaging company Cambridge Analytica revealed. It was discovered to have trawled through the most ostensibly trivial and throwaway postings – including the 'like' upticks users check while browsing the website – to gather sensitive personal information about sexual orientation, race, gender and even childhood trauma. In relation to using the collected data for 'psychographic profiling' to influence the outcome of the 2016 US presidential election, the company was accused of reducing the voter to 'a bundle of psychological vulnerabilities to be carefully exploited', and as no more than 'mathematical inputs' (Chen 2018: 8). It is evident that people are viewed simply as data, components of systems and as mere abstractions, by a range of designers, developers and editors who create and curate the media we consume. By being constantly audited, users are paternalistically nudged in the direction Facebook and its fellow manipulators, Google, Amazon and Netflix, deem best for them. This surreptitious process reflects the minds of the creators of their respective platforms and the motives of their trainers as they work tirelessly to turn our eyeballs into hard currency.

Even in this barren cultural landscape in which our self-image is largely media-dependent, as Aristotle observed in *Rhetoric*, 'all communication is persuasive communication' (1991: 57). By relieving humans of the burden of free choice and free will, the ideas of essential speech and necessary exchange, as well as silence and pause, are substituted by the incessant noise, chatter, gossip and excessive talkativeness of, for example, Twitter, Facebook and Snapchat. When swamped by a continual mass of sensory data, however, curiosity (the innate compulsion to make internal maps of reality) and fear comprise antagonistic emotions because satisfying one's curiosity about the detail and ramifications of a frightening occurrence or threat is impossible due to a lack of time to consult a broader and more eclectic set of information sources. Curiosity is further undermined by the immediate disheartening and crippling feelings of horror and fear elicited by sensory overload in relation to the incessant rapid communication of often macabre, sensationalistic and troubling news. Therefore, while fear may motivate us to find reliable sources of information, or a more logical solution to a perceived threat, our capacity to find that information or solution may simultaneously be limited by the same stimulus.

Meanwhile a diverse range of social movements and organisations attempt to convert public fears into participation in their various media undertakings and political objectives. In addition, emotional responses to reports of crime, rather than the experience of actual crime, impact on the ways in which individuals navigate their social worlds and respond to external stimuli. For example, a recent poll found that the 75% majority who were persuaded by the doomsday rhetoric of 'weapons of mass destruction' that it was necessary to invade Iraq in 2003 has since become a thin minority (Gallup 2017). In spite of double-digit percentage decreases in US violent and property crime rates since 2008, the majority of voters insisted crime had worsened in the last decade, according to another recent survey (Pew Research Center 2017). A similar trend was noted in the UK where, against the statistical evidence, 60% of people believed crime had risen across the country from 2009 to 2016, and almost 20% of the population expected to be a victim in the near future (Office for National Statistics 2017). This research demonstrates the danger of underestimating the persuasive authority of fear-empowered rhetoric to provoke public reactions which are disproportionate to the level of risk. In the digital ecosphere propaganda has become democratised, and the algorithmic maps used by social media news feeds pander to some of our worst prejudices, bad habits and irrational fears.

Just as emotions enable individuals to discern what standpoint towards particular risks corresponds with their own personal values, social influences and cultural norms play an important part in shaping the emotional reactions and sensibilities people form collectively towards existential and actual threats. Yet when digital media play a key determinative role in informing the public, the drive for more content and to keep feeding the news cycle means a relentless bombardment with compelling yet largely inscrutable images and text. The interminable regaling of lurid tales of tragedy, injustice and horror is irresistible, yet only serves to increase risk perception and intensify fear. Whereas a sound judgment may be made by someone who has had access to all pertinent information and time to reflect on competing interpretations of a relatively novel risk, the relentless stream of increasingly unverified instant information that drives our fears and anxieties provides an unreliable guide for regulation.

The indoctrinating and conditioning influence of the mass media not only adversely affects the individual's capacity for rational judgment; it also creates a 'them' and 'us' mentality. As a consequence, people become fearful of each other, and of an uncertain future which produces disharmony, discontentment and mistrust. This, in turn, forms the basis for powerful legitimating strategies which justify increasing levels of insidious and sophisticated public and private methods of surveillance and control. In this way, fear creates and reproduces relations of power which are connected to an excess or abuse of power. All governments, and not only governments but other public and private power elites, are capable of cruel edicts and actions. From state-sanctioned and private sector acts of cruelty comes fear, and from fear comes loss of freedom. Accordingly, to understand fully the circumstances of the creation, architectonic and utility of fear in a legal context, the focus must shift from simply juxtaposing those positive emotions which are in conflict with fear to examining the protagonists (legal institutions, government, corporate and media entities, state, non-state actors) as a whole, and interrogate their rationale, values and objectives in relation to rightful obligations due within the wider social context they inhabit.

Where judges fear to tread: law and the politics of fear

Fear is an intrinsic element of a variety of crimes, the nature and extent of which varies with the type of crime and severity of the threat of injury to person, property, character or reputation. Fear is also associated with risk, so that *caveat emptor, quia ignorare non debuit quod jus alienum emit* – or, in short, 'let the buyer beware' – was a familiar warning in the early days of trading that preceded legislative provisions such as the original UK Sale of Goods Act 1893 and the more recent UK Consumer Rights Act 2015. Historically, the weaker bargaining party had much to fear in the marketplace, as no mechanism for redress existed. In order to allay what was a legitimate fear of being tricked, mis-sold or becoming the victim of other fraudulent activity, the buyer needed evidence that his good faith would be backed by legal sanction and remedy, should something go wrong. The evolution of contract law in imposing legal limits on unconscionable behaviour can therefore be understood as driven by the need to remove the fear from contractual transactions, and in so doing stimulate the desire to enter into a contractual relationship. Other dyadic interactions, such as those occurring in the workplace concerning oppressive hierarchical relationships and disparities in pay, have been similarly addressed by employment law developments such as the Health and Safety at Work Act 1974, the Equality Act 2010 and gender pay reporting rules which came into force in the UK in 2017. While Parliament has enacted legislation to allay the fears of the general public by providing safeguards in key areas of criminal and civil law, the courts have responded less decisively in upholding the spirit of the rule of law in relation to the protection of human rights in the absence of statute.

In *Kaye v Andrew Robertson & Sport Newspapers Ltd* [1991] FSR 62, for instance, two reporters from the *Sunday Sport* took photos and held an interview with a then well-known but seriously injured actor in his hospital room, who was in no fit state to give his consent. The courts refused to acknowledge that this cruel invasion of privacy was an actionable wrong. Although they originally concluded that publication of the photographs and the reporters' account of what was said was not preventable, eventually an interim injunction was granted on the basis that the actor had legal rights in his own wish to tell his story at some future date, and that publication of the photos would lower the economic value of this right. Lord Justice Bingham noted that 'this case highlights, yet again, the failure of both the common law of England and statute to protect in an effective way the personal privacy of individual citizens' ([1991] FSR 62 at 70). Such invasions of privacy are now covered by the UK Human Rights Act 1998, which requires

English courts to take into account Article 8 (right to respect for private and family life) of the European Convention on Human Rights when making determinations. Nevertheless, the tort of intentionally causing harm could have been extended to cover this situation as it had previously been developed to deal with similarly contemptible behaviour in *Janvier v Sweeney* [1919] 2 KB 316.

The assumption of moral burdens and ethical duties associated with the increasing complexity of law in relation to a rapidly changing society has led to muted deliberations and allegedly poor decision-making by the judiciary. In such instances, fear is a dangerous emotion, at worst leading to decisions that lack context and reason, and at best resulting in an overly cautious approach, for example, in the application of burdens and standards of proof and in passing a custodial sentence. Although it is commendable for judges to be aware of the limitations of their knowledge and understanding of wider moral complexities, in recognition that so much depends on the accuracy of their judgment (including their choice of metaphor, degree of impartiality and justifications), difficult and controversial issues should nonetheless not be evaded; nor should questions be left unasked in order to avoid giving offence. A judge often does have a choice about whether to develop the law or leave it alone; but there is no possibility of establishing consensus if controversial beliefs and values are left unquestioned. Drawing on Kant's *Critique of Judgment*, Hannah Arendt suggested in 'Truth and Politics' that judgment does not mean the dismissal of another's personal beliefs for reasons of expediency or incompatibility; rather, 'the power of judgment rests on a potential agreement with others' (1977b: 220). Being unafraid to acknowledge plurality is argued to serve as a point of departure for meaningful dialogue, and the adoption of an 'enlarged way of thinking which, as judgment, knows how to transcend its own individual limitations ... needs the presence of others in whose place it must think and whose perspectives it must take into consideration' (Arendt 1977b: 221).

Previous studies have shown that judges are susceptible to numerous cognitive and emotional biases, along with extra-legal factors, when making decisions (Leibovitch 2016; Posner 2010; Wistrich *et al* 2015: 855). For Posner, although the judiciary are essentially rational in their thinking, 'few judges are fully inoculated against the siren song of an emotionally compelling case' (2010: 119). Quite often such biases exert an influence outside the conscious awareness of the judge; however, recent over-zealous attempts to refrain from harsh sentencing have led some members of the English judiciary to fabricate an entire vocabulary of euphemisms to avoid appearing unequivocal and blunt in their pronouncements. At the same time, accusations of erring on the side of leniency in a growing number of cases have led to a sharp decline in public confidence in the ability of the judiciary to dispense justice. Fears and doubts have been expressed in relation to the decision quality, the rigour of 'truth' or fact finding, and the appropriate application of the law to those facts. Consequently, in 2016 the UK Appeal Court increased a total of 141 jail terms after complaints over the application of soft sentences. These included 16 cases of robbery, 19 grievous bodily harm with intent, 41 sex offences and 14 sex offenders who were originally handed non-custodial sentences but are now serving time; also, one rapist and one attempted murderer had their original sentences replaced with life terms (Keating 2017: 3). The review was ordered under the Unduly Lenient Sentence scheme, which allows victims of crime and their families, prosecutors and members of the public to ask for decisions they consider too low to be reviewed. Although it is a moot point whether victims should be allowed to determine what the courts should decree or how a miscreant should be punished, clearly those who hold judicial office are performing a public service, and as such are accountable to, and importantly rely on, the confidence and respect of the populace. In 2018 more terror-related offences were added to the scheme, which operates in England and Wales, whereby 'soft' judicial punishments can be challenged and then reviewed by the Attorney General on request.

While these new vulnerabilities which permit challenge and appeal represent a new fairness and compassion for the victim, they also create uncertainty and further weaken public perception of the adjudication process. Of course, a judicial decision is a 'credence good' which makes it difficult for a lay person to ascertain the quality of a judgment, due to a lack of competence and information asymmetry. Like medical professionals, car mechanics and taxi drivers in unfamiliar cities, we cannot be sure of the quality or accuracy of the diagnosis and execution of the expert service provided. It is, however, apparent that the judiciary often lack more than a rudimentary comprehension of complex moral and ethical issues. In such usually non-routine cases, and being only too aware of their own limitations, the courts have looked to Parliament to implement the necessary legislative reforms; for example, in decisions relating to voluntary and involuntary euthanasia, removing life support or withdrawing artificial nutrition and hydration. This is not a new phenomenon. Some 25 years ago Tony Bland, an 18-year-old victim of the Sheffield Hillsborough football stadium disaster, suffered severe brain damage and was left in a persistent vegetative state. Dr James Howe and the Airedale Hospital Trust, with the support of Tony's parents, sought a declaration from the family court allowing the withdrawal of treatment so that he might be allowed to die peacefully. The case went through the Court of Appeal and the House of Lords before permission was finally given four years after the tragedy occurred. Lord Browne-Wilkinson commented:

> In my view ... if the judges seek to develop new law to regulate the new circumstances, the law so laid down will of necessity reflect judges' views on the underlying ethical questions, questions on which there is a legitimate division of opinion. ... Where a case raises wholly new moral and social issues, in my judgment it is not for judges to seek to develop new, all embracing, principles of law in a way which reflects the individual judges' moral stance when society as a whole is substantially divided on the relevant moral issues (*Airedale NHS Trust v Bland* [1993] AC 880).

A similar reluctance to address difficult and controversial moral and ethical dilemmas has been evidenced more recently in cases such as *R (Conway) v the*

Secretary of State for Justice [2017] EWHC 2447 (Admin), in which a man sought permission to be assisted by his doctors to die peacefully and with dignity before becoming entombed in his body from the cruel effects of amyotrophic lateral sclerosis (ALS), a form of motor neurone disease. His case, which was rejected by the High Court, was supported by Humanists UK and opposed by the Secretary of State for Justice, with the backing of Care Not Killing and Not Dead Yet UK, who also made submissions. The British Medical Association has likewise expressed its opposition to physician-assisted dying; yet, as Ronald Dworkin observed in *Life's Dominion*, 'Every day, rational people plead to be allowed to die. Sometimes they plead for others to kill them ... because they are unwilling to live in the only way open to them' (1993: 179). The latest attempts to challenge and update the law in this area, such as Lord Falconer's Private Members' Bill on Assisted Dying [HL] 2014–15 and the Assisted Dying Bill [HL] 2016–17, ended in failure. Progress has been hampered largely by arguments based on fear, superstition, slippery slopes and rudimentary dogmatic theological determinism. Of course it is only reasonable to protect vulnerable groups of individuals, such as the disabled and elderly, from being encouraged or coerced into killing themselves; however, providing such safeguards is well within the remit and capability of the law-makers.

Although the case for assisted dying was rejected, the judgment in *R (Conway)* [2017], *supra*, was successful on one significant point. It was confirmed that the English courts would now have the authority to make a declaration of incompatibility under s.4(2) of the 1998 Human Rights Act, on the grounds that s.2(1) of the 1961 Suicide Act is incompatible with human rights legislation, specifically the right for private life under s.8(1) of the European Convention on Human Rights. However, so far no such declaration is forthcoming. In the meantime, while equivocation and obfuscation continue to beleaguer UK parliamentary debates, countries such as the Netherlands, Belgium, Luxembourg, Canada, a number of US states and Colombia have legalised assisted dying, without endangering the vulnerable. Victoria became the first Australian state to pass a Bill legalising assisted dying for terminally ill people in November 2017. Italy passed its End of Life Bill by a vote of 180 to 71 in December 2017, which allows the refusal of artificial nutrition and hydration. Even Pope Francis is reported to have stated that 'the mechanical application of a general rule is not sufficient', and 'the teachings of the Roman Catholic Church [in relation to its] doctrine on the sanctity of life do not justify overzealous medical treatments to artificially prolong life' (Povoledo 2017: 1). In the meantime, an ever-increasing number of Britons with incurable and terminal illnesses travel abroad to clinics such as Dignitas in Switzerland, while they still have the physical and mental capacity, in order to be assisted to die 'well', with dignity and serenity.

Seventeenth-century Dutch Jewish philosopher Baruch Spinoza counselled that to be led by fear is not to be led by reason and, conversely, 'a man who lives according to the dictates of reason alone is not led by fear of death' (2001: 212). When law-makers fail to give adequate weight to the distinctly personal circumstances which are central to the assisted dying debate, it not only represents a lack of intellectual effort, but also the triumph of fear over compassion and reason. By surrendering to what is essentially an irrational fear of death *per se*, our judges, legislators, religious leaders and some medical professionals have been accused of impeding the advancement of informed 'end of life' debates in the UK. Since the debates are often framed as a battle between a crude conception of 'an ethics of autonomy' and 'an ethics of care', in the context of austerity and a funding crisis in the UK National Health Service, the needs of a growing number of patients with incurable diseases cannot be met by palliative care. Accordingly, the archaic and barbaric provisions of the Suicide Act 1961 condemn such people to a life of unbearable suffering, which frequently has complex medical, psychological, social and existential elements.

On the latter point, since suffering is not simply somatic, then allowing the possibility of assisted dying for those suffering from a terminal medical condition, but not extending the provision to those whose existential suffering arises from social factors, is inconsistent with both an autonomy-based stance and with an approach founded on compassion. In any case, the repeated refusal of the legislators to reform the Suicide Act 1961, and a deficiency of judicial creativity in this area, demonstrates a disregard for the individual's profoundly personal perception of their suffering, and the right of rational and autonomous individuals to be accorded respect for their own belief systems and aesthetic preferences for a 'good death', in the spirit of the *Ars Moriendi* or 'art of dying' from the late Middle Ages.

The importance of autonomy and self-determination, in what is the ultimate act of control and freedom, led Roman Stoic philosopher Seneca – in 'Letter 70: On the Proper Time to Slip the Cable' – to define the 'wise man' as someone who 'will live as long as he ought, not as long as he can', because 'mere living is not a good, but living well' (2016: 176). In examining our often conflicted relationship with dying, on anticipating and even embracing the moment of death, late French Renaissance essayist Michel de Montaigne recommended the only way to a meaningful life is for individuals to exercise insouciance in the face of the inevitable and, in particular, relinquish one's fear of death:

> For as it is impossible for the soul to be at rest when she fears death, so, if she can gain assurance against it, she can boast of a thing as it were beyond man's estate: that it is impossible for worry, torment [or] fear. … She is made mistress of her passions and lusts, mistress over indigence, shame, poverty, and all other wounds of fortune. … this is the true and sovereign liberty, which enables us to thumb our noses at force and injustice and to laugh at prisons and chains (Montaigne 1991: 94, 95).

For Montaigne, the folly of irrationality and the fear of death could be eradicated if the mind were to be disciplined by philosophy because the 'entire life of philosophers is a contemplation of death'; the business of learning to die is deemed necessary for learning to live 'free from all subjection and constraint' (1991: 92). Urging individuals to divest death of its unfamiliarity by habituating oneself to the idea of mortality, he advises:

> That same journey from death to life which you once made without suffering or fear, make it again from life to death. Your death is part of the order of the universe; it is part of the life of the world (Montaigne 1991: 103).

For lawgivers to engage in this kind of philosophical reasoning in relation to the hitherto impenetrable issue of assisted dying or, as it is often referred to, assisted suicide, requires imagination, and both personal and cultural resourcefulness. Moreover, addressing the conflict between the twin values of life and freedom requires a deeper interrogation of the traditional background assumption that all suicide is *prima facie* a sign of mental disorder or other psychopathological state.

As a modern response the commonly held opinion that suicide is always an indication of pathology, Joris Vandenberghe (Professor of Psychiatry at the University of Leuven and a member of the Belgian Advisory Committee on Bioethics) suggests 'there is a whole philosophical history of looking at suicide as a rational choice. We, as humans, have the possibility to weigh our own life and decide to end it' (Aviv 2015: 25). Existential and nihilist philosophers similarly argue that, in an absurd and unfair world, life has no intrinsic value or meaning; that there is no consensus on the 'greatest or supreme good', and therefore no reason not to commit suicide. Rather, individuals must justify not committing suicide by making choices that create a meaningful life, and fulfil their unique potential through this meaning. Otherwise, as Montaigne points out,

> if you have never learned to use life, if life is useless to you, what does it matter if you have lost it? … [However] if you have profited from life, you have had your fill, why not withdraw from life like a guest replete? (1991: 103).

In *Being and Nothingness* Jean-Paul Sartre stated that accepting responsibility for leading a reflective life begins with the realisation that 'we are alone', with no other purpose than the one we set ourselves and no other destiny than the one we choose to forge (Sartre 1956: 489). Besides, as he muses in 'The Metamorphosis', 'One is still what one is going to cease to be and already what one is going to become. One lives one's death, one dies one's life', in which case the entire meaning of life is contained in one's death (Sartre 2012: 2).

In his essay 'A Custom of the Isle of Cea' (Cos), which presented arguments on both sides of the debate, Montaigne concluded that suicide was a personal choice and a perfectly reasonable moral choice in certain situations, noting that 'pain and the fear of a worse death seem to me the most excusable incitements' (1991: 407). It follows that only by the application of emotion-based reasoning is it possible to imagine empathically the horror of a life of unabated pain, humiliation and unendurable suffering (either physical or existential), and a lack of social support when people frequently live alone, having few accommodating family members and friends to rely on. Under such circumstances, according respect for the ability and freedom of individuals to choose between competing conceptions of how to die is just as important as respecting how a person chooses to live their life, leading to the conclusion that 'making someone die in a way others approve, but he believes a horrifying contradiction of his life, is a devastating and odious form of tyranny' (Dworkin 1993: 217). In the modern world where technology can easily prolong a life of physical and mental suffering without improving the quality of that life, it is all the more important that individuals are able to exercise autonomy and free will over their final, yet most significant, expression of radical freedom, unimpeded by a timorous and intransigent legal profession seemingly bedevilled by various forms of irrational obscurantism.

In any case, legal judgment is largely premised on the often arbitrary and *ad hoc* application of universal rules, abstractions and the largely unreflective representation of an experience. Decision-making is therefore not an exact science. Accordingly, to prevent injustice and harm in an increasingly complex, rapidly changing society, it is necessary to question conventional hypotheses and theoretical assumptions; and perhaps judges would be well advised to adopt the attitude, approach or fearless 'way of an iconoclast', as described by Lord Denning:

> It is the way of one who is not content to accept cherished beliefs simply because they have been long accepted. If he finds that they are not suited to the times or that they work injustice, he will see whether there is not some competing principle which can be applied in the case in hand. He will search the old cases, and the writers old and new, until he finds it. ... Once found, this principle will be invoked to modify the old beliefs and to mitigate the injustice produced by them. Only in this way can the law be saved from stagnation and decay (1960: 220).

From the equivocation evidenced by Parliament and the courts in end of life matters to recent examples of a failure to apply what is considered to be fair punishment in cases involving serious sexual crimes in England and Wales, the consequences are troubling for both the individuals concerned and for public confidence in the administration of justice in general. Although the concealment and withholding of crucial evidence (for example, exonerating texts, emails and photographs) 'until the last minute' by the police, and procedural irregularities by the Crown Prosecution Service, has led to the recent collapse of a number of rape trials in the UK, this does not fully explain the current trepidation among members of the judiciary in relation to handing down appropriately punitive sentences in the presence of compelling evidence of guilt (Gibb & Brown 2018: 5).

In order for our judges and law-makers to be prepared to meet the emerging challenges of a rapidly changing world, they must embrace fear as an inevitable part of life; not least of all because when we think constitutionally about the moral and political outcomes of law, then 'we are afraid not only for ourselves but for our fellow citizens as well – we fear a society of fearful people' (Shklar 1998: 11). In this conception of liberal politics, the biggest fear is the politics of fear itself and, above all, collective concentrations of power that make possible institutionalised violence, particularly when justified by the politics of fear. Since time immemorial the primary function of a judge has been to dispense justice, free from the biasing effects of fear or favour. However, it is clear that those members of the judiciary or legislators who are reluctant to make unpopular decisions for fear of giving offence, and who assiduously avoid intellectual and rational-empathic engagement in complex moral and ethical deliberations, will find it almost impossible to be just, reflective and reasoned arbiters of matters that come before them.

Fear, fetish, fantasy and legal framing strategies

Our current era is a product of the political and philosophical project of modernity, which is typified by: *individualisation*, through the obliteration of outmoded earlier forms of communal life, traditional roles and structures committed to the social good; *massification*, through the assumption and enforcement of uniform behaviour and lifestyle, for example via mass media, mass production and mass culture; *desacralisation*, through the displacing of grand religious narratives by a scientific understanding of the world; *rationalisation*, through the pre-eminence of instrumental reason or means–end rationality, as evidenced in the free market model and technical competence, which replaces the quest for reason; and *universalisation*, through the global extension of a model of society or the 'common good' postulated implicitly as the only rational and best option, which fails to recognise a plurality of perspectives. The original essence of the Enlightenment idea of intellectual freedom and imagination, which purported to liberate the individual, has mutated into an ultra-individualism in which social bonds that were once delimited by various institutions have begun to collapse as loyalties have shifted from society to the individual.

As the old notions of family, workplace and nation have become less stable and permanent characteristics of people's lives, everything familiar has had to be reconsidered. Traditional gender roles, racial and religious biases, class consciousness and even the definition of what it means to be human in the age of artificial intelligence, are in the process of being reimagined. Consequently, rather than liberating the individual, a key characteristic of late modernity has been the neutralising of the individual, who is consumed by an interminable onslaught of information, a dizzying array of choices and the proliferation of material objects and devices (requiring continual adaptation and absorption) which mediate oneself and the real world of experience and human practices. The intensifying current of cultural anxiety, a dangerous focus on identity politics and other catastrophic disruptions in cultural life, aligned with an aesthetics of suspicion and insecurity, has produced isolationist attitudes and a contempt for 'otherness', which in turn provides the fuel for society's burgeoning climate of fear.

It is natural to fear what we do not know, what we do not understand and what we do not like – as such unknowns threaten to collapse our world of meaning and the key values that underpin various certainties and realities which attach to that world. Even when fear occurs at the preconscious level, it can still influence the development of particular dispositions, attitudes, opinions and preferences, and acts as a heuristic in making decisions. However, fear also has the function of distortion, by reanimating the ordinary and creating it anew. In so doing, it constitutes a form of fetishising or eroticising the perceived danger, giving it a newly charged significance. This is the difference between our personal experience of an actual threat or danger which is shared and corroborated by others and the representation of that threat in our minds. For Žižek, our fundamental fantasies constitute how we approach reality; but what precedes fantasy is not reality, but an absence or lack in reality, so that 'it is the way we picture the wholly Other that gives us insight into the nature of the repressed trauma, the fantasy, that makes the Other what he is' (1995: 1529).

In the psychoanalytic theory of Jacques Lacan the *objet petit a*, the object of fantasy (of delight or disgust) is not what we desire; rather, it is that which stimulates our desire for something that will resolve the lack or the void that occupies the place where a permanent foundation for identity and meaning would be discovered (1998: 67). It is not itself a signifier, but a conceptual point from which to organise one's signifiers. Described as a fundamental principle and key feature of the human condition of feeling incomplete or helpless, it stimulates a quest for fulfilment. However, being a property of the phantasmic and hallucinatory realm of unconscious desire, the *objet petit a* almost always corresponds to that which has no form or necessary existence. For example, even though we currently enjoy historically unparalleled levels of health and stability, there is a compulsion to experience the self as vulnerable and in a permanent state of peril. The eventual elimination of particular threat and fear objects, such as extremist groups Al-Qaeda and Islamic State (ISIL) as simulations of *object petit a*, will therefore always fail to satisfy the desire for safety and security which motivated their pursuit. Ultimately, to fulfil the object of one's desire by uncovering the lack is to threaten its persistence as the desired object; and because desire is articulated through fantasy, it is driven mostly by its own impossibility. Accordingly, the hallucinatory object can never satisfy the lack; rather, it forever circulates around the focal lacking point which traps and sustains our desires.

Lacan reimagined Descartes' famous *cogito ergo sum* as 'I am not where I think' to illustrate his view that the human mind is not simply a unified entity governed by reason, and that any pretension of self-knowledge is inevitably illusory. Although our fantasies and fears provide a framework through which we experience reality because we are defined by their (our) presuppositions, they deny us an objective interpretation of the world. Underscored by instant access to multiple images and stories, web life has further obscured the fine line separating fantasy from reality. A dizzying variety of online reality destabilising techniques has helped to propagate the fear and confusion necessary to systematically undermine mass belief in pluralist liberal democracy, and in the general goodness of humanity. For example, the perpetuation of post-disaster myths, particularly the myth of widespread looting and violence, not only hinders effective disaster response and recovery but also may justify military intervention and more mundane, everyday governmental exercises of power outside the disaster context by reaffirming that only authoritarian government stands between communities and chaos. Following Hurricane Katrina which devastated New Orleans in 2005, media reports initially framed victim behaviour negatively as urban warfare and civil unrest, on the basis of mainly repeated second-hand accounts of looting, rather than reporting on the overwhelming pro-social altruism and cooperation evidenced by the victims and wider communities. Since most people who would enter shops and homes in disaster zones are either looking for personal possessions belonging to friends and family or searching for clean water, food and clothing, the fear of looting has proven to be more of an issue than looting itself.

Once people are exposed to biased, misleading and especially alarming information they tend to:

> assimilate new information in a biased fashion; those who have accepted false rumours do not easily give up their beliefs, especially when they have a strong emotional commitment to those beliefs; it can be exceedingly hard to dislodge what people think, even by presenting them with the facts (Sunstein 2009: 9).

Adolf Hitler's Nazi regime Minister of Propaganda and Public Enlightenment, Joseph Goebbels, is often credited with stating 'A lie repeated often enough becomes the truth.' The spectral 'Dark Web' or 'Dark Net' (part of the 'Deep Web' and accessible via browsers such as *Tor*, derived from the original software name 'The Onion Router'), is commonly cited as the source of our ten biggest fears; and is routinely portrayed as a depraved marketplace where children, drugs and pirated movies can be purchased for cryptocurrency. Although also used for criminal activities, the Dark Web is claimed to represent the 'World Wide Web' as it was originally envisaged; namely, as a space beyond the control of individual states, where ideas can be exchanged freely without fear of censorship or undue state interference. Beyond the scaremongering, in order to evade censorship and surveillance, citizen journalists in repressive regimes like Iran and China use the Dark Web with good reason, to report local events or call for social change. Similarly, news organisations including the *New York Times* and *The Guardian* routinely accept documents from, and communicate with, anonymous sources secretly and securely over the Dark Web, to promote freedom of information. According to security experts, dissidents and whistleblowers such as Edward Snowden and Julian Assange have been prolific users of the Dark Web. Sites which have exposed government and corporate wrongdoing, such as WikiLeaks, could not exist without the anonymity and privacy provided by the hidden networks that lie beneath the public Internet.

Jennifer Granick, in *American Spies: Modern Surveillance, Why You Should Care, and What to Do About It*, debates the incompatibility of mass surveillance and routine invasions of privacy, with the rule of law and democratic government of, by and for the people:

> It is impossible to know whether judges, lawmakers, and presidents are acting out of principle and allegiance to their understanding of what the public wants

> or out of fear that spies will disclose embarrassing or illegal behaviour. Massive surveillance thwarts citizens pressuring for political change through the risk of criminal prosecution, blackmail, or other threats (2017: 8).

Legislative measures, such as the US Intelligence Community Whistleblower Protection Act 1998 and the UK Public Interest Disclosure Act 1998, fail to offer adequate legal protection against retaliation, discrimination or prosecution for individuals who make public allegations in good faith. Members of the European Parliament recently called for the European Commission to launch an 'EU-wide protection plan' to support and protect whistleblowers who reveal 'serious breaches of the public interest' including corruption, miscarriages of justice, tax avoidance, lack of protection for food safety or the environment and attacks on social, human or workers' rights' (Europa 2017). Currently, legal protections are not only weak but the rules also vary from country to country, meaning whistleblowers can face sanctions preventing them from speaking out and severe reprisals when they do. Given the precarious nature of whistleblowing, the Deep Web site *Dead Man Zero* even offers the possibility for informers to have their information automatically published if they are kidnapped, imprisoned, injured or eliminated.

By disparaging whistleblowers such as Assange and Snowden, advocates for unrestrained mass surveillance and bulk data collection can influence public opinion without having to engage with, or by diverting attention from, the real question which relates to whether governments are out of control in spying on their citizens, and whether there is anything to be done about what is, at the very least, a serious violation of human rights. As Snowden (using the code name 'Verax' or truth-teller) said in one of his emails to Barton Gellman of *The Washington Post*, 'at this point in history, the greatest danger to our freedom and way of life comes from the reasonable fear of omniscient State powers kept in check by nothing more than policy documents' (Gellman 2013). It is only because of the *Tor* network software, which allows anonymous access to the Dark Web, that Edward Snowden was able to send information about the surveillance program PRISM to both *The Washington Post* and *The Guardian* in June 2013.

In this post-truth age of the spectacle, hyperbole and fake news (characterised by differentiated truths and lies, clichés, omissions and distortions), it is becoming harder to contain the retributive fury swelling up in modern (un-) civil society. With daily reports of an agglomeration of angry, alienated and frustrated individuals resorting to extreme levels of violence, from road rage to serious gun crimes, the remainder of the population must increasingly rely on the fictions conjured up by their imaginations to maintain control over their darkest fears and illicit desires. As Manderson points out, it is impossible not to 'react to the images and sensory input to which we are constantly exposed and which, by their symbolic associations, significantly influence our values and our society' (2000: ix). A pertinent question then arises in relation to the nature of images and stories we choose (or are nudged towards by persuasive computer algorithms) to consume, absorb and share, along with what views and prejudices these choices affirm, construct or deny, as well as the means by which these are expressed and interpreted by others. Even so, the framing of events by the media and social institutions helps to shape and galvanise public opinion. The way in which an issue or event is framed, for example how the relevant facts are assembled, interpreted and applied, will often determine its status, how the problem is defined, probable causes and lastly construct a moral judgment which signifies a set of 'appropriate' reactions and solutions. As George Lakoff explains,

> Framing is critical because a frame, once established in the mind of the reader (or listener, viewer, etc.), leads that person almost inevitably to the conclusion desired by the framer, and it blocks consideration of other possible facts and interpretations (2004: 2).

Acquired knowledge, once selectively integrated into both the background and foreground as justification, then serves to provide a sound basis and framework for further deliberation or action on a particular issue. If the facts inconveniently fail to fit the established frames, the frames tend to remain while the facts are disregarded or reinterpreted. Disaster myths of looting, social disorganisation and deviant behaviour persist in spite of evidence that altruistic social behaviour and group bonding are the post-disaster norms, as communities rally around to help each other adjust to, and cope with, abnormal and adverse circumstances. The 'looting frame' – constructed and perpetuated by the US media who have tended to focus their reporting on the putative lawless behaviour of specifically young black males – has been instrumental in shaping post-disaster policy, and continues to be used to justify actions undertaken by military and law enforcement agencies in response to emergency situations (Tierney et al 2006: 61–66). At the same time, a fear of the possibility of looting has led community residents to ignore evacuation warnings and remain in their homes, risking injury and loss of life.

Although the law is a meaning-making institution and framing is often presented as merely a straightforward way of fixing the boundaries or organising the material facts of a case, it is an interpretive and dynamic process and the symbolic utility of particular legal frames cannot be underestimated. Skilful and imaginative use of language transforms an event, report of an incident or an impression, from the realms of the ordinary and mundane by providing a heightened concept of sensory associative experience which produces the mythic perspective. The associative, expressive, attitudinal and evaluative meanings transmitted by various narrative devices, including framing, necessarily serve as an essential part of an underlying, invisible organising principle of the legal institution, comprising a connotative order of signification. As Edwards elaborates:

> when we talk about legal authority, using the logical forms of rules and their bedfellows of analogy, policy, and principle, we are actually swimming in a sea of narrative, oblivious to the water around us. It is not surprising that we have

> failed to consider that narrative pervades the analysis of legal authorities. As the old Buddhist saying goes, we don't know who discovered the ocean, but it probably wasn't a fish (2010: 884).

This wider referential order also comprises legal fictions and facilitates the construction of 'myths', in the sense of the legal culture's conceptualisation of abstract ideas and principles which appeal to an aestheticised ideal of community. Most laws are not articulated in explicit form; nor are they carefully considered by the general populace. Rather, legal dogma operates invisibly in the community, being to the greatest extent uncritically accepted and shared by others as taken-for-granted, practical or self-evident common sense. The engendering of social feeling and a sense of partnership with others (characterised by the proximal interpersonal attachments of reciprocity, moral obligation, communal responsibility and trust), when far from being partners or equals, elicits a compliant self-conscious sociability. It is one thing when the myriad false intimacies, fake communal bonds and pretend friendships relate to the intentionally artificial and disembodied world of social media; however, when the inauthentic sense of community is applied to digitally unmediated lived experience it appears to legitimate, by failing to interrogate, truth claims – in this case the myth of a unified and equal legal community. For Foucault such legal fictions are part of what he describes as 'regimes of truth' in which reality is constructed, historically and politically, according to the singular vision of powerful institutions of civil society (1980: 131). These regimes or narratives of truth are claimed to control and monitor the production of discourse, including legal discourse. Accordingly, the individual is reconstituted in relation to a particular prevailing cultural or political ideology within which language creates and contextualises the social subject.

Produced 'only by virtue of multiple forms of constraint', regimes of truth are well-versed and practised at suppressing alternative truths, while simultaneously obscuring their own ontology (Foucault 1980: 131). This policing exercise legitimates the authenticity of law's truths as the only truth which allows the legal culture, its dogma, practices, traditions, principles and rules to be conceptualised in all aspects according to a singular vision. The presentation of law's truth as a timeless entity, resolutely ahistorical and having no discernible beginning or end is reminiscent of George Orwell's infamous Ministry of Truth which was tasked with 'reality control' in his famous dystopian novel *Nineteen Eighty-Four*. Reality control referred to the imperative to ensure that all language, art, literary works and the mass media echoed the approved narrative promoted by the state. The primary function of the Ministry of Truth was to promulgate the doctrine of the perpetual 'mutability of the past', meaning the past was to be erased and the erasure forgotten, thereby ensuring that 'the lie would pass into history and become the truth' (Orwell 1949: 164). Just as for the citizens of Oceania, the wilful destruction of all textual records and historical proofs meant 'the past was dead and the future unimaginable', the concerns of protagonist Winston Smith in relation to the denial of objective reality were irreducibly linguistic (Orwell 1949: 29). Similarly, in non-fictional modern society, structures of power such as law and the state set out what is true and false, the means by which each is authorised, how truth is acquired and the status of those entrusted with determining what counts as true; and it becomes difficult, if not impossible, to be defined outside of these discursive formulations (Shaw & Shaw 2016: 33, 34). Moreover, since law's narratives of truth are constructed through the artful manipulation of language, the corollary must be that language is the principal site of struggle and resistance within which the control of meaning is the winner's prize.

Legal truths and truisms, moral metaphors and moral panic

Law has often been referred to by legal scholars as an aesthetic enterprise. For Peter Goodrich 'law is a literature which denies its literary qualities'; and, according to Pierre Schlag, '[b]efore the ethical dreams and political ambitions of law can even be articulated, let alone realised ... aesthetics have already shaped the medium within which those projects will have to do their work' (1996: 112; 2002: 1049). Beyond simply recognising the aesthetic qualities of the legal institution, it is necessary to appreciate how legal dogma, principle, rules and argument are frequently motivated, maintained and confined by the aesthetics through which they are represented and performed. Much of English law is replete with lyrical and mythic imagery, which resonates from ancient times to modern life. The intellectual connection between myth and language is metaphor, as metaphors amplify the expressive nature of language. In *The King's Two Bodies* (1957), Ernst Kantorowicz traces the construction of theological metaphors by English common law jurists for secular political ends to reinforce the secular power of the medieval and early modern state, beginning with an analysis of one of the earliest legal uses of metaphor in the 1571 Reports of Edmund Plowden. Far from being mere embellishment, metaphor is still the main methodological tool in the formation of legal principle, and is fundamental to both the construction and critique of legal theory.

One of the most significant findings of modern cognitive science is that people tend to think in terms of the conceptual structures of frames and metaphors. Metaphors are a necessary part of thought itself, including legal thought, as they frame our conceptions into specific patterns and categories which, in turn, assist in the formation of judgment. They have a compelling representational function, standing in for or substituting the very things they merely symbolise, which is perhaps why metaphors are commonly taken for granted and treated as expressions of literal truth and reality. From this premise, reality can be understood as something we experience metaphorically, and 'legal truths' and legal truisms are therefore nothing more than metaphorical constructions which have become normalised to the point where their metaphoricity has been forgotten. As summarised by Nietzsche, in 'On Truth and Falsity in their Ultramoral Sense', there can be no literal truths because language comprises nothing but figures of speech, and so all truth is necessarily comprised of metaphors:

> What therefore is truth? A mobile army of metaphors, metonymies, anthropomorphisms: in short a sum of human relations which became poetically and rhetorically intensified, metamorphosed, adorned, and after long usage seem to a notion fixed, canonic and binding; truths are illusions of which one has forgotten that they are illusions; worn-out metaphors which have become powerless to affect the senses (1974: 80).

From this perspective, it would be impossible to imagine that a single interpretative framework, as proposed by the 'exact sciences', could explain all the nuances of our world of experience; for example, the aesthetic, historical and cultural relevance of music. In *Beyond Good and Evil*, Nietzsche professes the desire to have done with a 'will to truth' that ultimately prefers 'a handful of certainty' over 'an entire wagon full of beautiful possibilities' (1966: 10). That is to say, we sacrifice what makes us human, our imaginations, creativity and 'beautiful minds', when we opt for bare predictability, precision and an absence of doubt, usually distinguished by a paucity of expressive language.

While Nietzsche's claim that philosophical and legal enquiry can be grounded only on purely rhetorical foundations is open to challenge, it is evident that metaphoric speech is often used to express higher-order values. This led Aristotle to caution that a sense of 'appropriateness for the occasion, audience and situation' was essential, adding that 'the greatest thing by far is to be a master of metaphor ... since a good metaphor implies an intuitive perception of the similarity in dissimilars' (1995: 23.5). In response to his admonition to always choose a metaphor which is appropriate to its context, it is incumbent on lawmakers to consider carefully how a particular representation may communicate ideological bias; especially since the inopportune exercise of figurative language may result in some degree of moral ambiguity when implemented by ruling authorities such as judges and the government.

In *Law, Text, Terror* (2009), Ian Ward presents an eloquent argument for the inherent textuality of the law. He uses the example of 'terror' to explain how the use of figurative allusion, hyperbole and metaphor have been essential to crafting laws and policies which have framed 'terrorism' as a social construction rather than a physical fact. Recent research within critical legal scholarship has further suggested that the cultural embeddedness of fear within law and the current trend for catastrophic imagining, which has provoked often unfounded intrusions on civil liberties, can only be properly understood within the context of aesthetic expression, mythologies, fantasies and mystical discourses (Shaw 2013: 128–129).

Popular formulations of fear are framed and focused according to the idiosyncrasies of culture. The prevalent culture of fear includes fear of the unknown, fear of the stranger, fear of ageing (accompanied by the familiar exhortation to consume more products to 'fight' the signs of advancing years), fear of the future and, more recently, the fear of a 'zombie apocalypse' (Pettit 2017: 6). Such fears are asserting their increasing influence in myriad ways. Insecurity is one of the key drivers of modern society and, for example, the framing of the threat to security of global terrorism has emerged through specific social processes that have elevated what is a justifiable concern beyond the usual political logic. Consequently, everyday life has been subject to a radical restructuring in order to justify actions taken by ruling authorities beyond the legitimately established boundaries of political and legal practice, and in most instances these have eluded public debate.

The similarities between Franz Kafka and George Orwell, in relation to the controlling environment of constant fear and the panoptic discipline of the surveillance state, are centred on the struggle against a power that is too large for any individual to fight and too powerful for any one person to make a meaningful impact. The alacrity with which people willingly relinquish their rights in modern life, in the face of innumerable terrors, is more reminiscent of the surreal world of Joseph K in Kafka's *The Trial* (2009) than Orwell's *Nineteen Eighty-Four*. The sentencing for an unnamed crime at the hands of an unnamed court, along with a seemingly endless progression of judges and advocates who operate covertly, is not only reminiscent of the extension of secret trials into the main civil courts in the UK (sanctioned by the Justice and Security Act 2013); Kafka's novel seems to foreshadow the modern world in many other respects. Not understanding why or knowing who or what is influencing new laws, which seem in some instances to operate beyond the boundaries of the rule of law, or why there is a dearth of counterbalancing protective legislative measures, why we are often uninformed and which actors or agencies are to be held responsible for acts or omissions, we have no idea who or what organisations are really in control and how it is that we frequently seem to have few or no choices. Our only recourse as uninformed and unrepresented citizens may be to try and fight an unfair, opaque, incomprehensible and unaccountable system; but ultimately resistance may be futile.

Although public safety and crime prevention are legitimate aims, the imposition of Kafkaesque cybersecurity mechanisms (augmented by sweeping suspicion-less surveillance and monitoring) is driven primarily by the demands of an often exaggerated and orchestrated culture of fear, rather than as a response to the actual experience or corresponding incidence of crime (van Munster 2011: 147; Shaw & Shaw 2015: 239). As exposed by Snowden in 2013, the obsessive information-gathering activities of the intelligence services are typically beyond the reaches of law and regulation; and yet the profound implications for privacy and human rights, arising from the corporatisation of political power, tend to be disregarded. Intrusive and far-reaching legislative provisions – such as the US Computer Fraud and Abuse Act (CFAA) 1986 and proposed amendment to the US Active Cyber Defense Certainty Act (ACDC) 2018, the UK Regulation of Investigatory Powers Act (RIPA) 2000, the UK Data Retention and Investigatory Powers Act (DRIPA) 2014, the amended UK Computer Misuse Act (CMA) 1990 by the UK Serious Crime Act (SCA) 2015 and the UK Investigatory Powers Act (IPA) 2016 (the so-called 'Snooper's Charter') – are some of the more insidious examples of sweeping information-gathering powers given to government intelligence agencies and private actors such as local councils, law enforcement authorities and private security companies.

At the same time as various rogue states are hacking the servers of their adversaries in Western Europe or North America, intelligence agencies such as the CIA and GCHQ are creating vulnerabilities in their domestic communication networks by interfering with smart televisions and exploiting loopholes in our operating systems. Consequently, the growth and maintenance of the surveillance capabilities of democratic governments assumes a permanent structural insecurity of our own communication networks. As mentioned earlier, a significant number of acts, directives and regulations provide legal justification for private organisations, governments and their intelligence agencies to spy on individuals, to hack and collect personal data at will. However, in relation to the cyber activities of non-state sanctioned hackers, little account is taken of the ethical distinction between, for instance, *bricoleurs* or tinkerers, whose sole purpose is to find the ultimate hack or a disruptive but non-violent UFO obsessive motivated by curiosity, and those whose intentions are commercially damaging, or organised networks whose ambition is to kill.

The metaphors of disease, including virus, contagion and quarantine, are routinely employed in relation to individual hackers, and existing legal remedies relating to criminal activity such as theft, burglary and trespass are used to justify a range of severe punishments. Even though theft, burglary and trespass have an 'ordinary' meaning in the material world, and are subject to a clear, albeit broad interpretation in English law, when applied to the abstract realm of cyberspace they are often given a more generous interpretation to justify harsher treatment than their more measurable physical equivalent: there is a consistent tendency towards over-prosecution (Shaw 2017: 97). Under the CMA 1990, for instance, computer trespass is treated as a more serious offence than actual trespass, and carries a broader and more punitive range of sanctions.

While computer crime is an increasing menace in society and there is a need for national and international law that allows the possibility of strong sentences for serious online offences, such laws must be drafted in a way that does not harshly prosecute those whose cyber actions amount to no more than the metaphorical theft of a loaf of bread. Not only would this represent a significant move toward basic justice as fairness, but it would also enable law enforcement agencies to focus on serious computer crimes rather than nuisance events. At present, by metaphorically associating all hackers with contamination, infection and robbery, even inconsequential or ill-judged actions are routinely transformed into pathological and predatory behaviour, which often, inappropriately or disproportionately, demonises the perpetrator and legitimates a control ethos in law-making. Moreover, in relation to the 'war on terror', framing expansive and invasive legislation on the premise that electronic communication is the principal means of orchestrating acts of terror is a *non sequitur* as, after all, Attila and his marauding hordes of barbarian Huns, evil dictators such as Adolf Hitler, the ferocious Vikings and other terrorising aggressors managed to communicate efficiently before the World Wide Web. Also, more recently, so-called lone wolf attacks have proliferated where there was an absence of co-conspirators, and the only equipment needed by the perpetrator was a large vehicle or the necessary materials to fabricate a home-made explosive device. The assault on our freedom of expression, right to privacy and way of life by draconian legal interventions is considered by many within legal scholarship to be disproportionate under the circumstances. Ian Ward has described a juristic 'black hole', consequent upon a 'collateral absence of voice' by law-makers in relation to the insidious 'real war' which has intensified since 9/11. The objective of this real war is claimed to be 'to control our thoughts, constrain our expression and crush our sense of humanity' (2009: 179).

The socially structured idealisation of a world at 'war' with terror has, without doubt, stoked social fears and obsessions in relation to the likelihood of a violent, sudden death, and is responsible for triggering moral panics. Moral panics occur when a hyper-mediated representation of an action or event creates a 'spectacle' which intensifies negative emotions such as fear, confounds reason and galvanises public opinion (Debord 1994: 12). While major terrorist attacks, such as those which have occurred in France, Germany, Sweden and Belgium, signify global terrorism as an ongoing danger, the use of the metaphors of disease and contamination, and in this case enemies and other military metaphors, to accompany scaremongering stories in the media and political discourse has mass-encultured a fear of acts of 'terror' which is disproportionate given the fortunately infrequent occurrence of major incidents. The preoccupation with terrorism marginalises long-term, yet more endemic, mortality risks such as cancer, heart disease and dementia that require global political engagement and a greater commitment to national government research funding. Statistically, according to a report from the World Economic Forum (WER), there is also a greater likelihood of being killed as a result of homicide than by terrorist violence (Muggar 2016). As a former US National Security Advisor famously stated in respect of the 'war on terror', 'the damage these three words have done is infinitely greater than any wild dreams entertained by the fanatical perpetrators of the 9/11 attacks. It defines neither a geographic context nor our presumed enemies' (Brzezinski 2007: 3).

The culturally encoded, and often hysterical, imagistic representation of unsettling events not only creates lasting cultural traumas, but is also effective at fostering fear and suspicion of others and difference, leading to the creation of categories of people whom the law excludes. In response to ubiquitous calls for greater security measures to 'combat' the war on terror, continuous surveillance and categories of exclusion – referred to by Giorgio Agamben as *homo sacer* – have been imposed on individuals and social groups with particular characteristics. Reminiscent of the concentration camps of Nazi Germany, by separating the 'accursed' individual, or 'bare life', from the rest of humanity through various means of isolation, such as emergency legislation, rendition and detention centres, entire categories of people are relocated outside the protection of the law. Once a national crisis has been determined, civil liberties are readily eschewed, and deemed to be luxuries rather than basic human rights. The implicit adoption of a permanent 'state of exception', therefore, constitutes a paradox, as it elaborates a theory of law to account for the existence of a sphere of human activity not subject to law. This paradoxical formulation is alleged by Agamben to comprise 'a *fictio iuris* par excellence which claims to maintain the law in its very suspension'; however, instead it yields a violence that has in fact 'shed every relation to law' (2005: 59).

Counterterrorism measures such as the imposition of tighter controls on vehicle rentals, expansion of electronic surveillance, greater censorship of the Internet and, even more contentious, allowing the preventive detention of suspects and the installation of monitors on all laptops and mobile devices at the time of manufacture have all been recently proposed by domestic and external security agencies. Similarly, recent proposals to introduce extreme vetting in the US have attracted criticism, since there is a real danger that innocent people who pose no threat will be excluded, or even deported, due to bureaucratic errors and inaccuracies. Such harsh responses not only assume that all acts of terror can be prevented, but also perfectly evoke the spectre of an Orwellian police state. That is not to say there is no threat of violence in society – as a range of international treaties and laws have been drafted over the years to deal with many such instances and emergencies on both a large and small scale; rather, it is the impulsive and violent response of policy-makers which presents a real threat to objectivity, reason and the rule of law. As Ian Ward argues, the post-9/11 counter-terrorist rhetoric which urged 'trust' in the government to deflect the 'threat' of future acts of terror, elicits more fear than the terrifying acts of violence themselves (2009: 36–37).

Because of their reliance on legal justifications, counter-terrorism policies and practices proposed by the British government have encountered some, albeit limited, degree of jurisprudential resistance. Addressing the incompatibility of detaining terrorist suspects without trial with certain provisions of the European Convention on Human Rights (ECHR) in the Belmarsh Prison case, Lord Hoffmann stated in *A and others v Secretary of State for the Home Department* [2004] UKHL 56 at 97 that the word 'life', as in 'threat to the life of the nation', is to be understood only in a metaphorical sense because 'the life [or spirit] of the nation is not coterminous with the [actual] lives of its people. The nation, its institutions and values, endure through generations.' He warned against reactionary laws that are passed hastily, having been debated in a period of disorientation, arguing that they are likely to be based on clouded judgment and flawed reasoning. Legislation which amounts to a disproportionate interference with human rights – such as the now invalidated EU Data Retention Directive (DRD) 2006, enacted after the 2004 Madrid and 2005 London terrorist attacks – is too often the consequence of a purely emotional response, or fearful reaction to shock experienced in the wake of a crisis that seems to have transformed the familiar world. Milton Friedman stated in the preface to the reissue of his 1962 manifesto *Capitalism and Freedom*:

> Only a crisis – actual or perceived – produces real change. When that crisis occurs, the actions that are taken depend on the ideas that are lying around. … our basic function [is] to develop alternatives to existing policies, to keep them alive and available until the politically impossible becomes the politically inevitable (2009: 14).

Fear induces panic which, in turn, not only exaggerates danger or the threat of harm; as Nussbaum points out, 'it makes our moment much more dangerous than it would otherwise be [and] more likely to lead to genuine disasters' (2018: 34). However, maintaining an environment of fear, and creating moral panics, as a way of controlling society has been a habitual means of manipulation used by policy-makers to gain support for unpopular economic and social policies – such as the privatisation of national industries, social welfare cuts and draconian forms of legislation – that would otherwise have been rejected under normal circumstances. Because what we fear typically goes hand in hand with what kinds of laws we pass, Michael Williams recommends adopting a 'critically aware fear of fear and its possibility for strategic manipulation' (2011: 460). In this case, our policy-makers and lawgivers would ideally always be prepared to interrogate the claims and decisions that are made ostensibly to counter popular fears, and to be vigilant, circumspect and sceptical in relation to the possibilities created by the politics of fear. In both instances, the objective of the critical approach would be to compel discussion as to whether, and to what extent, such policies or practices can be legally and morally justified.

Reimagining the foundations for justice: overcoming the new politics of fear

In ancient Greek mythology, Phobos (fear or dread) and Deimos (terror) were the names given to the twins of Aphrodite, the goddess of love, and her lover Ares, the narcissistic, slow-witted and drunken god of war. While Deimos represented the terror brought about by humans by engaging in war, Phobos represented the systematic use of fear for political ends which has frequently been portrayed as an essential instrument of government. While ruling elites are small in number, they have the upper hand because they can control the masses through the cultivation of fear. As Machiavelli suggests in *The Prince* 'since some men love as they please but fear when the prince pleases, a wise prince should rely on what he controls, not on what he cannot control' (1950: 98). Even now, our social institutions – such as law, state, education and economy – use the politics of fear as a means of applying subtle force, to make people comply with otherwise unpopular government edicts and to instil civic obedience. This is often achieved by orchestrating a climate of fear in relation to the idea of some future apocalypse with which to strike terror into the hearts of a majority of the people. In our modern era of mistrust in authority when all the grand ideas have lost credibility, aside from physical restraint, manufacturing the fear of a phantom adversary is most likely the only effective way in which politicians can maintain their power.

Michael Crichton, in his novel *State of Fear*, describes a political–legal–media complex which is committed to promoting fear in the population under the guise of promoting safety. He refers to:

> the requirement of every sovereign state to exert control over the behaviour of its citizens, to keep them orderly and reasonably docile. To keep them

> driving on the right side of the road or the left, as the case may be, to keep them paying taxes ... [and] we know that social control is best managed through fear (2004: 454).

Functioning as far-reaching forms of social control and exploitation, it is unnecessary to coerce the collective will into compliance as people passively accept particular ideological conceptions validated by the law and instruments of legal authority. This not only applies to sovereign powers and governments, but in an age of artificial superintelligence and innovative new technologies, those who 'own' these vast networks of information and innovation, comprise the new 'structures of domination' (Fuchs 2008: 114). As our technologies continue to advance, and reconstitute the relationship between architectural constructions, urban territories, media, law, politics and social practices, our thinking and behaviour also adapts in response to the evolving technology- and media-driven environment.

Just as the economic capital accumulated by the knowledge industry is invested in the manipulation of reality and truth and the privileging of particular interests, the application of sensationalist metaphoric expressions by the media and in political discourse legitimates further draconian and intrusive legal interventions. The news media already acts as a proxy for public opinion, and its constant feed and endless supply of sensational events and breaking news – which often lack meaningful content, context or perspective – creates more fear and panic, which legitimates the imposition of further oppressive legislative reforms (Baudrillard 1995). Keeping people perpetually overwhelmed and confused means there is no need for physical force to exert control over society; it only requires the use of subtle tactics and techniques, including propaganda, suppression of information, obscurantism and the inculcation of implicit understandings of what counts as credible, and how credibility is measured. In *Welcome to the Desert of the Real* Slavoj Žižek suggests that the 'false terms' designated to fundamental concepts such as democracy, freedom, human rights and the 'war on terror' have been co-opted by law, mask their origins and only serve to mystify our 'perception of the situation instead of allowing us to think it' (2002: 2). In this precise sense, our freedoms themselves constitute a precarious autonomy and only sustain our deeper 'unfreedom'. Accordingly, the aim of the real 'war' would seem to be intellectual oppression, the constraint of free expression, and to crush our collective sense of humanity.

The erosion of the twentieth-century's political belief systems and social structures has left many people feeling disengaged, insecure and fearful. Unable to summon a positive outlook on a situation or imagine a positive future, fear is the most pervasive, and one of the key defining, political and cultural emotions of late modernity, and has affected political action, legislative reform and social relations. Since the arts and humanities often reflect and represent common sensibilities by presenting them in ways not yet articulated by discursive means, a clear indicator of the increasing incidence of fear is the proliferation of literary and cinematic narratives portraying the total collapse of civilisation, dystopias, disaster and impending apocalypse. The end of the world is a common theme in recent novels and movies, and for sociologist and philosopher Zygmunt Bauman this is the ultimate social fear. In *Liquid Fear*, the 'forced' openness and connectedness of the current globalised world order is blamed as the primary source of insecurity (2006: 97). The intensification of global (physical) interaction and (virtual) interconnectedness is stated to have produced not only positive outcomes such as the free movement of capital and investment, and the dissemination of knowledge and innovation, but is also perceived as producing negative consequences: for example, wage depression, greater competition for essential social goods and welfare services, the importation of contagious diseases and transnational organised crime (Andreas 2011: 407). Consequently, over the last few years, films about zombie uprisings have been especially popular – a phenomenon which speaks to common fears concerning epidemics and the porous nature of socio-cultural, political and physical boundaries in relation to a particularly dark depiction of 'illicit globalisation'.

Dystopian speculative literature and cinematic works have always blurred the line between fiction and reality in their vivid portrayal of the myths, alarmist misconceptions and anxieties conjured up by our worst imaginings. The recent television adaptation of Margaret Atwood's chilling yet plausible *The Handmaid's Tale* (2017) and Jonathan Nolan's *Westworld* (2016) presented two horrifying visions of a dystopian America, mired in chronic political corruption, violence, repression and misogyny. Similarly, US films such as *Pandemic* (2016) and *10 Cloverfield Lane* (2016) and the South Korean *Train to Busan* (2016) all describe a frightening end-of-days world of scarcity, lawlessness, social breakdown, disease and chaos. Considering the daily bombardment of real-life apocalyptic imagery which accompanies news reports, the popularity of films and dramas about ravenous strangers, bioterrorism, plagues and epidemics is hardly surprising.

From extreme weather events, genocides, refugees, cities in rubble, devastating viral outbreaks and the threat of nuclear destruction, these graphic representations provoke and exacerbate the feeling that all human life forms are teetering on the edge of the abyss. However, according to Ritzenhoff and Krewani:

> If you drive through America in certain areas it looks like you are in the apocalypse already; these rundown houses that are boarded up, people who are homeless, entire downtowns with one storefront after another that are empty, roads falling apart. The apocalypse is not these child-eating monsters or the comets that hit us. The apocalypse comes from inside. It really is all the choices we make as a society that render us uncivilised (2015: 5).

Such everyday realities of poverty, homelessness and inequality not only call into question the current 'order of things' or 'the fundamental codes of a culture'; they also negate the traditional belief in societal advancement (Foucault 2002: xxii). Consequently, these mundane and seemingly unremarkable occurrences represent more worthy and legitimate objects of terror, instead of the relative 'safe place' of cannibalistic zombie outbreak narratives from which to explore a set of (as yet) unrealised apocalyptic prophecies. The experience of genuine horror would, therefore, be more appropriately elicited by growing evidence of the inexorable rise of the urban poor, and the very wretchedness and precarity of ordinary life for those who live on the margins of society, along with increasing levels of inhumanity that challenge traditional humanitarian values. There is, for example, an increasing normalisation of, and desensitisation to, the atrocities and privations resulting from irresponsible economic and political strategies, and from the devastating effects of the policies and practices of often unaccountable regimes of governance on a wide range of individuals and communities. Dystopian literature nevertheless performs an important function by depicting a nightmarish future in order to launch a critique of the present which intrudes on our preconceptions, and disrupts our sense of security by challenging established beliefs and values. It lays bare the fragility of the human condition, and by articulating the pain and suffering of fictional characters for a wider audience, has the capacity to inspire greater empathy and a commitment to the promotion of a less divisive and, therefore, less dangerous world.

The contemplation of lives and scenarios which differ from personal experience expands the imaginative capabilities, so that people may make better decisions and our judges may produce better judgments, as the rapidly changing landscape of public life demands. In any event, judges have occasionally resorted to poetic flourishes and imagistic language, providing a distinctive aesthetic experience within which to further elaborate on a point of law or principle. Lord Denning was renowned for his mastery of evocative storytelling, as evidenced in *Hinz v Berry* [1970] 2 QB 40, a case relating to the award of damages for 'nervous shock', in which Mrs Hinz witnessed the death of her husband and injury to her children caused by a runaway car. His opening judgment began with the words 'It happened on April 19 1964. It was bluebell time in Kent', to creatively set the scene for the horrific spectacle of an intrusive 'alien' force, the Jaguar car, which violently devastated the 'natural' and quintessential pastoral idyll of English family life. In this particularly persuasive judgment, Denning relied on a dystopian reimagination of events to foreground a particular conception of English identity with the idea of English law as just, which no doubt helped to ensure this became the first case in which damages were awarded for nervous shock, unconnected with personal injury.

The law, and significantly a just law, is grounded in rational and ethical considerations, for which the core motivation for ethical action is empathy. Equally, 'imagination will often carry us to worlds that never were, but without it we go nowhere'; accordingly, finding new political and legal solutions is to a large extent dependent upon being able to envisage novel scenarios in which innovative methods and hypotheses can be safely tested (Sagan 1980: 57). It is suggested that without the application of the empathic imagination, which can extend itself into the widest reaches of human experience, the law is simply a tool for the powerful to rationalise their position rather than an instrument for social justice in the service of all. For our law-makers, and judges, to be able to meet the transformational challenges of a rapidly changing political, economic, social, cultural and technological world, it must be acknowledged that fear is an unescapable part of modern life. After all, a minimal level of fear is implied in any system of public governance. However, fears which arise in relation to non-interference in the application of unfamiliar scientific and technological innovations, especially where there is significant social impact and implications for civil liberties and freedoms, must be confronted directly by forceful parliamentary debate. Similarly, the type of cross-societally experienced fear which is produced by arbitrary, unexpected, unnecessary and unrestrained acts of force and habitually invasive laws – for example, as part of a shift towards 'security' in its more extreme manifestations – calls for an independent judiciary with the ability to speak up for basic human rights, and to resist and fearlessly challenge the worst excesses of coercive rule.

4 Law as hate

I was angry with my friend;
I told my wrath, my wrath did end.
I was angry with my foe:
I told it not, my wrath did grow.

And I watered it in fears,
Night and morning with my tears:
And I sunned it with smiles,
And with soft deceitful wiles.

And it grew both day and night.
Till it bore an apple bright.
And my foe beheld it shine,
And he knew that it was mine.

And into my garden stole,
When the night had veiled the pole;
In the morning glad I see;
My foe outstretched beneath the tree.

William Blake (1794)

The English legal system comprises an autonomous, rarefied, self-referential and essentially closed network of uniform rules and concepts within which the normative and binding character of legal rules holds sway because the legal institution says it does. While many of the core values, interests and power distributions comprising the legal institution originate from within the wider social community, according to formalists and legal theorist Hans Kelsen (1970) – who insisted on the absolute autonomy of legal thought and action – law finds its foundation entirely within itself. By providing the general categories through which its actions and interpretations are rendered intelligible, law conditions its own applicability. Even in a pluralist society containing smaller communities, each with their own normative order, only the legal system itself has the authority to declare which statutes, regulations and judicial precedents have validity, and which rules and principles must be followed. Inevitably, the claims and demands of this 'Imperial' legal order are deemed to be hierarchically superior and, therefore, are entitled to be definitive and unyielding (Cover 1983: 13). Such laws hold and remain true even if nothing and nobody is subject to them at any given time, and alternative laws or competing views are likely to be de-legitimised because only a limited amount of deviance from the overarching Imperial law can be tolerated.

For those accustomed to thinking of law as a domain of logic and reasoning which has produced a sacral tapestry of settled and consistent principles and rules, some legal scholars have offered alternative readings: for example, the 'indeterminacy of law' thesis, and the broad degree of interpretative leeway allowed to the courts which tends to undermine law's fabled predictability. As legal rules and standards are decided in advance, they are necessarily abstract, which means 'the very feature of law that allows it to operate at the wholesale rather than the retail level – its abstraction – limits its ability to guide concrete decisions taken in the law's name' (Dorf 2003: 883). More than this, for Derrida (1992: 47) '[e]very juridical contract, every *Rechtsvertrag* ("legal contract") is founded on violence. There is no contract that does not have violence as both an origin (*Ursprung*) and an outcome (*Ausgang*)'; and in his essay 'Violence and the Word' (1986), Robert Cover concurs that law is irrevocably linked to the organised violence of the state. State violence preserves the status quo and maintains dominant interests, but it is always exercised in the name of normative ideals – however abstract or general – such as Nation, Peace, God, Law or Humanity, thereby maintaining a veneer of legitimacy. Also the majority of legal systems are the outcome of violence, as a consequence of war, revolution, rebellion or occupation.

The act of law-making is argued by critical theorists to necessitate the assumption of power, via the use of force, in order to ensure law's efficacy. Without enforceability there is no law; this holds true regardless of 'whether this force is direct or indirect, physical or symbolic, exterior or interior, brutal or subtly discursive and hermeneutic, coercive or regulative' (Derrida 1992: 6). Therefore, any attempt to rationalise law must also endeavour to rationalise law's intrinsic violence. This violence is not merely abstract or hypothetical, but is actualised in law's yearning for expansion beyond itself and for purification within its domains. Accordingly, Cover applies the vocabulary of epistemic violence to the activity of legal interpretation, referring to it as practised on 'the field of fear, pain and death'. He elaborates:

> A judge articulates her understanding of a text, and as a result, somebody loses his freedom, his property, his children, even his life. Interpretations in law also constitute justifications for violence which has already occurred or which is about to occur. When interpreters have finished their work, they frequently leave behind victims whose lives have been torn apart by these organized, social practices of violence' (1986: 1601).

Although beneath the unifying claims of the legal order there exists a plurality of diverse peoples and groups, each constituted by their own beliefs and commitments, Cover recognises that neither law nor mainstream legal theorising perceives or accommodates such peoples and groups. Rather, although a legitimate normative ideal or aspiration, the claim that law is impartial and applies equally to all is nothing but a legal fiction and patently untrue (Beckett 2011: 3). From this viewpoint, in the act of affirming and imposing a single interpretation, idea or perspective, every other potential source of law-making is simultaneously destroyed, as the end or aim of law is none other than law itself.

For Goodrich, law is formed and applied by legal representatives who are essentially working with what might be described as 'memories' of law. From this premise, the question then becomes that of 'whose memory [and] whose order of reference does the law institute', as interpreting or 'reading [the law] is never innocent' (Goodrich 1990: 251, 253). Historically grounded in religion, superstition and ritual, law bears the scars of a past replete with ecclesiastical dogma, preconceived notions of what constitutes ordinary morality, along with a range of prejudices which have survived into modern life. The deployment of religious signifiers and rhetorical stratagems by law-makers has been practised throughout time as essential in order to maintain the legitimacy of law and compel obedience. In early European medieval culture, papal letters, court cases and learned treatises on enforcing the law reveal the emotion of hate and the principle of vengeance to be commonplace in judicial processes. Even in late medieval society, litigation and denunciation were often motivated by hate, envy, spite and the desire to ostracise and humiliate. Joan of Arc, for example, famously led the French army to victory over the English at Orléans in 1429; and, after being captured by Anglo-Burgundian forces a year later, she was tried for witchcraft, heresy and for 'dressing like a man', and burned at the stake. Arbitrary decision-making fuelled by vengeful reciprocity was an essential part of medieval law and legal culture, and considered to be a form of justice rather than merely lawless reprisal.

In modern society, many laws and judgments can still be considered to 'consist in a passionate reaction of graduated intensity' (Durkheim 1964: 96). For example, in relation to punishment, the principles of hate, anger and most of all vengeance survive in the already large and rising prison population, in the longer sentences handed down in England and Wales, and in the act of imposing the death penalty in countries such as the US and parts of Africa and Asia (Geoghegan 2018: 3). The infliction of capital punishment for murder is the typical articulation of *talionic* justice or *lex talionis* (an 'eye for an eye') – a form of Old Testament scriptural retributive justice – with the state acting as enforcer and taking vengeance on behalf of the injured party. Important questions arise concerning the application of negative emotions such as hate, anger and revenge which have been, and to some extent still are, responsible for animating oppressive laws, harsh legal principles and vengeful legal judgments. This chapter addresses the origins and character of these destructive passions – characterised by the permanent threat of institutional violence, endless revenge and collective hatred – which are alleged to comprise the clandestine cornerstone of society and are essential to the foundation, operation and legitimisation of law.

Law's symbolic violence: use of linguistic coercion in the constitution of the legal order

Power is the central organising principle of all social life, and all epochs are distinguished by their particular practices of knowledge and strategies of power, which are derived from regimes of truth-making, authenticity and the procedures of authoritative expression. Our sense of reality and of those laws which shape our experience of the real world by which we are determined and controlled is therefore constructed from the dominant standpoint. The dominant party determines appropriate forms of action and behaviour, and acquires legitimacy for the arbitrary configuration of power relations, through the complicity of the dominated. Yet, due to the subtlety of these practices and the disposition of the oppressed group, the bars of the iron cage are rendered almost invisible to those incarcerated within their confines. The concealment of the foundations of knowledge production industries such as law – which *inter alia* perpetuate the normalisation of particular stereotypes, nurture tolerance towards specific kinds of aggression and facilitate the legitimisation of certain power relations and hierarchies – allows for the construction of discriminatory practices that may become a breeding ground for hate and, in turn, legitimate the use of various forms of symbolic violence. Accordingly, the 'established order, with its relations of domination, its rights and prerogatives, privileges and injustices, ultimately perpetuates itself so easily' precisely because legal dogma is ingrained in the cognitive structures of individuals, to the point where it needs no justification (Bourdieu 2001: 1).

The force of law and legal culture is transmitted through its traditions, education and professional practices, and is resistant to competing forms of alternative legal practice in the wider social field. Notwithstanding the recent popularity and proliferation of informal and social means of resolving conflicts beyond the limits of the courtroom – for example, what is now commonly referred to as 'appropriate' or 'proportionate' dispute resolution processes, incorporating agreement-based alternative dispute resolution (ADR) (mediation and conciliation) and adjudicative ADR (arbitration and tribunals), also online dispute resolution (ODR) – their wider reach and impact is limited (McGregor 2015: 607). Even these new forms of 'arbitration' are still viewed as a lesser alternative to litigation, and tend to focus on the relatively narrow economic and private-commercial aspects of disputes rather than public policy concerns. This is because the determination of public standards of justice is outside the remit of this 'privatised' system of justice. As such, the courts remain the chief arbiter of disagreements, since their decisions alone set legal precedents and affirm law's supremacy as the only state-sanctioned body capable of articulating wide-ranging societal standards of justice.

That assumptions relating to the unrivalled rationality and infallibility of law go unchallenged testifies not only to law's veiled 'symbolic violence' but also to the conflicted relationship between law and justice. Justice is considered by many legal scholars to be an inherent part of the law, not separate or distinct from it; and, more significantly, the law of necessity incorporates considerations of justice. In his introduction to *A Theory of Justice*, following H.L.A. Hart, John Rawls (1999) distinguishes *concepts* of justice from *conceptions* of justice. While the former relate to formal ideals of law, such as equal treatment, absence of bias and impartiality, the latter are commonly bound together with notions of ethical justification and moral motivation, providing the perfect non-juridical principle (Shaw 2018a: 26–27). Sometimes referred to as the law-of-law or the conscience of law, it is always compromised by its own legal form which, for Derrida, destroys the very possibility of justice as a non-normative transcendent concept (1992: 3–67).

An *aporia*, the expression of doubt between law and justice, is particularly evident with reference to ethical and moral duties purportedly owed to the Other, in light of the disjunctive force of suffering and aggression simultaneously perpetuated in the space of power occupied by legal force. It is, therefore, the enterprise of law as control, often with menaces, which comprises 'the monopoly and codification of authorised and organised public violence', and 'prescribes what constitutes a reasonable order, by accepting and validating some parts of collective life … while excluding others, making them invisible' (Goodrich 1990: 174; Douzinas 2007: 298). Derrida describes the authority of law as an 'authorised force, which is founded on 'mystical violence', and finds '*there is no such thing as law that does not imply in itself, a priori, in the analytic structure of its concept*, the possibility of being "enforced," applied by force' (Derrida, 1992: 6, emphasis in original). For lawyers, particularly those working within the formalist tradition, justice is reduced to a simple matter of legal enforceability; and, for Derrida, this means that the law becomes a useful instrument of oppression to be employed by dominant external political forces.

The relationship between law and violence is complex. For example, Bourdieu's use of the term 'violence' drives our ordinary understanding of violence to its limit; however, his argument that 'symbolic violence' is more significant than actual violence is justified on the grounds that:

> Force acts directly, by physical constraint, but also through the representation that those subject to it have of this force; the most brutal and violent force obtains a form of recognition that goes beyond mere submission to its physical effect … there is no physical effect in the social world that is not accompanied by a symbolic effect … the strange logic of human action means that brute force is never only brute force: it exerts a form of seduction, persuasion, which bears on the fact that it manages to obtain a certain form of recognition (Bourdieu 2014:192).

The exercise of exclusionary 'symbolic violence' is argued to be necessary by law-givers, since they must maintain and continually reinforce their powerful image as the socially recognised and rightful interpreters of 'a corpus of texts which sanctify a correct or legitimised vision of the social world' (Bourdieu 1987: 817). Not only is it impossible to separate the hateful practices of the material/physical from the ideal/symbolic characteristics of force; rather, these latter aspects take precedence. They comprise a more insidious type of rhetorical violence which, in turn, establishes a hierarchical framework that sustains future violence.

Symbolic violence is rarely explicit; rather, Bourdieu suggests that it constitutes more often a subtle or 'gentle violence, imperceptible and invisible even to its victims', and is exerted for the most part 'through the purely symbolic channels of communication and cognition (more precisely, mis-cognition), or even feeling' (2001: 1, 2). Particular interpretations are inculcated through state education and legal training for example, and each competing idea or contention is played out in terms of the implicit and explicit assertions of the pedagogical authority. Some ideas are rendered 'unthinkable', such as the connection between morality and law; also, the imposition of a 'cultural arbitrary' masks the nature of its contribution to prioritising dominant interests (Bourdieu & Passeron 1990: 22). The latter may include the concealment of notions such as revenue enhancement (and the centrality of profit as a motive) in relation to, for example, imposing exorbitant fines for exceeding arbitrarily imposed speed limits on motorways.

In the UK, from 2017, revisions to the Road Traffic Regulation Act 1984, s.89(1) mean the fine for 'speeding' offences may comprise up to 175% of the driver's weekly income, in addition to a claim for court costs. A victim surcharge of up to £170 is also levied in the case of all 'victimless' motoring offences. The reason given for the new 'fine structure' was to show 'a clear increase in penalty as the seriousness of offending increases', in light of a reported 44% increase in speeding in the preceding five years (Sentencing Council 2017). This decision was taken in spite of no corresponding increase in motor vehicle accidents caused by 'speeding'. No alternative approaches were considered, such as switching off the 'safety cameras' on empty motorways at night; conducting motorway repairs in smaller sections rather than imposing a 50-mph restriction on a 14-mile busy section of a major motorway over 3 years; or revising the speed limit upwards, as on German autobahns where many rural sections have no general speed limit. Rather, once the 'pedagogic authority' has been established, reinforced and 'naturalised' through the exercise of arbitrary power, it is thereafter perpetuated 'in the practices and principles of the internalised [cultural] arbitrary' (Bourdieu & Passeron 1990: 31). Preferred interpretations, (mis-)understandings or 'mis-cognitions' constitute the process by which power relations are understood; not for what they are objectively, but in a form which renders them legitimate to those who are subject to their force.

As it is not assumed to be aggressive or threatening, rather presenting itself as 'natural' or inevitable and benign, or even benevolent, this subtle form of violence has a greater possibility for imposing itself successfully than if it were direct or overt. For Bourdieu, the 'symbolic' comprises fundamental instruments of knowledge production, such as art, science, religion and language, which assist in constructing worlds of meaning. This symbolic capital is neither secondary nor complementary; rather, it coexists with cultural, economic and social capital, and together they comprise a system of social classification that operates as a principle of exclusion and selection, which has the capacity to falsify, distort and conceal. Consequently, law's characteristic and symbolic violence – experienced most keenly by those whose interests are disregarded and whose voices are not heard – is communicated through language, and via a series of emblems, signs, icons and values that convey relations of domination and inequality.

Law's truth and the Tinkerbell Effect

It has been suggested that to seek the truth is an ideal of reason (Lynch 2014: 126). However, reason is located in the private and subjective consciousness, and incapable of fully communicating the richness of its experience to others. While reason provides the structure or form of what we know, the senses provide the content; so reason can only be described, at best, as a mechanism for the discovery of truth. To express the truth of a matter is, rather, an ideal of rational discourse since humans are not only rational beings but also possess the superior endowment of language. Yet only members of the legal community are given the power, and right, to originate moral categories by means of which to justify their claims to authority and legitimacy. As Walter Benjamin stipulates in *Critique of Violence*, violence is the means by which law is founded and preserved, and 'when not in the hands of the law, [violence] threatens it not by the ends that it may pursue but by its mere existence outside the law' (1999: 239). The monopoly on law-making as an act of symbolic violence is furthered in a variety of forms, including the 'architecture of the courtroom and the choreography of the trial process [which] converge to restrain and physically subdue the body of defendant' (Douzinas & Warrington 1991: 116), and via the unjust imposition of a rarefied legal language:

> And their judges spoke with one dialect
> but the condemned spoke with many voices.
> And the prisons were full of many voices,
> but never the dialect of the judges.
> And the judges said,
> 'No-one is above the Law'. (Leonard 1995: 17)

In literal terms, with language operating as disadvantage, individuals before the courts are often judged in a language or an idiom they cannot comprehend. For example, immigration officers routinely request asylum seekers to recount their experience of brutality and torture in a language with which they are unfamiliar, whereas legal empowerment requires having 'access to the language of [the] rights-holder and duty-bearer' (Purkey 2013: 270). The privileged language of law relates not only, as in the poem above, to 'dialect', lexicon and syntax, but also to the symbolic capital of legal discourse articulated by those with legal authority. Alternative voices, such as those of the witness or accused in the courtroom, are not allowed to stand alongside or above the standard legal discourse, and nobody has the right to refute the validity of the 'truths' implied by the designated legal representatives.

The illocutionary force of law – its forms of enunciation, utterance and reiteration as practised by the judges in their 'theatres of justice' – not only determines the fate of the defendant but also delineates the institutional site of legal discourse. In this way, legal judgments constitute determinative statements and deeds which both interpret the law and act on the world. Since the position of the judge and the judged has representational significance, the legal spectacle is mapped according to 'places of ascension'.

> [B]oth physically and verbally all points look up to and are directed towards the bench, upon which, after the ushers have demanded silence and respect, it is the Law that sits down in the place of merely human demands. Consider too the forms of dress, the apparel of justice, the order of its coming and going and the restriction upon the forms in which it can be addressed, the various metonymies as well as the sacral appellations: the court, the bench, your honour, your worship, your lordship (Goodrich 1990: 223).

For the legal community it is necessary to ensure the continuing primacy of its rituals and masks, and legal thought conveyed by the law's sacral language, as these are instrumental in maintaining the social influence of law. Consequently, articulated by those with privileged position, specialist knowledge and linguistic superiority, and proficiency in applying the language of law, gives very real power to the 'authorised interpreters' – namely, judges and advocates – within the juridical field. For this reason, and in light of the indeterminacy of legal doctrine, critical legal theorists have explored the use of language (textual analysis) and the importance of narratives and stories in formulating critical alternatives to prevailing legal practices. Committed to the ideas of social and political reform, they have sought to prioritise individual agency (autonomy) and social diversity – with a respect for difference at its core.

In his 1979 seminal work *The Postmodern Condition*, Jean-François Lyotard maintained that advancements in knowledge, politics, the sciences, education and technology have all been language-related (1984a). Since language is constantly evolving and meaning is often fluid, he suggested that understanding the use of language demanded consideration of a text as 'an event' – being alert to its uniqueness and peculiarities, rather than adopting the universalistic process of reducing a text to its pre-existing or settled meaning in already familiar concepts. For Lyotard, the most important elements of language relate to its intensity and energies, rather than simply its bare meaning; for example:

> What [language] does: the affective charge it contains and communicates; what it causes to be done: the transformation of these potential energies into something else – other texts, but also paintings, photos, film sequences, political actions, inspirations to love, refusals to obey, economic initiatives (Lyotard 1984b: 6).

In exploring the language pragmatics and aesthetic philosophy by means of which the legal culture and community are shaped and defined, one of Lyotard's chief objectives was the unmasking of all pretensions of hegemonic master narratives. So the meaning of a universal rule can never be understood, as it were, 'in itself' because it belongs to a complex unity, which includes the moment of application. In relation to seeking justice, therefore, this is always deferred – in the sense of being indeterminable in advance – since competing discourses apply different criteria against which truth claims are judged.

> As distinguished from a litigation, a differend [*différend*] would be a case of conflict, between (at least) two parties, that cannot be equitably resolved for lack of a rule of judgment applicable to both arguments. One side's legitimacy does not imply the other's lack of legitimacy (Lyotard 1988: ix).

From this perspective, the absence of a universal genre of discourse, accompanied by authoritative texts with which to impose the same rule of judgment, means it would be impossible to take one position over another, since the correct one could not be easily determined. In any event, for Lyotard, the prioritisation of efficiency and search for universality only served to suppress difference, to ignore the *différend* and avoid conflict – all of which are of necessity implicated in the search for justice.

Preferring the option of adjudicators having to think or philosophise anew in relation to equal consideration of each viewpoint, they are urged to embrace their role as 'thinkers', and make a commitment to 'deepen what language there is, to critique the shallow notion of information [and] to reveal an irremediable opacity within language itself' (Lyotard 1993: 27). In most circumstances, irrespective of disparate identities and languages, adherents of different genres of discourse are still able to communicate without any major difficulties. However, Lyotard refuses the authority which would pursue reconciliation between diverse voices at the expense of silencing them. Accordingly, the *différend* (in the sense of dispute) arises in those contexts where there is a lack of refinement in adjudication or insensitivity to differences. In such cases, the *différend* was argued to be a necessary challenge to the established order, and communicated via language; more precisely, the language of resistance. This resonates with Nietzsche's opinion that individuals flourish best under 'conditions of disorder', having asserted themselves against the repressive rule of the prescribed order (1982: 570). Therefore, the idea of disorder or dissent – as resistance against the centralised and oppressive force of law, constituting the non-legitimate and 'mystical foundation of authority' – is equated with freedom and agency; with language at the heart of a commitment to address the question of injustice.

The ability to participate in the construction of rules and the evolution of legal interpretation is, therefore, dependent on a communicative relation, and would entail non-dominant agents having a voice and being acknowledged as differentiated individuals. Ideally, then, at the very simplest level, realising justice is simply a matter of conversation – with each party as an equal participant. However, since language is a significant factor in the exercise of symbolic power, in that 'symbolic power is expressed through language' – even as body language, gesture and accent, which signify class and origin – it has a significant connotative and performative quality (Swartz 2013: 86). Furthermore, as the ontological norms deployed in, and performed through, discourse adhere to particular principles, power structures and conventions, the discursive constitution of the person is indivisible from their social constitution. Thought and expression are, in this way, reduced to the level of commodities – mere competences to be packaged and managed by dominant groups.

> The principle of the magical efficacy of performative language which makes what it states, magically instituting what it says in constituent statements, does not lie ... in the language itself, but in the group that authorises and recognises it and, with it, authorises and recognises itself (Bourdieu 1990: 109, 110).

It is the logic of performance, and particularly the maximisation of self-legitimating performance, which allows for the privileging of efficiency over the ideals of truth and justice.

Performativity is one of the powerful and insidious ways in which subjects are formed and reformulated according to a pre-given authority. For this reason, the syntactic and lexical semantic norms and conventions of language make an important contribution towards the achievement of the overall communicative purpose of an ideology. As a primary means of signification, most professional languages have explicit denotative vocabularies. The medical and business professions, for instance, have adopted a relational classification of extra-linguistic practices. Yet the legal lexis not only has rhetorical significance; it is also moralistic and emotionally aware. Legal practitioners have strategically co-opted a pious emotionality for their own purposes, and the routine use of a connotative vocabulary – a standard of expression that is a language in its own right – elevates otherwise prosaic legal terms to internal or latent ideological signifiers (Shaw 2014: 53). The hidden and admitted moral assumptions which comprise law's meta-discourse constantly re-inscribe the limits and content of law, how it is to be understood and applied, and that it is able to declare itself as the only authentic voice in advance of its latest pronouncements.

This top-down approach is particularly evident in the courtroom, where judges customarily employ expressions such as 'having heard all the evidence the court deduces that ...', 'it is evident that ...', 'it is agreed that ...' and 'after thorough consideration the court concludes ...'. Even so, too often the final ruling follows an imbalanced or poorly informed debate on the facts, as evidenced in English court cases on physician-assisted dying. In many instances it was clear that the judges were ill-equipped to contend with the competing complex philosophical and moral arguments, and were keen to gloss over these. Instead, there was a tendency to offer a standard set of rehearsed opinions, based on canon law or outmoded strict legal authority, followed by an insistence that 'Parliament is best placed to take a decision on the issue in question in light of the sensitive issues, notably ethical, philosophical and social, which arise' (*R (Nicklinson and Lamb) v Ministry of Justice* [2014] UKSC 38 at 84). Arguably, in this case, after the necessary finding of fact and consideration of applicable rules, the judges could have chosen to exercise their discretion as to what would be a fair and just outcome. The English courts also have the power, under s.4 of the Human Rights Act 1998, to declare legislation incompatible with ECHR rights. Declaring the Suicide Act 1961 incompatible, while not going so far as to decriminalise assisted suicide, would nevertheless have put political pressure on Parliament to change the law. Although the primary role of the judiciary is to apply and not to create the law, the function of the courts as 'truth-finders' and 'policy-makers' – especially at the level of the Supreme Court – is necessarily political due to the profound influence their decisions may exert on public policies and social values. However, the reluctance of the judiciary to use their discretionary powers to realise a just decision in morally complex cases constitutes the manifestation of law's overarching organisational hierarchy. Of course, beyond the competing claims of judicial versus parliamentary supremacy, a critical question is how to facilitate a more inclusive dialogue on such issues which takes into account a broader range of diverse perspectives and alternative truths.

By means of a process of sifting and ordering of disparate voices and groups, legal discourse is able to impose, unchallenged, a set of hierarchically defined narrators, and promote specific authorised texts and stylised rhetorical settings of legal communication, in isolation from non-legal society (Poulantzas 2000: 88–92). The monologic, or closed, nature of legal discourse enables, and even encourages, the exclusion of semantic intertextuality by removing the possibility of any challenge to the stratified legal language system. Not only does the incestuous legal verbalism of legal code make it occlusive and obscure to other discourses within the society it governs, but linguistic and discursive exclusion also effectively justifies the hierarchical semantic social, political and ideological options perpetuated and expressed by that discourse (Goodrich 1990: 158–204). Accordingly, the manipulation and debasement of language comprising 'law's truth' continues to be a potent stratagem for establishing the legitimacy of legal hierarchies and maintaining structures of power while simultaneously having a stymieing effect on public debate and functioning as a vehicle of oppression.

Where discourse functions as authoritative discourse it ceases to function as information, rules and paradigms and, rather, attempts to determine the foundations of our ideological relations with the world as:

> located in a distant zone, organically connected with a past that is felt to be hierarchically higher. It is, so to speak, the word of the fathers. Its authority was already acknowledged in the past. It is a prior discourse … [There is no] question of choosing it from among other possible discourses that are its equal. It is given in lofty spheres, not those of familiar contact. Its language is a special language. It can be profaned. It is akin to taboo, i.e., a name that must not be taken in vain (Bakhtin 1981: 342, 343).

Although in disagreement about the importance of writing over speech, both Saussure and Derrida proposed that all societies legitimate themselves primarily through language, and these discourses produce truth claims that present themselves as 'narratives of truth'. Foucault similarly referred to 'regimes of truth', which are able to reimagine historical and political realities according to the singular vision of authoritative institutions (1980: 131). These linguistic preferences set up as objective truths – which offer a partial perspective and effectively blur the line between truth and illusion – demonstrate the 'relations of symbolic power in which the power relations between speakers or their respective groups are actualised' (Bourdieu 1991: 37). Consequently, meaning is reduced to the raw material of beliefs shared between, and repeated by, members of the legal community of interpreters; the truth being grounded essentially in the individual legal advocate's own institutional allegiances, and within a limited and pre-judiced body of written legal text.

A regime of truth has the capacity to mask, and even repress, other truths while at the same time its own ontology is obscured; this further establishes its authenticity, putting itself beyond question by having no identifiable beginning or end (Shaw 2013a: 109). The creation of a collective illusion that subjective representations of reality are, in fact, objective and truthful is reminiscent of the tale of Tinkerbell, the fairy who was revived from near death by poisoning in James Barrie's play, *Peter Pan*. Peter was able to save Tinkerbell by utilising the imaginative force of a sufficiently sympathetic audience, of whom he entreated, '"if you believe [in fairies], clap your hands ... don't let Tink die". Many clapped. Some didn't. A few beasts hissed ... but already Tink was saved' (Barrie 2011: 244). Just as, in the story, fairies exist only because many people are inclined to believe in them, the selective application of a privileged narrative of truth – or discourse of illusion produced by the legal imagination – fulfils an overarching ordering function because people willingly accept its authority. It then becomes possible, with minimal opposition, to determine the position of various actors and their interrelationships by means of an arbitrary classification which assists in the identification of all possible modes of being, both before the law and in relation to the wider social world of associations.

The (in-)visibility of law: 'secret' justice is justice denied

Having the power of definition, classification and closure, law's gaze is not neutral; rather, it has been described as contemptuous, violent and engaged in reshaping the possibility of meaning and controlling the behaviour of members of its community (McDonald 2011: 154). As Cover explains, 'on the one hand, law participates in the generation of normative meaning; on the other, [it] plays in the domain of social control and uses violence to enforce just one (namely its own) conception of order' while simultaneously denying individuals the right to interpret their own suffering and shape their own meaning Cover 1986: 1602). The core or standard definition of hatred refers to an intense or extreme dislike, aversion, loathing, antipathy, enmity, hostility or feelings of violence toward or against something or someone. This type of violence has figurative or metaphorical connotations, referring also to textual or narrative violence and not simply that which relates to actions. Since 'law's violence is manifest not only through the capacity to punish, but in the capacity to draw and enforce distinctions and to impose meanings', the text is much more than a mere supplement to the legal institution (Moran 2001: 341). The 'violence of words' is illustrated in *Titus Andronicus*, opening act IV, scene ii, where Aaron, Chiron and Demetrius entered at one door and through the other door Young Lucius entered, carrying what was referred to as 'a bundle of weapons [with] verses writ upon them' (Shakespeare 2017: 78).

Slavoj Žižek refers to the subtle form of violence embodied in the language that underpins the operation of our economic, political and legal systems as 'objective violence' (2008: 1). The rhetoric of objective violence includes an assumption about the infallibility of the state and adherence to the legal fiction of law's infallibility, both of which are claimed to pose a threat to democracy since state authority, and particularly legal authority, are presumed to be beyond all doubt. Yet, as Terry Aladjem points out in *The Culture of Vengeance and the Fate of American Justice*, doubt is a necessary component of democratic thought and legal judgment, and 'where democratic justice pursues the truth in the awareness of its own fallibility, then it is no absolute authority and does not embody a uniform morality' (2008: 155, 175). In such cases the contingency of legal authority is emphasised, as words and meaning are open to interpretation, and an environment typified by coercion is transformed into one characterised by persuasion. The presence of doubt or vulnerability, therefore, acts as an assurance that the pursuit of truth trumps the self-assured authority that conflates truth with power, as there is always the possibility of an error of judgment, and with it the likelihood of amendment or appeal.

Accordingly, the visibility of law and legal processes, as a reversal of the panoptic gaze of the 'surveillance society', is a necessary requirement of justice in exposing errors of judgment and by providing the basis from which to challenge institutional power asymmetries. Open justice forms the bedrock of the rule of law, and is a fundamental feature of any modern democratic society. According to Bentham, 'publicity is the very soul of justice [and] the keenest spur to exertion and the surest of all guards against improbity' (1789: 316); yet, according to recent statistics, 'secret' or private court hearings have proliferated in the UK. The Justice and Security Act (JSA) 2013 extended 'closed material procedures' (CMPs) into the main civil courts in England and Wales in order to deal with ongoing discovery issues in current litigation arising out of recent terrorist and political threats to national security. This procedure permits the State to disclose sensitive material to the judge without having to disclose the material to its opponent. Some security-sensitive cases resulted in closed judgments where the full decision was not published, which potentially deprived claimants of important information in relation to the reasons why they either won or lost their case. CMPs were already used in employment tribunals, Special Immigration Appeals Commission hearings and investigatory powers tribunals, which handle complaints about the intelligence services; however, the JSA 2013 has extended these into the main civil courts. This allows the government to exploit intelligence material to defend itself in secret against claims for damages over alleged mistreatment such as detention, extraordinary rendition and torture. As decided by the UK Supreme Court in *Belhaj and another v Director of Public Prosecutions and another* [2018] UKSC 33 (4 July 2018), such cases have clear public interest and human rights implications.

In its current form, the JSA 2013 is in conflict with the constitutional tradition of open justice and the right to a fair trial, a common law principle in the English legal system which dates back to the Magna Carta. Since justice conducted behind closed doors often amounts to justice denied, public bodies have a legal and moral duty to be accountable to their citizens, and open hearings are vital in order to ensure that our courts operate fairly. So there is a need for greater transparency, not less. Yet over the past few years the number of cases heard in private, and the range of issues they concern, have escalated. Judgments delivered in the Court of Protection (CoP) and family courts have led to children being removed from the parental home, and the elderly being deprived of their liberty and forced into care homes against their wishes and those of their families.

The Court of Protection (set up under the Mental Capacity Act 2005) has jurisdiction in all areas of decision-making in relation to the health, wealth and liberty of individuals who lack capacity. *Stoke City Council v Maddocks* [2012] EWHC B31 (COP) is thought to be the first case of a person being jailed 'in secret' by the CoP, for trying to remove her father from a care home where the family believed he was in danger of dying. Essentially, family members concerned for their elderly father were pitted against professionals and state employees, who insisted only they knew what was in his best interests. Wanda Maddocks was also condemned for taking the 80-year-old Alzheimer's disease and vascular dementia sufferer to a court hearing, and to see a solicitor. The court ordered she desist from trying to remove her father from the care home, disregarding the family's concern over his ill-treatment there. When she ignored the court order, a judge ruled that the 50-year-old woman should receive a custodial sentence and be sent to prison for five months for contempt of court, even though she was not present at the hearing or represented by a lawyer. It is significant that the facts of this case were only revealed due to the persistence of a UK media outlet, the *Daily Mail*, as part of its campaign for 'open justice' (Doughty & Dolan 2013: 4, 5). Moreover, although Maddocks only served six weeks of her sentence, where a prison sentence is involved the arguments for privacy in such cases are largely unconvincing.

There is a different standard of proof in the family courts; the dispute must be proved according to the balance of probabilities, rather than beyond reasonable doubt. There is also no jury, only a judge. Although there are often good reasons why the deliberations of family courts are hidden from public scrutiny (such as where commercially sensitive financial information is divulged, or the identities of children in cases where there are allegations of sexual, physical or emotional abuse), when judges withhold information they can also conceal the basis of their own decision. Consequently, the lack of transparency may serve to conceal a mistake or an unjust decision, and even cover up biased or malevolent decisions that may well constitute a serious abuse of power. Although the 2014 Transparency Guidance requires that a judgment should be published whenever the judge decided it was 'in the public interest' to do so, recent reports have indicated this has not been happening. Furthermore, there are still many barriers to applications from, for example, family members who might wish to challenge decisions made by the CoP or family courts (Series et al 2017: 102).

Too many cases which involve minors and disputed medical treatment, for example, are still discussed in closed courts, hidden from the public gaze, with a guardian appointed to represent the child's best interests. The case of *Re Ashya King* [2014] EWHC 2964 (Fam) illustrates the disregard, and even contempt, which is commonly shown for the views and perspective of the parents and other close family members. Following the removal of a four-year-old child's brain tumour, his parents disputed the hospital's proposed post-operative medical treatment of radiotherapy and chemotherapy, which they argued would cause their son further pain, unpleasant side effects and adversely impact his future quality of life. They proposed transferring him to a medical facility in Prague for pioneering proton beam therapy which was, at the time, generally unavailable in the UK. On application by the local authority, the judge made the child a ward of the court and ordered a further hearing. In the meantime, the parents removed Ashya from the UK and they became the subject of a European Arrest Warrant. Assuming the parents to be guilty of 'wilful neglect' in defying the authority of the healthcare professionals, in spite of overwhelming evidence to the contrary, their sick child was made a ward of court and his parents incarcerated. The National Health Service (NHS) later agreed it was an appropriate treatment in this case, and not only arranged to fund Ashya King's proton beam therapy but also revealed plans to open several cancer-fighting proton beam treatment centres throughout the UK. As Bridgeman states, 'child protection proceedings are not appropriate when there is a genuine difference of opinion between the parents of a seriously ill child and caring professionals on the question of the best medical treatment' (2015: 477). The healthcare professionals and public authorities demonstrated a lack of respect for the perspective and concerns of, what were, loving and caring parents in seeking to secure the best possible care and outcome for their seriously ill child.

A similar case, *Great Ormond Street Hospital v Yates and Charlie Gard* [2017] EWHC 1909 (Fam Case No: FD17P00103), concerned an infant with mitochondrial DNA depletion syndrome, a rare genetic disorder that causes progressive brain damage and muscle failure. His parents wished to take him to the US for experimental nucleoside therapy, but permission was denied by Great Ormond Street Hospital and upheld by the family court, with tragic consequences. Although in such instances there is a need to balance privacy (or at least anonymity in certain cases) with the public interest, as Lord Scarman clarified in *Harman v Secretary of State for the Home Department* [1983] 1 AC 280:

> Justice is done in public so that it may be discussed and criticised in public. Moreover, trials will sometimes expose matters of public interest worthy of discussion other than the judicial task of doing justice between the parties in the particular case.

According to the Children and Family Court Advisory and Support Service, between April 2017 and March 2018, there were a total of 42,058 new private law cases brought before the family court, which may involve one or more children (Cafcass 2018). This represents a 3.8% increase in referrals compared with the previous financial year. Even though reporters are now allowed more access to family court hearings, family courts are still largely secretive bodies that lack accountability. Also, since recent figures show the number of children taken into care has soared, it is a matter of concern that the family courts and the CoP still tend to focus on procedure and defer to the authority of the health and social welfare 'professionals' as a default position, rather than adopting a more holistic appraisal of the 'best interests' of individuals. This should arguably include, and perhaps even prioritise, consideration of the opinions of close relatives and significant others, who have at least an equal interest in promoting the well-being of their loved ones.

Despite the symbolic violence inherent in adjudication, for Cover it remains true that our legal interpreters and judges are not obliged to defer to the violence of state administrative machinery; rather, they have choices. This is because:

> The creation of legal meaning is essentially a cultural activity ... and is not naturally coextensive with the range of effective violence used to achieve social control. Thus, because law is the attempt to build future worlds, the essential tension in law is between the elaboration of legal meaning and the exercise of or resistance to the violence of social control (1983: 1602).

Appealing to an 'aesthetics of welfare' – from the root word *aesthesis*, which refers to 'our sensuous engagement with the world' – Gearey recommends a 're-worked notion of welfare' as an 'institutional form of care and compassion', founded on our shared world of 'being with others' (2012: 149, 159). Against the arbitrariness of a 'uniform morality' imposed by the state, the courts or individuals, Emmanuel Levinas (1969) similarly appeals to the emotional and relational sphere in order to ascribe a binding moral imperative which is premised on a meditation on the human face. An encounter with opacity in the face-to-face relation with the Other is constituted as the primary way in which the immeasurability and uniqueness of each individual can be discovered. It acts as a metaphor for the authentic presence of another person, representative of those aspects of human individuality and culture which resist and overcome objectification. However, it is much more than a mere metaphor; rather, Levinas refers to our quintessence, our physicality, the way in we touch others and how we look at people and see or experience their humanity. The ethics of 'alterity', or otherness, is a challenge to all attempts to reduce the Other to self, because the face of the Other is itself beyond any process of signification. Levinas proposes emotional identification with the human face as an act which transcends oneself, and is not contingent on any previously experienced appearances. The Other is only disclosed in their unique alterity, which appeals 'not [to] an experience of values but to the anarchic (*an-arche*, without beginning or principle) domain of responsibility and the obligated answer to the Other's demand' (Douzinas & Warrington 1994: 167).

The opaque specificity of the face dissipates any prior notions of belonging, loyalties, orientations and boundaries. This Other-prioritising ethical encounter is the basis of Levinas' pre-rational 'ethics as first philosophy', which forbids any resort to equivalence or standardisation, since responsibility is assumed by, and within, the self for the distinctive Other. We are transformed by the moral experience of both the visibility and proximity of the face-to-face relation: 'Immediately it summons me, claims me, recalls me to a responsibility I incurred' (Levinas 1993: 93–94). To gaze on the face of the Other is to accord respect without desiring to possess, judge, dominate or impose – as the face of the Other is itself beyond any signifier. The face of the Other is resistant to our control and rejects our potential to absorb that person into mere information; it is a 'relation with the other, absolutely other. which I cannot contain, with the other in this sense infinite' (Levinas 1969: 197–199). Encountering the Other as a separate individual, with unique concerns and interests, elicits a self-conscious impulse as moral obligation towards this stranger. Because of our emotional sensibilities, it is possible to experience the face, or ethical position, of the Other as distinct and worthy of our involvement and engagement: 'respecting someone, we take care not to do various things to them or to let various things happen to them; loving someone, we are open to caring about them in all sorts of ways' (Velleman 2008: 201).

Whilst individuals are capable of communicating a moral order based on a shared understanding of injustice which recognises and rejects inhumane laws or outcomes, legal codes alone cannot prompt ethical behaviour because they arise from developmentally pre-social categories and ontological assumptions about right or rational conduct. Mechanically deterministic, legal categories are formulated on the pre-ethical basis of supposition and hypothesis relating to facts or things rather than forming an ethical basis; therefore it is impossible to construe moral actions as predicted and codified in advance. Rather, the impetus for right actions towards others is based on the challenge of recognising the Other, their freedom and integrity as a 'first philosophy', and to feel motivated to selflessly assume responsibility out of unavoidable and irreducible concern. This unashamedly idealistic conception of justice focuses on the connection between oneself and the often unknown, yet contemplated, Other, on the basis that there is something special in our encounter with another person and their appearance to us.

The legal world presents itself as a closed system of expert knowledge, based on principles which are always arbitrary and are themselves abstractions rooted in a contested past. At the same time, the oral and written tradition of law operates in a sensory environment where other communicative forms continually augment, adapt, reinforce and often purposefully challenge each other. Given that society is constituted by every one of its members and all events are defined by their associations with other actors and undertakings, for actions to have any meaning, they must enjoy the widest recognition and validation (Shaw 2014: 56). This essential connection to the social world of individuals and groups requires law to be an adaptive and reflexive system. However, whilst ostensibly striving for a fair and just outcome, too often the legal community not only fails to address the best interests of all parties but also its dispassionate gaze can lead to the very outcome it seeks to avoid, namely injustice.

Law as hate: killing in the name of the law

The rule-dominated determination of legal meaning is considered to be the distinguishing characteristic of legal language which, with few exceptions, excludes a defining role for any alternative political, moral or other positions within the semantics of legal validity. Yet it is evident that law comprises not only the legal system proper; its reach also extends to the political, social and economic institutions which give form and substance to law, and which formally and informally influence the development of a variety of rights and responsibilities. Although principal laws and customs in areas such as marriage and property ownership have evolved from original canon law and Roman law models, their wider social effects have influenced subsequent judicial decisions, and legal thinking is revealed to be a key driver in the production of social meaning. As Susan Silbey states, 'law does more than reflect or encode what is otherwise normatively constructed; ... law is part of the cultural processes that actively contribute in the composition of social relations' (1992: 41). Accordingly, as a major producer of 'truth', the influence of the law and its interpreters flows through a wide range of public organisations, and in so doing transforms reality in a number of innocuous and insidious ways: 'When they need to, these are the people who can put the most skilful exercise of formal rigour (*summum jus*) to the service of the least innocent ends (*summa injuria*)' (Bourdieu 1987: 850).

As a social organisation and under the conditions of the rule of law, the law has a duty to be epistemically accessible so that its rules and principles are public knowledge, and its institutions and processes are available to all in providing safeguards against abuses of public and private power. Because the act of law-making and dispensing justice is a public affair, the legal institution seeks to preserve its status and esteem via performance and publicity, such as by allowing visitors to the public galleries of the Houses of Commons and Lords so that they can hear MPs and Peers debate current issues. In ensuring the visibility of law, many parliamentary debates are also televised. The spectacle of justice being done extends to the public display of justice being served; for example, in the UK details of a person's bankruptcy are still published in the *London Gazette* and the Insolvency Register, both of which are publicly available. In addition, a bailiff or enforcement agent may make a home visit if debts are not paid, such as Council Tax bills, parking fines or court fines. A court summons used to be hand delivered by a messenger of the court, so the notification of the court's requirement for presence could be witnessed by one's neighbours. Even further back, public shaming rituals included the stocks, the ducking stool, flogging and branding.

In *Discipline and Punish*, Foucault equated the public nature of punitive legal practice with the will of a state or sovereign authority to wield power over its subjects, so that 'the body of the condemned man [became] the place where the vengeance of the sovereign was applied, the anchoring point for a manifestation of power' and at the same time affirmed 'the dis-symmetry of forces' (1991: 55). For Cover, law's 'organised, social practices of violence' are embodied in the act of criminal sentencing, which comprises 'the deliberate infliction of pain in order to destroy the victim's normative world and capacity to create shared realities' (Cover 1986: 1601–1603). To this end:

> law is the mechanism by which a society either recovers the individual for collectivity, or places him or her in an alternative social category. What we call a trial can therefore be interpreted as a rite of passage whose purpose is to take the suspect individual, previously joined to the social body, and to separate him or her in custodial space (Hanson 1996: 57).

The act of imposing a criminal sentence and punishment, therefore, has an ambiguous communicative function; for instance, the death penalty metes out violence not just to transgressors but also to the law itself. In inflicting isolation or suffering without sufficient meaning and pain without reason, justice is undermined by the violence that defines the law. As suggested by David Gurnham in his discussion of Kafka's *In the Penal Colony*, 'the condemned man's guilt and his punishment bypass the individual offender himself', since 'the sentence is left to the punishment alone to communicate every aspect of the relationship between him, his crime and the law' (2016: 75). In the act of sentencing, separation and the exacting of just punishment, the court attempts to make sense of the suffering produced by violence even as it creates yet more suffering. The judges maintain a veneer of equanimity and righteousness while imposing judgments that inflict pain, hardship and death, in part because they are able to abdicate moral responsibility for 'the collective perpetuation of cruel acts' – which 'is made all the easier by the fact that responsibility is essentially "unpinnable", while every participant of these acts is convinced that it does reside with some 'proper authority' (Bauman 1989: 163). Meanwhile, the motivational force of archaic yet mundane negative passions – such as hate, anger, indignation and contempt – which lie beneath the vengeful self-certainty of, say, capital punishment remain unacknowledged or repudiated. Consequently, there is a risk that the criminal law may, itself, fail to make sense of the suffering with which it is inextricably involved.

In the case of the harshest punishments, the retributive urge – rooted in contempt for wicked wrongdoers – routinely determined how lawyers thought about causation and blame. For example, the causal links between crime and macro-level social forces, such as extreme poverty, were ignored in the enforcement of the 'Bloody Code' in the eighteenth century, when criminals could be hanged for a vast range of property crimes, including shoplifting and pickpocketing. Irrespective of the type or seriousness of the criminal act, it amounted to an attempt to sabotage the state or, at least, question the authority of the state; and so between 1770 and 1830 some 7,000 men and women were executed on public scaffolds. That sacrilege, scrumping (stealing fruit from an orchard) and spending a month in the company of gypsies were also included in the list of more than 200 capital offences illustrates a reluctance to 'forget' even the lesser injuries to the sovereign authority and an unwillingness to 'forgive' those, many of whom were children, who inflicted the injury.

As Austin Sarat points out in *When the State Kills*, it is possible to adopt a pragmatic approach to criminal violence and believe in the retributive or deterrence-based rationalisations for the death penalty, and yet still take a stand against the death penalty itself:

> One can be as tough on crime as the next person yet still reject state killing. All that is required to generate opposition to execution is a commitment to democracy, the rule of law, and a mature engagement in responding to society's most severe social problems (2001: 253–234).

Rather than consider responses which included reconciliation and social reconstruction, the state used the rituals of execution to assert its claim to power, which included the monopoly of judicial violence and strategic use of the coercive force of the gallows. As British historian Vic Gatrell suggests in *The Hanging Tree*, 'the sanction of the gallows and the rhetoric of the death sentence were central to all relations of authority in Georgian England' (1994: 56–57).

Although executions were first suspended in 1965 and then finally abolished for the crime of murder in the UK in 1969,[1] it was not because of an institutional turn away from violent state punishment. There was no moment of recognition that the death penalty was a relic of a more barbaric era and did not allow for the redemption of the criminal. The state has always struggled to distinguish its own deadly violence from the deadly violence that it condemns in the wrongdoer; and in 1948 and 1956 the House of Lords rejected proposals to abolish capital punishment. Rather, the catalyst for change was popular outrage at miscarriages of justice evidenced in the controversial cases of, for instance, Timothy Evans, Ruth Ellis and Derek Bentley. Widespread objections and mass demonstrations on moral and humanitarian grounds meant that places of execution became increasingly susceptible to being appropriated by protestors who sympathised with the accused, in defiance of sovereign authority. It may be concluded, therefore, that there is a latent vengeance within legal institutions which is akin to hatred; and so the intervention of law does not disrupt, but rather might be said to rationalise, the logic of revenge.

On ideology and language in the classification of legal subjects: 'them' and 'us'

When individuals appeal for equal treatment or for fair representation in law, it is frequently from the standpoint of a pre-formed foundational basis in which a single feature of a person is taken to represent the whole; for example, their sex, gender, ethnicity or age. The individual exists then as a bare legal concept, a legal norm even; as independent from the concept of a free-standing, autonomous self. Such prior significations form the cornerstone of legal discourse within which the subject is represented in advance, classified and fixed according

1 It was not until the enactment of the Crime and Disorder Act 1998 that the British government finally abolished capital punishment for treason, mutiny and piracy with violence, replacing it with a discretionary maximum sentence of life imprisonment.

to the interests privileged by law's regime of truth; these arbitrary assumptions function as normative reference stereotypes (Foucault 1998). The phenomenon is summarised by Žižek as 'there is no ideology that does not come into being without asserting itself in the guise of one truth against another' (1999: 54). It follows that a decision made by the judicial body is invariably influenced by an emotional inclination towards not only the perceived rightness, wrongness or seriousness of an offence, but also by a fixed idea of the pre-judged protagonist, which in turn helps to determine the appropriate course of action. Nietzsche provided this summary: 'People whom we cannot tolerate [or understand], we try to make suspect' (1996: 243).

Law constitutes a distinctive literary genre, within which metaphoric imagery continues to infuse and inspire the legal imagination. For this reason, metaphors are often used by the legal community to ascribe morally evaluative descriptions of individuals and groups. Their words, actions, inaction, intentions, motivation, personality traits and imputed predisposition are attributed a moral value, and gauged against an objective standard of 'good' behaviour. Ascriptive characteristics such as race, ethnicity, religion and social class are often associated with typical behaviour or attributes, which can be used to stigmatise and exclude someone from being treated as an equal member of society, and disqualify them from an entitlement to basic justice (Shaw 2015a: 95). Attendant figuration, such as scum and dirt, induce associated feelings of disgust and revulsion; for example, the metaphor of filth has functioned as a powerful determinant of criminal justice policies. Law commonly responds to the threat and incidence of actual or environmental filth or pollution in three different ways: by tolerance, prevention or avoidance. Because 'a polluting person is always in the wrong', however, the perception of criminals as vermin (both contaminated and contagious) has prompted the implementation of various pollution-avoidance measures, such as segregation, and a tendency to detain and incarcerate offenders in dirty, fetid pest holes (Douglas 1988: 113). Equating wrongdoers with filth hides their humanity, and encourages the perception of such persons as objects and less than human.

In relation to aspects of human subjectivity and notions of social and cultural value, there is a rich critical history that tackles the legal, ethical and political significance of the vocabulary of waste, degradation, disgust and abjection. In the nineteenth century, for example, many cases relating to pollution, under the common law of nuisance, treated the foul odours and noxious gases emanating from a neighbouring farmyard, factory or city streets strewn with horse manure as a physical invasion of person and property. The nuisance or inappropriateness of the polluting agent depended on the relation of 'substance' to 'space', constituting a social construction of stink and filth which founded the legal doctrine. Norbert Elias explored the evolving concepts of cleanliness and disgust in relation to the 'civilizing process', in his eponymous monograph (2000). The management of dirt and smell was not only a breeding ground for modern environmental rules, but also of more general *them* (the polluters) and *us* (the good citizens) politics of the modern state.

Aesthetics often functions as the minor premise underpinning social syllogisms embedded in discourses of legal justification, which is unsurprising given its root meaning. The Greek *Aesthesis* refers to the entire domain of human perception and our engagement with the material world. It describes the activity of making sense of those objects which arouse the senses and shape experience due to our 'biological insertion into the world', aside from the absolute rule of reason and conceptual thinking. This territory is said to comprise:

> nothing less than the whole of our sensate life together – the business of affections and aversions, of how the world strikes the body on its sensory surface, of that which takes root in the gaze and the guts and all that arises from our most banal, biological insertion into the world (Eagleton 1990: 13).

The aesthetic sensibility assists in the formation of ethical values and notions of, for example, moral obligation, duty and responsibility, which cannot be understood by logical sense alone. However, in addition to being unifying and inclusive, the sensorial can also produce imagistic language which is divisive and excluding, but yet underpins the emotions and sentiments which animate public life. The metaphors of pollution and disease, for instance, are influential rhetorical devices which inform social values, legitimate draconian laws and create moral panic when used to signify violation, perversion and the corruption of moral standards. For Lakoff and Johnson, the main issue is 'not the truth or falsity of a metaphor but the perceptions and inferences that follow from it and the actions that are sanctioned by it' (1980: 157). Jeffrie Murphy discusses this point in *Punishment and the Moral Emotions*, suggesting that not only ought 'our legislatures and public officials be less inclined to exploit the fears of citizens', but also the symbolic foundations of attitudes towards, for example AIDS – formerly referred to by the media as 'the gay plague' – need to be acknowledged for their role in manipulating social consciousness (2012: 228). A set of fixed assumptions and, barely concealed, moral imperatives are often used to construct a division between the 'us' and 'them' of the legal world; namely, its legitimate subjects against those identified as beyond law's normative framework.

The legal lexicon presents itself as complete, and is capable of privileging one set of group interests whilst prohibiting those of another. Projecting only its own values and experiences as authentic and universal, the dominant legal discourse not only marginalises but also pathologises, even criminalises, antipathetic discourses. Those individuals or groups who do not share the experience of the dominant culture, who do not match the idea of what is considered normal, are marked out as 'Other' – often as an abomination, and ultimately an object of hatred. For example, suicide and homosexuality were once considered deviant acts and outside of law's contemplation, meaning in the latter case that England's sodomy laws were no more than a licence for blackmail (Moran 1996: 198). This was the theme of the then controversial 1961 film *Victim*, which tells the story of a successful and seemingly happily married barrister, Melville Farr, who is about to be become a QC and is also a covert homosexual. After his presumed lover, 'Boy' Barrett, commits suicide, Farr attempts to uncover the blackmail ring that led to the young man's death. The film was intended, by the producer Michael Relph and director Basil Dearden, to be an open protest against the statutory proscription that being a homosexual was a criminal act; and many believed it had a significant influence on liberalising the law in this area (Greenfield et al 2001: 118).

Dramatising the main themes of the *Report of the Departmental Committee on Homosexual Offences and Prostitution*, published on 3 September 1957, the film shared the same point of view; namely, that 'contrary to suggesting homosexuals exist only among a low-life criminal group ... homosexuality may be found in otherwise completely responsible citizens in every strata of society' (Relph 1961: 3). As the report concluded:

> Homosexuality cannot legitimately be regarded as a disease, because in many cases it is the only symptom and is compatible with full mental health in other respects. It is not, in our view, the function of the law to intervene in the private life of citizens, or to seek to enforce any particular pattern of behaviour (Wolfenden 1957: 14).

Both suicide and homosexuality were 'out-lawed', to some extent, until 1961 and 1967 respectively. In the case of the latter, once decriminalised and the emotion of hate was inverted, discrimination or hate speech directed against a person on the grounds of sexuality came to be viewed as abhorrent. More recently *MacFarlane v Relate Avon Limited* [2010] IRLR 872 and *Hall & Another v Bull & Another* [2011] EW Misc 2 (CC) evidence the law's intolerance to what are now described as 'hate crimes'. Under current law, someone who murders an LGBTQ person out of feelings of revulsion or hatred will receive a harsher judgment and sentence than if they were killed in the course of, say, a robbery. The emotional state, the unsanctioned expression of hate, renders the perpetrator more culpable.

A danger of the 'personalisation' of the criminal justice system and extension of a 'victim culture', however, is that it embeds the notion that punishments should appease aggrieved victims as a priority, rather than reflect a balanced judgment about the public interest or satisfy a principled respect for all individual rights. Ignoring the motivating circumstances behind a person's actions, and the appropriateness of suffering imposed via the punishment, for example, shows a disregard for the pursuit of just ends. It also absolves the state from any accountability for what may be the foreseeable consequences of wider social forces, such as the endless hardship caused by austerity measures, or governmental failures. So while significant inroads have been made in transforming the law so as to acknowledge and respect the profound otherness of individuals, as George Herbert Mead suggested a century ago:

> Hostility toward the lawbreaker inevitably brings with it the attitudes of retribution, repression and exclusion. These provide no principles for the eradication of crime, for returning the delinquent to normal social relations,

> nor for stating the transgressed rights and institutions in terms of their positive social functions (1918: 590).

In the courtroom there is a tendency not to think beyond the confines of good and evil, and praise and blame, and so the focus of the judges and jury is inevitably fixed on the facts and the account of the victim. This may be due to the moral incongruence of framing the criminal as a kind of victim when, at the same time, confronted by the awfulness of their crime. For the greater part, however, a court is primarily a blame-apportioning rather than a problem-solving forum. While not excusing the crime or the criminal, taking a nuanced view of human behaviour and recognising the constraints which may have shaped individual choices could be viewed as part of the essential role of judges as agents of change; supplementing their function as impartial and independent arbiters of justice.

A useful starting point would be to consider the relationship between rhetorical strategies and violence, in particular reconsidering our assumptions about the explicit and implicit role of violence in attributing certain characteristics to specific categories of individuals in society. Within a modern legal context, negative emotions such as vengeance, disgust and hate tend to occur mostly in relation to criminal law and human rights atrocities. Retributive punishment is sometimes interpreted as an expression of hatred for the aggressor or perpetrator, to a large extent, by appealing to a base desire to make them suffer. The desire to respond to the crime, to the collective insult, elicits the rise of 'vengeful passions' – rendering it 'necessary, in order to allay the one and the other, to inflict an evil upon the malefactor. The hatred directed towards the criminal always brings with it the desire that he should suffer' (Oppenheimer 1913: 39). For Aristotle, hatred is a much colder emotion than anger, and in certain ways more committed and resolute in its determination to satisfy its hunger for an outlet. Furthermore, anger is said to focus on individuals, while hatred, although it can be directed against individuals, is more frequently targeted against classes or types of persons. In addition, one who is angry wants the other to suffer in turn or in kind (Aristotle uses the word *antipathein*, meaning to 'feel in return'), whereas one who hates wants in some way to obliterate the other and quite literally ensure 'that they do not exist' (Aristotle 1998: 1382a1–15).

Justice is said to 'reside in truth alone', and the pursuit of justice as truth, as opposed to the arbitrariness of law's truth, demands we interrogate the narratives behind legal principle and seemingly simple acts of judgment because the business of law-making is not disconnected from the world of aesthetics in its liberal appropriation of symbolism and sensuous expression (Zola 1903: 519). In the case of partial truths relating to, for example, the ubiquity of terrorism, these not only promote a climate of fear along with a hatred and suspicion of others and otherness; they also serve to legitimate a series of intrusive laws curtailing personal freedom. Consequently, Ben-Dor suggests that, in the interests of transparency and legitimacy, it is necessary to put on trial the so-called 'actual' facts, as depicted by the symbolic order of law, about those who are alleged to have committed criminal acts and those who claim to 'fight' criminal activities (2011:

22). Aesthetic representation has the ability to alert our senses to injustice; but, equally, in the wrong hands it can be a tool for legitimising savagery and may constitute an abuse of power against the displaced, the unwanted, the outsider and those otherwise categorised as *homo sacer* (Agamben 1998). These are individuals who are designated outside the law, are reviled and may be killed without consequence; they are deemed unworthy of the protection of law or even recognition. Even so, law's protection may be considered to be a double-edged sword, since its protection appears to be inseparable from punishment.

Legal violence is always contradictory, as it is always a means to an end; and the means is not always justifiable and the end is not necessarily a just end. To a large extent, the level of hatred for the perpetrator, and thirst for vengeance, depends on the moral contours of the individual judge's character. It is contingent on their pre-rational and moral identification with the criminal as a fellow human being, an appreciation of the diverse perspectives that constitute our shared world, along with an awareness of the limitations which inevitably attach to their own judgment. Rousseau addresses the lack of a sympathetic association with the unfortunate, and a hardness of the privileged toward the poor, among the nobility, clergy, lawgivers and upper bourgeoisie, in *Émile*. On discovering that the spread of 'civilisation' had not made human society more fair or just, but instead more corrupt, he poses a series of rhetorical questions:

> Why are kings without pity for their subjects? Because they count on never being mere men. Why are the rich so hard toward the poor? It is because they have no fear of becoming poor. Why does the nobility have so great a contempt for the people? It is because the noble will never be a commoner. Why are the Turks generally more humane and more hospitable than we are? It is because, with their totally arbitrary government, which renders the greatness and the fortune of individuals always precarious and unsteady, they do not regard abasement and poverty as a condition alien to them (Rousseau 1979: 224).

The corollary of this observation is that the exercise of judgment without empathy, forsaking the perspective of the judged, becomes a failure of judgment. When the one judged is excluded from the 'community of judgment', the judged will not see the judgment as valid; rather, they will see it as an imposition of power, and that will in turn breed fear, resentment and hostility. According to Francis Bacon, judgments motivated by hate and a desire for vengeance are said to threaten the very existence of the legal structure because, 'as for the first wrong, it doth but offend the law; but the revenge of that wrong putteth the law out of office' (1999: 10). Also, law's primary function is to regulate justice, and so the employment of negative emotions in adjudication is described as 'a kind of wild justice', which 'the more man's nature runs to, the more [such inclinations] ought to be weeded out' (Bacon 1999: 9). For Martha Nussbaum, to overcome a hatred for the Other, or at least to avoid a 'them and us' mentality, it is necessary to cultivate

> the ability to think what it might be like to be in the shoes of a person different from oneself, to be an intelligent reader of that person's story, and to understand the emotions, desires, and wishes that someone so placed might have (1997: 10–11).

Reimagining the Other as self: the promise of justice fulfilled

William Blake's 1794 'A Poison Tree', from his *Songs of Experience* collection, is a short and deceptively simple poem about repressing anger and the consequences of doing so. The speaker tells of how they fail to communicate their wrath to their foe, and how this continues to grow until it develops into poisonous hatred. The extended legal metaphor, 'fruit of the poison tree', originates from the poem and refers to the inadmissibility of evidence obtained illegally, or 'derivative evidence' – most commonly applied to US legal cases and some Continental judgments as an extension of the 'exclusionary rule'. The doctrine has no application in England, where English judges have been willing to consume the fruit no matter how poisonous the tree. In a wider sense, however, Blake likens the process of cultivating one's emotions to cultivating a tree, and his allegory serves as a moral caution. Hate and anger set in motion the events of the poem, which suggests that any idea, plan or judgment nurtured with hate, fear and silence is dangerous no matter how appealing its appearance. Following this logic, the closed, intractable and inflexible nature of law which forcefully imposes its own system of meaning, along with the power to silence alternative narratives – while simultaneously appealing to a conception of equality, fairness, order, certainty and stability – comprises a toxic combination. The interpretive acts of lawgivers, which are performed within an institutional setting for violent behaviour, are likely to lead to poor or unjust decisions.

The imposition of what Walter Benjamin referred to as 'divine violence' may be understood to represent those decisions which can only be made by the solitary sovereign authority, as the ultimate and only legitimate source of power. In the spirit of *fiat iustitia, pereat mundus* (let justice be done, though the world may perish), the irreducible and transcendent divine authority of law is not accountable to any exterior influence, is entirely justified and lies beyond censure or criticism. The 'learning of the law' was described by early Roman jurist Justinian as inculcation into 'the science of what is just or unjust', and 'the knowledge of all things divine and human' (Justinian 1955: 3, Code 534). Lofty and inaccessible, the quintessential superiority projected by the legal community, and accentuated by the sacred aura surrounding its long-held traditions and rituals, is illustrated in Prague novelist Franz Kafka's story *Before the Law*, published in Germany in 1916 as *Vor dem Gesetz*. In Kafka's parable, the protagonist is without a name or identity, and referred to only as 'the man from the country'. He spends his entire life waiting 'before the law', hoping for admittance through the gate to the law which is guarded by a doorkeeper, who is 'the only thing stopping him from gaining access to the law'. Unwilling to let him in, but in an act of mercy, eventually the doorkeeper gives the man a stool to sit on, which he gratefully accepts while continuing to wait humbly and patiently 'for days and years'. When advanced in age and nearing the end of his life, and having failed to remove the chief obstacle to gaining entrance to the law, he wearily asks the doorkeeper:

> 'Everyone strives to attain the Law'... 'How does it come about, then, that in all these years no one has come seeking admittance but me?' The doorkeeper ... bellows in his ear: 'No one but you could gain admittance through this door, since this door was intended only for you. I am now going to shut it' (Kafka 1961: 65).

Even though the man from the country has lived his life as a subordinate and obedient subject, in respectful acknowledgement of the absolute and sovereign authority of the law, his patience, hope and longing for the promise of justice to be fulfilled never materialised. The bureaucratic world depicted by Kafka finds law's presence everywhere; yet the door which opens on to the transcendent source of legitimacy of law, namely justice, remains firmly shut.

As caretakers and curators of the ancient codes by which we live, our law-makers and legal practitioners construct barriers and obstacles which operate to exclude those who are unprepared and undeserving before their supreme authority; and in this way maintain an absolute monopoly over the law and its sacraments. Representing itself as immutable and transcendent, legal dogma isolates itself from the diverse contexts (social, political, philosophical and aes-thetic) in which it exists; rather, assuming a purity and inviolability which puts it beyond the reach of any challengers. Perceiving itself as only subject to itself, all criticism of legal rules, regulations or principles takes place within the majority tradition which is the subject of criticism. For Zartaloudis, this comprises 'an antilegalism-legalism, a being-against-the-law that ends up, whether consciously or unconsciously, as a being-within-a-(new)-law' (2010: 304–305). The mono-polistic creation and control of boundaries is, therefore, both internal to law (the public vs private divide) and external, in the construction of a constitutive 'out-side' from which it separates itself, of which violence is an elemental part (Agamben 1998: 18).

All enquiries relating to law's own inherent violence are answered by reference to the extra-legal violence that makes law essential; justifying the increasing use of emergency powers of arrest and detention, non-jury courts and the erosion of parliamentary legislative power. Yet all definitions of criminal acts are historically, spatially and politically contingent. While non-legal judgments describe the world of reality or what *is*, legal judgments deal with the prescriptive ethical realm of what *ought* to be, from which moral judgments fall into two distinct categories: namely, prescribing what *ought to be* done prior to an action, and what *ought to have been* done after the fact. Accordingly, law both implies and requires its own transgression; it gives particular acts their quality of criminality and counts on acts of deviance in order to exist and, therefore, the object of this fateful regime is to bring about the very offences it forbids.

Given the power of naming, and actualised as inflexible and purposive, law is able to dominate and oppress with impunity – having been 'endowed with its own discrete history, its own science and its own values, which are all treated as a single block sealed off from general social theory, from politics, from morality' (Shklar 1986: 2, 3). So, any discussion of the law is instantly complicated by the idea of justice, and any discussion of law and justice is instantly complicated by the problem of violence. The violence fuelled by the legal culture's hatred of the 'outside' of law – which serves to inhibit agency, restrict choice and curtail freedom – is described by Slavoj Žižek as 'objective violence'; as opposed to 'subjective violence' which is outwardly manifest and easily recognisable. He describes the embodiment of objectively violent conduct via rhetoric, and the functioning of our legal, political and economic systems, as 'precisely the violence inherent to the "normal" state of things. Objective violence is invisible since it sustains the very zero-level standard against which we perceive something as subjectively violent' (Žižek 2008: 2). The 'overpowering horror of violent acts' and our feelings of 'empathy with the victim' are argued by Žižek to 'inexorably function as a fascinating lure, which prevents us from thinking' about the role of the adjudicators (2008: 4). For this very reason we are urged to pause, think and 'perceive the contours of the background which generates such violence' before taking action; to contemplate, for example, the interplay of legal authority and justice, power relationships and the politics of knowledge production, and rhetorical modes of persuasion (2008: 1).

For many legal theorists, the problem of violence is inseparable from the problem of law and its binding force. This tension is illustrated in the dialectic between law and conscience, between rules and the ethical requirement of the jurist called upon to apply the rules, and particularly in the relationship between law and language. Law, like literature, is grounded in language and narrative; but it is also argued to be 'a literature which denies its literary qualities' (Goodrich 1996: 112). Yet law is logocentric and depends on a variety of linguistic modes of signification and representation, along with other modes of cultural discourse, which aim to make it relevant and generate a distinct field of meaning. As Bourdieu writes, 'It would not be excessive to say that law creates the social world, but only if we remember that it is the world that first creates the law' (1987: 839). So law is synonymous with the symbolic order and is, therefore, produced 'in the dialogue and discourse all around us: in all the things that we read and say, in the music we listen to, and in the art we grow up with' (Manderson 2003: 93).

Like literature, law claims to uphold the notion of a 'good society'; however, by tapping into our 'narrative emotions', it may be possible to overcome feelings of hatred and resentment and, rather, nurture the capacity for compassion, which is an ideal of law as justice.

> Citizens cannot relate well to the complex world around them by factual knowledge and logic alone. The third ability of the citizen, closely related to the first two, is what we can call the narrative imagination. This means the ability to think what it might be like to be in the shoes of a person different from oneself, to be an intelligent reader of that person's story, and to

> understand the emotions and wishes and desires that someone so placed might have (Nussbaum 2010: 95–96).

The notion that literature can facilitate the development of empathy and compassion is based on the premise that, like the people portrayed in a story, humans are essentially much alike and easily recognisable per se. It is only because of our interactions and experiences in relation to other individuals that it is possible to define our own identity and social status. By engaging the reflective faculties, we are better able to judge the particular situation of ourselves and others in the context of competing interpretations of the nature of community, its purposes and ends. Also, being open to considering a more diverse set of possibilities and alternative world views may increase the likelihood that many of the violent realities of power structures, which continue to subjugate and oppress, may be exposed and submitted to critical scrutiny. As well as having a knowledge and understanding of the facts, and the capacity for logical argumentation, it is suggested that the judges ought to hone their natural ability to think what it might be like to be in the shoes of a person different from themselves, to be an intelligent reader of that individual's story, and to understand the emotions, motivations and desires that someone so placed might experience.

The reclusive and initially misunderstood character Arthur 'Boo' Radley from Harper Lee's *To Kill a Mockingbird*, echoing the earlier wisdom of neighbour and lawyer Atticus Finch, suggested that 'you never really know a man until you stand in his shoes and walk around in them' (2010: 279). In the novel, Boo transforms from monster to hero through a simple shift in perspective. By meeting Boo in person, one of the Finch children, Scout (Jean Louise Finch), is able to visualise how traumatic events of the last few years have impacted on his life and feel sympathy for his situation. The revelation illustrates how an empathic understanding of the standpoint of others is only possible by exercising the imagination. Later in the novel, Scout makes reference to a wrongly maligned character in a story, *The Gray Ghost* by Robert F. Schulkers (which was read earlier to her sibling), as 'real nice … when they finally saw him', to which her father Atticus replies, 'most people are, Scout, when you finally see them' (2010: 292). In other words, the misunderstanding or mistreatment of people is frequently justified by unfounded suspicions, preconceived ideas, unjustified hatred and fears, and negative stereotypes. Throughout the book, children are shown to be less susceptible to the prejudices of their elders, and they make better use of their imaginations; hence, the opening quotation by Charles Lamb – 'Lawyers, I suppose, were children once.' The corollary of the story is that perhaps lawyers should learn to think like children once more, without spite, guile or bias.

The narrative imagination is important for public life and for anyone engaged with lawgiving; and particularly for judges, in order that their judgments will be less dogmatic and more empathic, and so have greater depth and meaning. By applying the narrative imagination and assuming an ethical role for literature, it becomes possible to understand the constitutive nature of law, the reality that law is constituted by more than constitutions, rules and rigid legal dogma alone and, most importantly, the constitutive relation of a constitution and its people.

As a consequence, legal principle may be understood as more fluid, malleable and relatable; and may even come to be perceived as a potentially revolutionising entity in service to the ideal of full participatory democracy, in order to achieve a more complete realisation of civil rights and human flourishing.

5 Law as compassion

You felons on trial in courts,
You convicts in prison-cells, you sentenced assassins chain'd and handcuff'd with iron,
Who am I too that I am not on trial or in prison?
Me ruthless and devilish as any, that my wrists are not chain'd with iron, or my ankles with iron?

You prostitutes flaunting over the trottoirs or obscene in your rooms,
Who am I that I should call you more obscene than myself?
O culpable! I acknowledge – I expose!
(O admirers, praise not me – compliment not me – you make me wince,
I see what you do not – I know what you do not.)

Inside these breast-bones I lie smutch'd and choked,
Beneath this face that appears so impassive hell's tides continually run,
Lusts and wickedness are acceptable to me,
I walk with delinquents with passionate love,
I feel I am of them – I belong to those convicts and prostitutes myself,
And henceforth I will not deny them – for how can I deny myself?

Walt Whitman (1881)

Individuals do not occupy an undifferentiated social space; rather, they are socially and discursively (re)constituted by an agglomeration of powerful meaning-producing social institutions and practices. Aside from technological and economic criteria, the cultural and symbolic distinctions comprising modern discourses of knowledge – such as literature, history, science, religion, economics, politics and law – tend to constitute discrete worlds characterised by their own policies and modes of authority. These distinct fields are historically conceived and, through various acts of interpretation, have acquired autonomy in the social sphere over important considerations such as whether to prioritise scientific rigour and originality above commercial gain, political expediency or social harmony. Over time, each field has developed the ability to insulate itself from external forces and maintain its own standards of evaluation above and against those of alternative or intrusive fields. These discursive processes constitute the local socio-historical material conditions that support and constrain disciplinary knowledge traditions, in relation to identifying what is meaningful and what counts as 'truth'. For Foucault:

> 'Truth' is centred on the form of scientific discourse and the institutions which produce it [and] is subject to constant economic and political incitement … it is produced and transmitted under the control, dominant if not exclusive, of a few great political and economic apparatuses (university, army, writing, media); … it is the issue of a whole political debate and social confrontation (ideological struggles) … and an essential political problem for the intellectual [in the sense of being the bearer of values and significations in which all can recognise themselves, as the consciousness and conscience of everyone] is that of ascertaining the possibility of constituting a new politics of truth (1980: 131–133).

Within this complex network of institutional, social and cultural power relations, the self is constantly reimagined and reconstructed by both normalising discourses and practices as well as by internalised, self-disciplining impulses. Such power/knowledge regimes of truth not only marginalise the moral subject; the practice of 'cultural exclusion' and silencing of 'alterities' or 'others' also militates against the formation of spontaneous moral relations. Rather, the moral capacities tend to be channelled towards socially designed purposes constituting an often extravagant display of public compassion, which too often aligns instrumentally with the narcissistic desire of the ruling elite to feel good about itself as opposed to a natural expression of tender feelings towards the stranger. Since, unlike other disciplines, law is unique in being mandatory, it compels human behaviour primarily through retribution; and the idea of punishment, in most Western societies, is intimately connected to specific notions of justice, forgiveness and compassion.

The Greek word for the expansive concept of justice, *dikaiosis*, is connected with moral rightness, acting rightly or as one should; it is the virtue which is sought after and advanced by the rule of law. Whilst the administration of law demands abstraction and purports to treat all people the same in a general sense, justice might be described as a matter of compassionate ethics which relates to each individual situation according to its unique properties and every person in terms of their 'otherness'; with a respect for difference at its core. The complex relationship between law, justice and humanity is a constant source of debate between legal theorists and moral philosophers.

There is an abundance of theories of justice which can be explained by the diversity of the concept in its application to individuals, institutions, decisions, processes, laws and actions; with each version having its own distinctive standards of justification along with a set of authoritative texts and mantras. Legal positivists, for example, do not judge the nature and merit of laws by questions of justice or humanity, but rather according to the manner in which the laws have been created, illustrated by the old joke where a petitioner demands justice, only to be admonished by the judge: 'Silence or I will have you ejected – this is a court of law.' Nevertheless, it is often stated that when people appeal to law what they really seek is justice, described as:

> a complex set of passions to be cultivated, not an abstract set of principles to be formulated, mastered, and imposed upon society ... our sense of justice is first of all our emotional response to a world that does not always meet up with our expectations and demands (Solomon 1990: 172).

Enquiries into the kind of society we want to live in and how to determine the appropriate limits and justifications for law give rise to the consideration of moral values and ethical issues, which lie at the heart of law. A decision to penalise or condemn is, therefore, ideally influenced by reason and the noble emotions such as compassion, mercy and forgiveness, underpinned by the rhetoric of justice and a concern for the common good.

In *Political Liberalism*, John Rawls called for substantive restraints on law-making on the grounds that law is not simply an instrument of social order; rather, it must recognise 'basic equal rights and liberties' which conform to the ideal of 'justice as fairness', as a 'higher law to which ordinary law-making is beholden' (Rawls 1996: 233, 284–299). Influenced by Aristotle, Aquinas defined justice as 'a certain rectitude of mind whereby a man does what he ought to do in the circumstances confronting him', determining justice to be a natural duty owed by one individual to another (1947: 848). Sir Edward Coke, early champion of the common law whose ideas influenced the American Revolution, referred to justice as 'the daughter of the law, for the law bringeth her forth'. Many contemporary Western philosophers have promoted justice as a necessary condition for a stable society, whilst others have even considered justice to precede law (Derrida 1992: 24–26). Levinas argued that only an irreducible 'ethical proximity' of one human being to another is capable of creating the metaphysical desire for goodness, as responsibility and obligation. Through that ethical encounter, experienced physically and emotionally, a corresponding relation to all others realises the possibility of a 'call to justice' which goes beyond the limits of ontology, of the human essence and the world (Levinas 1981: 61–94). There are also those who would rank justice alongside compassion. For American novelist and poet Wendell Berry, 'rats and roaches live by competition under the laws of supply and demand; it is the privilege of human beings to live under the laws of justice and compassion' (2002: 212). This chapter will explore the historical origins and continuing relevance of compassion within legal processes and adjudication, with particular emphasis on its ability to inform the notion of moral obligation in the context of what justice requires.

From vengeance to compassion: the two faces of 'justice'

The idea of justice originates in philosophical discourse but is widely used in everyday speech and legal language, often without being clearly defined. Comprising a vast and imponderable concept, there are various intra-legal and extra-legal formulations which all aspire to promote some form of rightness and equity. In ancient times, the Old Testament and Homeric idea of justice had a personal character; a person seeking justice did not want an apology or recompense – they wanted revenge. Justice as vengeance was a matter of restoring one's offended honour by a forceful response to the insult or disgrace, which, although personal, had also transgressed social rules and norms of conduct. Homer was an extremely influential figure and considered to be the moral educator of the Greeks; his works *The Iliad* and *The Odyssey* both portray heroes who ferociously pursue and inflict excessively violent revenge on their adversaries. To avenge the death of Patroklos, it is not enough for Achilles to kill Hektor; he goes on to mutilate the body of his enemy by mercilessly hauling it around the walls of Troy. Odysseus returns to Ithaca after a 20-year series of struggles and (mis)adventures following the Trojan War, and immediately slaughters all 108 of wife Penelope's noble suitors (even though none were successful), after which he then kills and mutilates his own disloyal servants.

The ritual retaliation of hubris, revenge and vendetta are common themes within the Homeric poems, and considerations we would commonly associate with justice, such as motive, culpability or willingness, are conspicuously absent. Some 400 years later Aristotle's formal conception of justice simply required treating equals equally and unequals unequally; somewhat complicated by how to determine which criteria are morally relevant to differentiate between these two groups. The biblical articulation of justice as *lex talionis* – 'an eye for an eye, a tooth for a tooth' – although still defined by the motive of exchange and concerned with reprisal, introduces boundaries and balance; the violence that may be inflicted in retaliation is bounded by the notion of equivalence. These early guiding principles evidenced a degree of succumbing to the negative passions and, whilst a millennium away from contemporary Western theories of justice, they emphasised reciprocity which formed a key stage in developing the modern conception of retributive justice.

In the eighteenth century, in a world that was being transformed through modernity, moral sentiment theorists began to consider the relation between the positive passions and moral contexts, specifically the moral significance of compassion. Jean-Jacques Rousseau connected the legitimacy of law to the moral imagination, describing the essential connection between 'justice and kindness' as 'no mere abstract terms'; rather, they comprise the 'true affections of the heart enlightened by reason, the natural outcome of our primitive affections' (1979: 235). Throughout his writing Rousseau affirms our first spontaneous impulse as goodness – we want to be kind; 'the first impulses of the heart give rise to the first stirrings of conscience' and so emphasises his belief in our innate predisposition for empathic concern (1979: 196). The belief that our natural inclinations and sensibilities could be compatible with the formation of valid moral judgment reflects the influence of English philosopher Anthony Ashley Cooper, the Third Earl of Shaftesbury:

> the affection of a creature towards the good of the species or common nature is as *proper* and *natural* to him as it is to any organ, part or member of an animal body, or mere vegetable, to work in its known course and regular way of growth (Shaftesbury 1999: 192).

A person who intuitively performs their duty for the good of the organisation of which they are part is purported to act as naturally (and self-interestedly) as their stomach in digesting food for the benefit of their body. When the original propensity for good is linked with a capacity for self-reflection on what is right and wrong, honest and worthy (so that our moral judgments are directed towards right actions), this instinctive inclination tempered by moral evaluation means our 'sense of morals' becomes virtuous.

Like Rousseau, Kant privileged natural human impulses, morals and virtues, the non-cognitive origins of morality – although he did not accredit compassion with moral value. Only kindness motivated by duty for duty's sake or the moral law (as the determining ground for the will) was considered to be capable of having moral worth and of fulfilling the objective conditions of morality. In his pre-Critical 1764 aesthetic work *Observations on the Feeling of the Beautiful and Sublime*, Kant repeatedly and explicitly differentiates between 'true virtue' (sublime) and the 'adoptive virtues' or 'assisting drives' (beautiful), locating compassion and benevolence in the latter and lesser category. Later, in his 1785 *Groundwork of the Metaphysics of Morals*, Kant even alludes to 'melting sympathies' in a cynical sideswipe at some of his British sentimentalist predecessors, particularly Hume – renowned for his reversal of the Platonic relationship in which 'Reason is, and ought only to be the slave of the passions, and can never pretend to any other office than to serve and obey them' (Hume 1967: 415). Nevertheless, in the introduction to the 'Doctrine of Virtue' in his last published work on moral philosophy in 1797, *Metaphysics of Morals*, the ability to experience compassion in relevant situations is expressed by Kant as instrumental to understanding what 'a respect for the duty of beneficence' requires of us:

> while it is not in itself a duty to share the sufferings (as well as the joys) of others, it is a duty to sympathise actively in their fate; and to this end it is therefore an indirect duty to cultivate the compassionate natural (aesthetic) feelings in us, and to make use of them as so many means to sympathy based on moral principles and the feeling appropriate to them. … For [compassion] is still one of the impulses that nature has implanted in us to do what the representation of duty alone might not accomplish (1991: 6.457).

Whilst imposing no direct obligation to feel compassion, the 'moral predispositions of the mind' provide the subjective conditions for receptiveness to the duty of beneficence, which requires our emotional participation in the sadness and sorrow of others. This gives rise to a conditional or limited and indirect duty to utilise naturally occurring feelings of compassion as a means of promoting 'rational benevolence', under appropriate circumstances. Cultivating these natural propensities is encouraged, therefore, only on the condition that they are acted upon in compliance with the moral law, so that the actions such feelings would motivate are always morally correct. After all, emotions of fellow-feeling such as sympathy or compassion might lead to morally dubious or even immoral actions, such as assisting someone struggling with a heavy package leaving by the back door of the

Museum of Fine Arts in the dead of night, when we ought to be calling the police (Herman 1993: 4–5). On the other hand, if lying is without exception always immoral, then telling a lie out of a compassionate impulse to protect and save another's life, such as hiding Jews from the Nazis in WWII, would also be morally wrong. Kant's moral philosophy has attracted much criticism on this point, and it might be argued that just as there is a perfect moral duty to always tell the truth, there is also a moral duty to preserve one's life and, by extension, the lives of others, especially given his prohibition on suicide as an expression of self-love which debases the moral self. In any case, the ability to act morally would seem to be largely dependent upon cultivating and refining our natural inclinations, such as compassion and love, so as to assist in finding the proper object for the motive of duty; and, despite his repudiation of moral sense theories as heteronomous, moral impulses and feelings continued to feature in Kant's moral thought.

As an alternative to, what Husserl termed, Kant's 'extreme intellectualist' and 'absurd rationalist' moral formulation (1988: 412, 415), Rousseau asserted that emotional feeling was not only useful but also necessary for moral motivation. In *On the Social Contract* he claimed that individuals can only escape experiencing pain at the suffering of others because the structure of society allows them to persist in the illusion that they are special and indestructible. Such abstract reasoning was said to undermine a more natural system of values as it imposed no duty on the fortunate to alleviate the suffering of less fortunate others or help in creating a more just society. For Rousseau, the passions guide us in questioning what is really important about the distinctions we encounter in society, such as divisions based on class, and compassion reduces the distance between individuals. His moral sentimentalism was in response to a decaying society, the values of which he believed were being distorted by the commercial and economic priorities of the Enlightenment along with their corrosive influence on the arts and sciences.

Scottish contemporaries Francis Hutcheson, David Hume and Adam Smith similarly placed moral sentiment at the core of their respective moral theories. For Smith the influence of the passions in law-making cannot be underestimated; he proposed that ethical judgments relating to right and wrong, just and unjust are as much a property of feeling as of intellectual understanding or reason (2002: 22–25). He further argued that all humans have the innate desire for realising a 'mutual sympathy' of sentiments; even the 'greatest ruffian' or the 'most hardened violator of the laws of society' gains pleasure from seeing their own sentiments reflected in the thoughts and behaviour of others. The impetus for imaginative identification with, and pursuit of, those with reciprocally held sentiments is claimed to provide the basis for certain acts of benevolence and greater social cohesion, as people seek to create sympathetic social relations with others in groups and communities:

> How selfish soever man may be supposed, there are evidently some principles in his nature, which interest him in the fortunes of others, and render their happiness necessary to him, though he derives nothing from it, except the pleasure of seeing it. Of this kind is pity or compassion, the emotion we feel for the misery of others, when we either see it, or are made to conceive it in a

> very lively manner. … it is by the imagination only that we can form any conception of what are his sensations [and] by the imagination we place ourselves in his situation (Smith 2002: 11–12).

Smith stressed the moral importance of recognising these interweaving natural networks of interdependencies with embodied human beings, rather than privileging only a pure abstract or rational concern for their universal essence. Inspired by Hutcheson's theory of 'moral sense' (2003), Hume's thesis extended this proposition by asserting that the ability to empathise with the suffering of others, so as to respond in an ethically appropriate manner, was not only posited as a necessary attribute of moral agency; it was also the source of moral agency without which we are only capable of a limited social existence (1975: 289). His sensible anti-rationalist conclusions proposed that reason is inert and incapable of exercising causal influence as 'morals excite passions, and produce or prevent actions. Reason of itself is utterly impotent in this particular; the rules of morality, therefore, are not conclusions of reason' (Hume 1967: 457). In light of the relational and social nature of humankind, the determination of compassion as a first principle of moral judgments (and the prerequisite for moral action which could not be learned) is worthy of consideration; however, the claim that the emotions can completely rule reason is perhaps spurious. Most moral sense philosophers supported the idea that there must be critical and constructive engagement between reason and the passions.

The turn of the twentieth century marked the beginning of a scientific interest in studying the emotions evidenced in, for example, the works of Sigmund Freud and his claim that self-knowledge is a precondition of empathy necessary for moral judgment, and William James' explication of the virtues of gratitude, remorse and compassion as emotions which motivate appropriate actions. In the 1950s and 60s John Rawls wrote a series of articles which reimagined the role of political and moral philosophy in relation to a modern conception of social justice; this approach, by his own admission, was influenced by Rousseau's social contract arguments in the formulation of his reflective equilibrium methodology. This forms an integral part of his *A Theory of Justice*, published in 1971, in which Rawls asserts we utilise our ordinary faculties of thoughts, desires, feelings and inclinations (our intuitions) to make moral judgments. He emphasised the importance of critically ordering our moral 'intuitions' as these were purported not only to assist in the composition of moral thoughts which lead to moral theories but also, for philosophers, they play an important role in making a choice between competing normative theories.

In order to determine the content of principles of justice, our pre-theoretical intuitions must be reconciled with moral theories by means of a deliberative process of back and forth critical reflection towards revising, modifying and amending both intuitions and beliefs until all judgments are consistent (Rawls 1999). The right theory of justice imposes a duty of compassion and humanity which any rational individual would choose to regulate their actions and to ground moral commitments relating to justice as fairness. Rawls constantly refers to the sentiments – a predisposition for particular feelings, behaviour and beliefs – in connection with honing our 'sense' of justice; however, this is too frequently no more than a spontaneous instantiation of abstract rational principles or casuistic evidence for them. It seems to be a somewhat weaker formulation than the philosophies of Hume, Rousseau and Smith, for whom moral sentiment, in particular empathy, underpinned all moral judgment; this was the fundamental starting point for formulating ethical principles pertaining to justice, equality, impartiality and rights. In contemporary law, although the utility of emotion is still central to much debate between legal scholars and moral philosophers, compassion continues to be an endangered and often ridiculed sentiment.

Compassionate justice and the ethical significance of vulnerability

To philosophically advance the notion of the possibility of, or desire for, justice in law, it has been suggested that compassion must be advocated as a basic concept of humanity and ethical judgment which transcends the centralised force of the given law. That is not to take a narrowly sentimentalist view of justice; rather, an authentic call to justice demands a constant resolve to commit oneself to the common good, on the basis that a civil society can only survive if maintained by an emotional, and intellectual, commitment on the part of all members in relation to all other members. Nussbaum's 2013 work *Political Emotions: Why Love Matters for Justice* considers the utility and value of public emotion to critical reasoning and practical justice, along with the significance of compassion and how it may be possible to develop this noble emotion out from its narrow roots to a much wider embrace. She argues that, although our evolutionary history has bestowed on humans the capacity for altruism, compassion and feelings of unanimity, these feelings commonly only attach to group affiliations. Such personal proclivities are said to comprise a particularised subjective 'circle of concern', rather than a concern which extends unconditionally to all persons; and so Nussbaum proposes a broader conceptual understanding of empathy, as 'the imaginative reconstruction of another person's experience [irrespective of] whether the imaginer thinks the other person's situation good, bad or indifferent' (2001: 302). The driving force of empathy is therefore about fostering compassion, not for friends and family members or for those in which we share common interests and values, but for those who have no pre-existing relation to us, who bear no resemblance to us and whose circumstances lie far beyond our own realm of experience. In *Political Emotions*, rejecting the 'Romantic idea that emotion is not worthy unless it comes unbidden', Nussbaum urges the co-option of government rhetoric and state-sponsored public activities, public art and corporate-sponsored events comprising, *inter alia*, 'symbols, songs and sculpture' in order to foster a new civic culture of 'enhanced empathy' (2013: 65, 381–386).

Whilst the imposition of any political initiative to influence or manipulate public emotions towards supporting liberal goals may be construed as a threat against autonomy, the postmodern tradition considers the grand metanarratives of law to be already an unacceptable expression of power relations. In the late eighteenth century, for example, the conscious promotion by law-making authorities of the hierarchical notion of the 'natural self' as male meant that Western European single women were taught accomplishments such as music, needlepoint and etiquette rather than academic subjects, and had few political, employment or educational rights. Married women possessed no legal identity; they were unable to retain the services of a lawyer, make contracts and they had no rights even over their own children. Feminist philosophers, including Luce Irigaray, Hélène Cixous and Judith Butler, have deconstructed the overarching patriarchal model, highlighting the application of a phallocentric ideology and socially defined gender categories with which to exclude women from participation in active civil life – rather reserving power and privilege for men (Irigaray 1999: 82–91; Cixous 1976: 875–893; Butler 2004: 134–151). In the opening words of *The Posthuman*, contemporary philosopher and feminist theorist Rosi Braidotti claims:

> Not all of us can say, with any degree of certainty, that we have always been human, or that we are only that. Some of us are not even considered fully human now, let alone at previous moments of Western social, political and scientific history (2013: 1).

The tendency to prioritise masculine virtues such as rationality, objectivity and totalising narrative over context and nuance means modern law-making is not geared towards empathic understanding and judgment (Smart 1989). Law commands our obedience because of carrying the weight of authority, as distinct from justice which compels us to challenge and enhance the law. In this case, in order to realise a call to justice it is first necessary to deconstruct the metanarratives of politics, economics, culture and ideals of progress, according to which those with power would seek to 'write' or dictate the conditions under which the rest of us should live:

> There is a history of legal systems, of rights, of laws, of political laws, and this history is the history of the transformation of laws … you can replace laws by other ones. Each time you replace a legal system by another one, or a law by another one … it is a kind of deconstruction, a critical deconstruction. Deconstruction is a call for justice [although] justice is not reducible to the law, to a given system of legal structures. That's why the call for justice is never, let's say, fully answered … no one can say 'I am just' [because] justice cannot be reduced to a calculation of sanctions, punishments or rewards (Derrida 1997: 16–17).

The deconstruction of law's inherent universalism, privileging of reason, conceptual knowledge and concern with the past releases the potential for future social and political reform by making it possible to focus on the particular politics which constitute a specific context or situation in the present. Doing justice is arguably more than adhering to a process that simply requires obedience to following the letter of the law, as formulated by the impartial spectator. It is, rather, an expression of moral responsibility to differentiated others which must take place outside legal principle and constitutes the code beneath the code of law. At an individual level, we are all situated within different echelons of a vast range of economic and institutional relationships which give rise to varying degrees of anxiety and conflict, privilege and hardship. It is, therefore, an unjust legal system which would dilute the wants and needs of all persons into 'one coherent system of desire'; rather, for Rawls:

> Justice is the first virtue of social institutions, as truth is of systems of thought [in which] each person possesses an inviolability founded on justice that even the welfare of society as a whole cannot override. For this reason justice denies that the loss of freedom for some is made right by a greater good shared by others. It does not allow that the sacrifices imposed on a few are outweighed by the larger sum of advantages enjoyed by many (Rawls 1999: 3–4, 27).

The principle of *sensus communis* or socio-moral sense of the common good, which influenced Rawls' idea of reflective equilibrium, is described by Kant in *Critique of Judgment* to be the location from which it is possible to extend compassion as meaningful engagement with the full range of others, who constitute a particular community of diverse judgments. Within this community, each person is considered to belong to a 'kingdom of ends' because they have an inner value or dignity that has nothing to do with their comparative market value, irrespective of their usefulness to someone or for something. Imbuing common sense with a moral compass and contrary to feelings of self-importance and superiority, the principle embodies the notion of empathic kindness derived from an awareness of the commonality all have with each other as human beings. It demands the recognition of a moral imperative to acknowledge and address the interests of each individual participant within the public sphere, on the basis that it is only possible to sustain the idea of community by cultivating a reciprocal appreciation for, and sympathetic identification with, differentiated others.

In compassion, a state of emotional resonance means the condition of the Other is empathically experienced, and their well-being becomes a matter of concern evoking our heartfelt consideration and support. Conforming to the Kantian principle of human dignity precludes, therefore, the instrumentalisation of human beings for economic, social, religious or political ideals. To this end, all those in Western society who are often considered to be 'outsiders' – such as the elderly, minority ethnic groups, homosexuals, women, the poor and the disabled – would be recognised as being equal members of the *sensus communis* with an identical ability to participate in the construction of rules and the interpretation of law. A concern for their well-being and suffering constitutes a decidedly moral discourse that involves questions of compassion, ethics, obligation and action, and is intimately linked to history and political economy. This ideal of a shared sensibility not only facilitates the formation of successful individual relationships but also, by creating mutual dependencies, gives rise to natural affections, improves social cohesion and further ensures the stability of society.

Political, philosophical, religious, legal and literary figures – from Mahatma Ghandi, Winston Churchill and Fyodor Dostoevsky to Pope John Paul II and

John E.E. Dalberg, aka Lord Acton – have all suggested that a nation's character or greatness is measured by how it treats its weakest members, the vulnerable and easily forgotten. In a lecture delivered in 1877 on 'The History of Freedom in Antiquity', Lord Acton insisted that 'liberalism cannot approve an extreme selfishness of the wealthy at the price of dire poverty for the poor'; rather, there is a duty to take care of 'the crippled child, the idiot and the madman' (Dalberg 1877: 41, 42). Vulnerability, although historically understated and overlooked in formal thinking in favour of the model of the individualistic, self-determined and autonomous agent, has often played a central role in formulating legal and ethical principles. In her essay 'The Vulnerable Subject: Anchoring Equality in the Human Condition', Martha Fineman conceptualises a positive form of vulnerability, describing an unavoidable and 'inevitable co-dependency', which includes the cooperation of the state, on which every person relies for the pursuit and attainment of various ends, particularly those which attach to the gratification of significant needs and desires. In this case, vulnerability is both 'individual and institutional', as well as 'universal and constant' (Fineman 2011: 168). This constant state of vulnerability, to which all are susceptible, is identified as a useful heuristic device which can help uncover the negative origins of the concept, and examine hidden assumptions and biases that shaped its original social and cultural meanings. Since the possibility of harm or suffering due to unpredictable events beyond our control is said to constitute 'a universal, inevitable, enduring aspect of the human condition that must be at the heart of our concept of social and state responsibility', vulnerability is identified as a powerful conceptual instrument which is capable of justifying the case for a more responsive state and egalitarian society (Fineman 2011: 166). In this analysis vulnerability is, therefore, an outcome of our physical embodiment and a consequence of the profound interdependence we all share with one another.

Poor health, disability, accidents, economic hardship and the inevitability of death result in human fragility; however, the fluctuating disparities in power relations between and among people create many forms of social, political and economic vulnerability. The latter vulnerabilities and variances contribute to the way in which our relationships with others are outlined and expressed, modifying these relations as power shifts. The legal system responds to such fluctuations by a constant process of refining its classification systems and narrative structures to accommodate the newly pathologised or sanctified discourses; implementing, for example, refocused standards of fairness, justification or proof. All regimes of power are legitimated by laws and, whilst ascribing to the principle of legality and some version of justice often as 'the rule of law', have produced a variety of 'rule*s* of law' – many of which have the potential to exacerbate human suffering in one way or another. Totalitarianism, for example, imposes hardship and inequality for the benefit of those who govern in their quest to seek control over both the minds and bodies of their subjects; theocracy imposes hardship in the name of a divine being, whilst liberal democracy imposes hardship so that those who are deemed to be entrepreneurial, privileged or affluent can better attain social and economic advantage over the less-fortunate masses (Shaw, H.J. 2014: 3). It is unrealistic, however, to expect society's institutions to eradicate every instance of individual vulnerability as all institutions, including the legal institution, have their own vulnerabilities, often as a result of economic constraints. The UK Constitutional Reform Act 2005, for example, had major institutional implications, and more recently the UK Legal Aid, Sentencing and Punishment of Offenders Act 2013 has had a significant impact on the English Civil and Criminal Bar. In addition to the imposition of additional hardship on vulnerable people by replacing the ethos of access to justice with 'justice by wealth', the lack of available funds has meant smaller law firms have closed, creating 'legal advice deserts', and efforts to increase diversity across the legal profession have been set back. Under such circumstances, the acknowledgement of vulnerabilities is complicated because, as Judith Butler elucidates in *Precarious Life*:

> Vulnerability must be perceived and recognised in order to come into play in an ethical encounter, and there is no guarantee that this will happen. Not only is there always the possibility that a vulnerability will not be recognised and that it will be constituted as the 'unrecognisable', but when a vulnerability is recognised, that recognition has the power to change the meaning and structure of the vulnerability itself (2006: 43).

As well as often being invisible or denied, the omnipresence of vulnerabilities such as adversity and suffering, and institutional responses to both, are inextricably allied to local, national and international histories, politics, economies, institutions and cultures that are not easy to unravel. As an alternative standpoint, the strength of the vulnerability critique lies in its capacity to constitute the necessary prerequisite for interpersonal ethics because it expresses the finitude and fragility of life which grounds the possibility of all morality. As those with power routinely engage in making judgments about others, it is important to recognise that all judgment has an inherent social dimension which inevitably relies on mutual interdependence and a duty of care; towards the actualisation of a more just society in pursuit of the flourishing of all members. So then, rather than muse on more complex formal and seemingly irresolvable questions of intrinsic value such as virtue, goods or particular moral imperatives for action, it is more useful and appropriate to articulate a set of rules and conditions of reciprocal engagement. It would then follow that social institutions such as the court system must assume a moral responsibility to mediate, compensate and otherwise address our individual vulnerabilities in an equitable manner and with compassion, in the knowledge that all members of the moral community have interests that are capable of being harmed; we are all vulnerable.

'Truth waits for eyes unclouded by longing': 'enlarged' (empathic) perception motivates compassionate judgment

Compassion has been referred to as a 'basic social emotion', worthy of being nurtured as a necessary virtue of legal rationality and key characteristic of good judgment because of its ability for sympathetic identification with the situation of others (Nussbaum 1996). Legal Realists Oliver Wendell Holmes, Roscoe Pound and Benjamin Cardozo all claimed that law is full of gaps, holes and contradictions; and, whilst good judgment is therefore an essential skill, it does not conform to any precise formulation, set of general rules or algorithms, and cannot be taught. In his famous treatise *The Nature of the Judicial Process*, which describes a variety of conscious and unconscious practices responsible for influencing the adjudicative process, US Supreme Court Judge Cardozo adopted a typically Aristotelian position. He emphasised the role of insight and understanding in being able to determine the lacuna between a rule and its application, along with the use of 'good judgment' in those circumstances where there are no clear rules. Discussing the role of good judgment in deciding difficult cases, he advises:

> If you ask how [a judge] is to know when one interest outweighs another, I can only answer that he must get his knowledge just as the legislator gets it, from experience and study and reflection; in brief from life itself (Cardozo 1921:112–113).

He later elaborates on 'other forces of which judges avowedly avail to shape the form and content of their judgments' that reside 'deep below consciousness', comprising 'the likes and the dislikes, the predilections and the prejudices, the complex of instincts and emotions and habits and convictions, which make the man, whether he be litigant or judge' (Cardozo 1921: 167). Where the application of a strict legal rule is not possible, experience, understanding and reflection are necessary for fulfilling the promise of the law in seeking to diminish human suffering and promote universal human dignity.

Rather than privileging mere knowledge of *what* may be the right answer, good judgment is practical judgment and is a matter of knowing *how* to determine the most appropriate course of action; and there are an infinite number of factors to consider. So where the facts fall outside prescribed legal criteria, a good judge will resist any compulsion to rely on personal opinion; instead they will look to apply practical wisdom underpinned by persuasive narrative. Applying practical wisdom to judgment requires imaginative and empathic identification with another person, in attempting to understand the world from another's point of view and the particular values at stake. It not only demands a compassionate outlook, whereby the beliefs, desires and motivations of those seeking justice are taken into consideration, but also requires an awareness that a particular interpretation of 'facts' and circumstances inevitably influence the decision-making process and impact the final judgment. Accordingly, being based in practical considerations emerging from a dynamic social context, the law is further developed as a responsive, flexible and reciprocal mode of organisation which, while not grounded in political confrontation, recognises social struggle – as opposed to simply acting as an autonomous and abstract body of rules and doctrines divorced from the real world. By acknowledging the role of both cognitive and affective components, legal practice is rendered both *just* – being rooted in ethical proximity – and *justified*, as a legitimate expression of self and society.

A social order is founded on a complex web of connections in which our relationships to others are instrumental in helping us to understand who we are; and so the moral and legal self is constituted in relation to others rather than individuals standing alone under a system of rules. It is hardly surprising that the role of emotions, and particularly the significance of mercy and compassion, have commonly featured in a diverse range of historical and contemporary legal formulations – in relation to either their presence or absence. Property law, for example, has evolved slowly; but even as modern surveying practices, record-keeping technologies and statutory reform have largely eroded the rationale for the doctrine of adverse possession, the relation between property and community continues to be an emotive topic (Fox 2007: 137). Profound feelings of individual self-worth and autonomy, a sense of safety, shelter, security, control and identity, are bound together with the notion of ownership in which our rights in a thing are enforced and protected by the state. Accordingly, 'if land is part of the self' the reallocation of state-sanctioned rights in land from owners to non-owners, without the consent of the owner, by the state 'is akin to physical or mental punishment' (Stake 2001: 2456). Bearing in mind the proverb 'an Englishman's home is his castle', recent research questioning the modern relevance of the ancient English doctrine (which has been around since Roman times) explores the application of loss aversion theory, focusing on the complex emotional attachments an adverse possessor has developed in relation to a particular property. It has been recommended that possession is awarded to the party who is most attached, and therefore would bear the greatest emotional injury, because 'the law refrains from depriving people of lands they have long occupied as doing so would cause them too much pain' (Stake 2001: 2473). This opinion, which resonates with the adage 'possession is nine-tenths of the law', also echoes Holmes' classic articulation of the adverse possession doctrine:

> It is in the nature of man's mind. A thing which you have enjoyed and used as your own for a long time, whether property or opinion, takes root in your being and cannot be torn away without your resenting the act and trying to defend yourself, no matter how you came by it. The law can ask no better justification than the deepest instincts of man (Holmes 1897: 477).

Yet property law remains an area which is dominated by rules and legal formalism; and, consequently, contested land claims commonly elicit a dispassionate (in the sense of uncaring or unfeeling) response from the courts.

Although the UK Land Registration Act 2002 attempts to militate against the negative emotions connoted by adverse possession claims, it still only represents a slight improvement to the arguably limited protections afforded to vulnerable owners. In *Best v The Chief Land Registrar & Anor* [2014] EWHC 1370 (Admin) (7 May 2014) a squatter was handed a landmark victory in spite of residential squatting being criminalised in s.144(1) of the UK Legal Aid, Sentencing and Punishment of Offenders Act 2012. Justifying the decision, Mr Justice Ouseley explained:

> Parliament should be taken to have thought that the public policy advantages of adverse possession at common law meant that the mere fact that the adverse possession was based on criminal trespass did not and should not preclude a successful claim to adverse possession (*Best* [2014] EWHC 1370 at 86).

In taking a dispassionate view of the circumstances, the Chief Land Registrar privileged the public policy benefits of adverse possession – namely, the prevention of economic and public disadvantages of land remaining unused and unclaimed – against the interests of the 'owner' who, in this case, is living in sheltered accommodation. The decision not only represents a slavish adherence to rules contrary to good sense; it is also tantamount to sanctioning land theft, by turning a material and moral wrong into a legal right. An uncritical adherence to unbending universal rules eliminates the importance of context and proportionality in decision-making, which can lead to absurd legal consequences as well as fuelling negative emotions – namely, a collective sense of disgust, resentment and public outrage at the injustice of those decisions which fail to consider relevant emotional attachments.

Although 'the law speaks universally', it is clear that under certain circumstances equity requires the law be set aside because the 'moral contours' of the case situate it outside the universal formula. In such instances, which require a more tailored or nuanced response, specific actions by individuals in specific situations are better accommodated by equity resulting in a judgment which may even, to some extent, be 'better than just' (Aristotle 1998: 37). The corollary of this view is that the central principles of a legal system, such as liberty, justice and equality before the law, are not vitiated by the more lenient treatment of a driver who exceeds the statutory speed limit to take their convulsive child to hospital, as opposed to handing down a harsher sentence for the speeding hard drug dealer who has an urgent meeting with his supplier. As a principle of justice, against arbitrariness, a judge would have to demonstrate moral consistency in the exercise of morally compassionate or merciful judgments. Moral consistency, however, would be dependent upon the personal and 'pre-rational' characteristics of the judge in advance of any application of the law. The ability to make extra-legal moral evaluations would require the development of a sense of justice which expresses a particular emotional cognition founded on value judgments. This would ideally, even rightfully, be informed by an *a priori* intuitive understanding and an intentional feeling towards impartial judgment so that, rather than imposing a superior standpoint, this form of impartiality would be able to take into account the viewpoints of others in acknowledgement of the plurality of society. For Hannah Arendt, judgments which evince such an inherently subjective dimension are only possible because of our human capacity for 'enlarged thought':

> The 'enlargement of the mind' plays a crucial role in [Kant's] *Critique of Judgment*. It is accomplished by 'comparing our judgment with the possible rather than the actual judgments of others, and by putting ourselves in the place of any other man.' The faculty that makes this possible is called

> imagination … Critical thinking is only possible where the standpoints of all others are open to inspection. Hence, critical thinking, while still a solitary business, does not cut itself off from 'all others'. To be sure, it still goes on in isolation, but by the force of imagination it makes the others present and thus moves in a space that is potentially public, open to all sides … To think with an enlarged mentality means that one trains one's imagination to go visiting (Arendt 1992: 42–43).

The expanded mindset that imaginatively considers the standpoints of others breaks free from the restraints of self-absorption and adapts itself to the world, firstly, by rejecting the ideology and indoctrination of any communal group alignments and, secondly, by understanding humanity through the eyes of an abstracted generalised Other. As fifth-century poet and philosopher Lao Tzu advised in the *Tao Te Ching*, 'Truth waits for eyes unclouded by longing', which entails suppressing one's own desires in order to facilitate a more compassionate response to the needs of others. It is possible to see, with 'eyes unclouded', the reality of the Other's existence which is not fully aligned with one's own needs or personal desire system. Such empathic reasoning constitutes the recognition of a shared right to human flourishing and justice, and in turn acknowledges a fundamental interdependency which affirms one's deepest humanity. For Judith Butler, beginning in infancy 'no subject emerges without a passionate attachment to those on whom he or she is fundamentally dependent … this situation of primary dependency conditions the political formation and regulation of subjects' (1997: 7). Whilst there is always a danger of exploitation, the state of initial dependency or 'primary passion' lays the groundwork for subordinating one's personal desires to a wider sense of good as the common good. As a consequence, the individual becomes a moral agent and, ideally, gains membership of a reciprocal ethical community of 'judges' who are able to appreciate the perspectives of each other. This does not mean adopting one or the same world view; rather, each person is required to appreciate the particularity and originality of the Other's views and seek to respond in novel ways:

> The power of judgment rests on a potential agreement with others, and the thinking process which is active in judging something is not, like the thought process of pure reasoning, a dialogue between me and myself, but finds itself always and primarily, even if I am quite alone in making up my mind, in an anticipated communication with others with whom I know I must finally come to some agreement. From this potential agreement, judgment derives its specific validity. This means, on the one hand, that such judgment must liberate itself from the 'subjective private conditions', that is, from the idiosyncrasies which naturally determine the outlook of each individual in his privacy and are legitimate as long as they are only privately held opinions but which are not fit to enter the market place, and lack all validity in the public realm. And this enlarged way of thinking, which as judgment knows how to transcend its individual limitations, cannot function in strict isolation or

> solitude; it needs the presence of others 'in whose place' it must think, whose perspectives it must take into consideration, and without whom it never has the opportunity to operate at all (Arendt 1977a: 220–221).

As the law is an entirely human invention, the always ongoing and ever-changing construction of specific rules and interpretation of founding principles by particular legal actors to fit a certain set of circumstances depends on their individual training, experience and values. Utilising the Kantian concept of the 'enlarged mentality' or what she refers to as 'representative thinking', Arendt provides a model for intersubjective validity in the public sphere which she claims is capable of overcoming narrow preconceptions, self-referentiality and the reliance on outmoded categories of judgment (1977b: 247). This is because plurality is the most significant political fact and judging is one of the most important activities (by engaging with politics, the social and morality) in which the idea of a shared world arises. However, to fully inhabit a 'common world' in the Arendtian sense is precisely *not* to share a world view because the common world is constituted by a multiplicity of different world views which shape its meaning. Such encounters begin with a dialogue between oneself and the impersonal, imagined Other(s) on a matter of mutual concern or interest. The enlarged mentality model cannot guarantee impartiality or correct distortions of power as it relies on the willingness of individuals with influence to consider alternative perspectives and even to optimally exercise their ability to judge by seeking out diversity, or 'train one's imagination to go visiting' (Arendt 1992: 43).

Although legal texts seek to exemplify and entrench the ideal of 'civilised' humanity by proclaiming a commitment to respect for difference and tolerance of diversity, lurking just beneath the surface is an underlying dynamic of self-justification and homogenisation. Perhaps limited by their personal experiences and presuppositions, decision-making power elites decide what counts as normal in society and use their own identity as the benchmark. The inevitable corollary of this is that other identities are often considered to be deviant, abnormal or alien. In the case of sexual identity, for example, more often than not difference constitutes a threat to the precepts determined and controlled by society, and so tests the limits of tolerance. However, the kind of toleration hoped for is not simply that which allows minorities the freedom to express themselves as they wish; rather, it must 'accord recognition to minorities so that they cease to suffer humiliating assaults upon their self-respect and self-esteem, and are enabled to function as full members of the society to which they belong' (Jones 2006: 127). This is because, not least of all, when the perspective of the judged is excluded from the community of judgement they will not accept the judgment as valid, but as a hostile imposition of force which may be met with violence.

The implication for law is that all individuals need to feel part of a 'community of judgment' rather than merely the object of judgment, so that their unique position and perspective is considered rationally and empathically – and perhaps even imaginatively worked out in advance. Like the angel sitting in the middle of a construction site surrounded by measuring instruments in Albrecht Dürer's

Melencolia, the deliberations and decisions of lawyers must be, as near as possible, a true and just representation of the world and its people. In turn, the community is able to evolve as a more cohesive and inclusive social, political and moral unity, by mitigating some of the anxiety, humiliation, resentment and precariousness that is inimical to the exercise of legal judgment.

Compassion and the criminal justice system

By theorising the essential role performed by moral emotions in adjudication with regard to punishment and other types of condemnation, it is possible to explore them in a variety of important and meaningful ways. The exercise of forgiveness and mercy motivated by compassion, for example, may reduce the severity of the sentence and penalty; however, the complex and conflictual relation between law, justice and compassion provides a variety of enduring conceptual conundrums. Recent times have witnessed the retreat of penal welfarism, the growth of carceral culture and increase in the prison population, including a rise in the incarceration of non-violent offenders, along with a popularisation of the rhetoric of insecurity or 'populist punitivism' and a loss of moral legitimacy of the rehabilitative ideal. In *The Culture of Control*, David Garland identifies, and offers a critique of, new techniques involved in the organisation of security and the characteristics of, often controversial, attendant crime control measures. Although published before 9/11, the conceptualisation of the threat to national security by criminal activity as an omnipresent and commonplace occurrence meant that the priorities of securitisation, prevention, harm reduction and risk management have become the norm. Garland outlines the transformative stages of the increasingly commercialised and objectifying criminal justice systems in the UK and the US, identifying the 12 key 'indices of change' as:

> (1) the decline of the rehabilitative ideal; (2) the re-emergence of punitive sanctions and expressive justice, (3) changes in the emotional tone of crime policy; (4) the return of the victim; (5) the protection of the public as paramount; (6) the politicisation of crime, and populist rhetoric and policies; (7) the reinvention of the prison; (8) the transformation of criminological thought; (9) the expanding infrastructure of crime prevention and community safety; (10) the commercialisation of crime control; (11) new management styles and working practices; and (12) a perpetual sense of crisis (2001: 6–20).

Differentiating between 'criminologies of the self' and 'criminologies of the other', Garland accuses the latter of representing criminals as menacing outcasts or 'super-predators', many of whom are said to be 'evil', 'wicked', 'beyond all human understanding' and 'barely human' (2001: 135). In many US murder cases, a variety of highly emotive and pejorative terms – such as 'cruel, heinous and depraved' or 'hardened' or being stated to have a 'malignant heart' – have been applied to the accused's character in order to justify the application of a harsher sentence. The retributivist idea of a morally permissible deserved punishment, or 'just deserts', is at the same time both a retrospective and interpretative concept. Being motivated by vengeful emotions, those who are inclined to rationalise the excessive punishment impulse also tend to view criminals as monsters and vermin, as members of a different species, and as something less than human that cannot be subdued.

Simultaneously, the capacity of such individuals for introspection is often limited due to a kind of self-righteousness which engenders an unforgiving nature and a propensity to demand draconian punishments. The modern American resource-starved penal system exemplifies this predisposition because of its attitude towards criminal punishment, prison conditions and the unduly harsh treatment of those accused of criminal acts – leading to the US earning the dubious distinction of having the highest imprisonment rate in the world. Currently the United States, with about one-twentieth of the world's population, locks up approximately one-fourth of the world's prisoners. This outstrips even Russia, Cuba, Rwanda, Belarus and Kazakhstan, and with almost no constructive outcomes to justify such mass incarceration – especially as many leave prison as career criminals or, at least, harder, enraged, resentful and less willing or able to assimilate in society. As the old African proverb explains, 'the axe forgets what the tree remembers'. Little has changed since Johnny Cash composed and performed his song 'San Quentin', written from the point of view of a prisoner, in a concert for the inmates of San Quentin state prison in 1969:

> San Quentin, what good do you think you do?
> Do you think I'll be different when you're through?
> You bent my heart and mind and you warp my soul,
> And your stone walls turn my blood a little cold.
> San Quentin, may you rot and burn in hell.
> May your walls fall and may I live to tell.
> May all the world forget you ever stood.
> And may all the world regret you did no good.

A recent report claims the American criminal justice system holds more than 2.3 million people in 1,719 state prisons, 102 federal prisons, 901 juvenile correctional facilities, 3,163 local jails, and 76 Indian Country jails as well as in military prisons, immigration detention facilities, civil commitment centres and prisons in the US territories (Wagner & Rabuy 2017). Non-violent drug convictions are a defining feature of the federal prison system due to over-policing the residents of particular ethnic and racial communities; with longer sentences being imposed on African American and Latino males, of whom a disproportionate number are more likely to be stopped, searched, arrested, shot, incarcerated and executed by the state. This leaves an increasing number of children effectively orphaned by the criminal justice system. One in five are imprisoned for minor drug offences such as possession; many of these are youths who then acquire a criminal record, with implications for job prospects and the increased likelihood of a longer sentence for any future misdemeanour or felony. In the spirit of 'too many laws means too many criminals', as well as too many incidences of over-criminalisation in particular cases and often ridiculously excessive punishments in the penal environment in general, white-collar criminals tend to be punished with excessive leniency. Meanwhile, others are punished for actions that should never have been criminalised in the first place or at best ought to have been treated as less serious offences, such as running away, truancy, incorrigibility, a delinquent act or the habitual disobedience towards a parent, guardian or custodian.

Once incarcerated, assault, rape and various forms of violence and degradation meted out to prisoners by guards are commonplace, such as the recent case of a Georgia inmate forced to wear a dog lead. The photographs of him covered in bruises and being surrounded by a menacing prison gang aptly encapsulate the cruelty and loss of humanity in American jails and prisons as places of unaccountable power (Simon 2015: 21). In spite of the Eighth Amendment of the US Constitution which bans 'cruel and unusual punishments', the prison system ethos conflicts with the basic human rights accorded to all human beings; and the extraction of labour and social ostracisation of an outcast group has more in common with slavery. Although the Thirteenth Amendment abolished slavery, this was not universal or unconditional; rather, an exception is made for the treatment of prisoners: 'Neither slavery nor involuntary servitude, *except as a punishment for crime* whereof the party shall have been duly convicted, shall exist within the United States, nor any place subject to their jurisdiction' (emphasis added).

The paradoxical reality of human rights abuses committed alongside a rhetorical commitment to human rights protections comprises one of the most disturbing dimensions of post-9/11 politics. For Žižek, the demonisation of the Other, aligned with an aesthetics of suspicion and insecurity, also represents an isolationist attitude; and the contempt felt for the outsider provides the fuel for society's deep uncertainties, anxieties and burgeoning climate of fear:

> It is the way we picture the wholly Other that gives us insight into the nature of the repressed trauma, the fantasy, that makes the Other what he is. For example, in the hated Jew lies the split-off, uncanny double of the Nazi's repressed unconscious fantasy, the destabilising taint that haunts him. This 'conceptual Jew' symbolises the perennial threat to an opposite fantasy, a fantasy of undisturbed desire. Only the (fantasied) Other's extermination allows (fantasised) desire to be fulfilled (1995: 1529–1530).

The nexus between law, crime, crime fiction, web life and the media, underscored by instant access to multiple images and stories, has obscured the fine line separating fantasy from reality. As a result of this misrepresentation, the impression that television and the offerings from a variety of web streaming services gives is of a more lawless and dangerous world, populated by far more violent criminal predators than is actually the case. Not much has changed since George Gerbner's study on television and social behaviour almost 50 years ago, when he found that a majority of dramatic themes represented by the media concerned a threat to, and the preservation of, the moral, social and global order – as well as communicating the necessity for strong social control. He concluded that:

> The [portrayal of violence] appears to project the fears, biases, privileges, and wishful thinking of dominant institutions onto a cosmic canvas ... The fundamental function and social role of ritualised dramatic violence is, then, the maintenance of power. The collective lessons [taught by these fictionalised accounts] tend to cultivate a sense of hierarchical values and forces. Their conflicts expose the danger of crossing the lines, and induce fear of subverting them (1970: 76).

The social and political environment, and institutional setting in which the courts operate, are profoundly influenced by the images circulated by the media. It follows that the media, the technological infrastructure and interests of those who 'own' and control them, are embedded into what Fuchs describes as 'structures of domination' (2008: 114). The absence or presence of specific physical properties means the emphasis has shifted from *who* has the capacity to influence the structures of power and principles of control, to *what* mediums are capable of maintaining or changing a particular representation of reality in their mediation of human experience and social interactions (Shaw & Shaw 2015: 239). People have been encultured into a variety of habits and understandings which are a source of both assimilation and alienation, and so the dramatisation of crime and criminals does more than simply reflect popular opinion; rather, it is worked into the popular consciousness and via cumulative exposure actually shapes the beliefs and values of the audience. Consequently, in this age of the spectacle, hyperbole and fake news (characterised by differentiated truths and lies, clichés, omissions and distortions), it is difficult to constrain the peremptory and retributive fury raging within people, and manage the counter-fictions conjured up by their imaginations in order to maintain control over their deepest fears, illicit desires and vengeful animosity towards the weaker Other.

For Nietzsche, the 'spirit of revenge' or *ressentiment* – as vengefulness, spite and rancour –signifies one of the most intractable and deeply internalised human emotions: it 'has so far been the subject of man's best reflection; and where there was suffering, one always wanted punishment too' (1978: 140). As it is claimed to be predicated on a malignant form of self-deception, he warned against those who hide their simmering *ressentiment* behind the rhetoric of justice and the common good. By demonising and dehumanising the wrongdoer so that they become a target for the infliction of cruel punishments, there is a danger of rendering both parties inhuman. The personal and social consequences of failing to act with compassion were illustrated by Nietzsche's aphorism in *Beyond Good and Evil*: 'Whoever fights with monsters should see to it that in the process he does not become a monster. And when you look long into the abyss, the abyss also looks into you' (1966: 98). Similarly, in Orwell's satire *Animal Farm*, the animals depose the tyranny of human control only to find that the oppressed become the oppressors and are indistinguishable. In the last paragraph of the book, the pigs are wearing trousers, getting drunk, smoking cigars and gambling: 'The [once again, enslaved] creatures outside looked from pig to man, and from man to pig, and from pig to man again; already it was impossible to say which was which' (Orwell 1996: 139). The allegorical message expresses the danger of malevolently contemplating the darker elements of humanity by gazing into the abyss, an action which is capable of irrevocably altering one's mindset and may even culminate in the perpetration of our own monstrous acts against the monsters, rendering both them and us interchangeable.

Contemplating whether there can be an honourable emotional basis for retribution, in *Punishment and the Moral Emotions* Jeffrie Murphy suggests that there is an incumbent moral responsibility to look with compassion for the decent core of the wrongdoer in the spirit of moral humility (2012). This 'rightful disposition of the soul' acknowledges one's own cognitive limitations in being incapable of knowing either the heart of others or our own capacity for evil. A measure of what psychotherapists refer to as 'cognitive restructuring' is, therefore, necessary in the behaviour of those making moral judgments against others, in order to avoid over-dramatising or over-moralising. In the context of being aware of our own biases and deficiencies – the 'dark double' that we carry hidden within ourselves – it is imperative that individuals acknowledge their own motivations to avoid the imposition of false moral judgments. This requires being aware of the often flawed foundations of our own predispositions and reconnecting with our innate sense of justice.

Rawls describes a method known as 'reflective equilibrium', by means of which it is possible to test the appropriateness of a moral theory against a consensus of opinion in a particular culture and through a process of deliberation on a wide range of beliefs and judgments (1990: 393). Inspired by Kant's theory of judgment, the autonomous moral agent chooses from amongst principles it is considered everybody could choose from. Their ethical incentives for determining a moral principle capable of grounding a 'moral law' for action arise from the agent's own internal practical reason, as opposed to the external incentives for considering a 'legal law' where, for instance, if you park in a forbidden area you pay a fine. Although for Kant 'moral feelings' alone amount to an inadequate standard of good and evil or lawgiving (as these differ from person to person), they are nevertheless 'the basis for the execution of laws'. Kant further explains in *The Metaphysics of Morals*:

> while it is not in itself a duty to share the sufferings (as well as the joys) of others, it is a duty to sympathise actively in their fate; and to this end it is therefore an indirect duty to cultivate the compassionate natural (aesthetic) feelings in us, and to make use of them as so many means to sympathy based on moral principles and the feeling appropriate to them … For this [compassion] is still one of the impulses that nature has implanted in us to do what the representation of duty alone might not accomplish (Kant 1991: 6:457).

Compassion, when tempered by empathy and moral humility, can lead to developing punitive retributive legal practices with a reformative character that promote the moral and spiritual rebirth of criminals and ease their reintegration into society. The US prison dog training programme is one such example, of which there are more than 290 correctional facilities across the United States that have implemented dog training programmes with a great degree of success (Cooke & Farrington 2016). The initiative matches abandoned, abused and neglected animals with inmates who prepare the dogs for adoption, and train dogs to assist people with mental or physical incapacities, such as disabled veterans, and to sniff out illegal drugs in airports or other public areas. Importantly, the inmates have a unique opportunity to interact with another living being in prison who will not judge them for their past wrongdoings, and have the opportunity to stimulate the kind of caring that is not tainted or inhibited by the prisoners' prior experiences with people. Through a process of habituation, by caring for their designated dog, prisoners forge strong emotional attachments with lasting behavioural benefits, as they learn to develop the virtues of empathic kindness which may have been absent from their former lives. The change produced in the attitudes, general disposition and emotions of the inmates demonstrates not only how emotions are essentially personal and have special significance by being experienced by the bearer, but also that compassionate concern for the moral welfare of other beings can be nurtured.

On the wider problem of addressing the institutional inertia and criminalisation patterns, traditions and values which have originated the principal expressions of punishment, Arendt dismisses the potential of passion as the primary driver of change on the grounds that:

> Compassion, by its very nature, cannot be touched off by the sufferings of a whole class or a people, or, least of all, mankind as a whole … Its strength hinges on the strength of passion itself, which, in contrast to reason, can comprehend only the particular, but has no notion of the general and no capacity for generalisation (2006: 75).

It may be true that, particularly in this technology-mediated age, a large-scale response to suffering can obscure from view the specific suffering of the individual so their cry for help is unheard. For example, the so-called modern phenomenon of virtue signalling tends to emphasise the 'virtuous' disposition or 'moral superiority' of the sympathiser, rather than focusing on the plight of the person(s) appealing for justice. However, in the case of mass imprisonment on a scale almost unparalleled in human history,[1] a degree of compassionate identification with the individual – and the individual as part of a class of similarly disadvantaged individuals – is arguably necessary, along with a concomitant demand for ameliorative action on behalf of the entire incarcerated population.

1 There are more black men in the grip of the criminal justice system – in prison, on probation or on parole – than were in slavery at its peak in the US in 1850. Overall, there are now more people under 'correctional supervision' in America – more than 6 million – than were in the Gulag Archipelago under Stalin at its height (Liss 2012: 16).

It is suggested that only a commitment to a wide-ranging series of socio-political and economic initiatives by government bodies can help to lessen the conditions of poverty, and feelings of alienation responsible for breeding crime and dangerous people in the first place. This would require addressing the often brutal foundations of authority that provoke violence and the shared discontent that inflames public anger which, in turn, threatens social and political cohesion. However, legislative reform is also needed in order to combat the prevailing unsympathetic and moralistic invective which reflects the current fearful and unkind attitude evidenced on the streets and in the courts towards criminals and punishment in the penal system, and the rhetoric of retribution towards what are essentially urban ills and socio-moral disorders. As a convenient answer to inconvenient questions, it is maintained that by imposing a system of mass incarceration, the punishment industry provides the US with a source of employment; a means of dealing with addiction and mental illness by removing them from public view, an economic ameliorative; and has been described as a useful form of social control, particularly in what Wacquant refers to as 'the carceral management of poverty':

> Against the backdrop of unfettered markets and enfeebled social-welfare programs, when the penal system has become a major engine of social stratification and cultural division in its own right, the field study of the prison ceases to be the province of the specialist in crime and punishment to become a window into the deepest contradictions and the darkest secrets of our age (2002: 389).

The treatment of the poorest and weakest in society, and especially the 'criminal class', is a good barometer of a civilised society. Describing prisoners dying of tuberculosis, frostbite and exhaustion as a result of neglect in a remote Siberian labour camp, Fyodor Dostoevsky suggested, in his 1862 novel *The House of the Dead*, that 'the degree of civilisation in society can be judged by entering its prisons' (2004: 76). This is because the meaning of criminal punishment and forms of condemnatory expression are derived from the values of the community. In this case, Murphy urges a modicum of compassion even for the serial killer in acknowledgement of the innocent child he once was, quoting the musings of protagonist Felicia from William Trevor's novel, *Felicia's Journey*: 'lost within a man who murdered, there was a soul like any other soul, purity itself it surely once had been' (2012: 17–19). That is not to trivialise criminal behaviour and the harm done – the injury to self-respect, respect for the victim and for the moral order itself are not to be trivialised or overlooked; rather, it is proposed that the moral judgments of individuals and our law-makers are appropriately tempered by compassion. The advice given by novelist Henry James, in a conversation overheard by his nephew Billy James in 1902 and recorded by biographer Leon Edel, is suggested as a corrective to the dominant values of the criminal justice system: 'Three things in human life are important. The first is to be kind. The second is to be kind. And the third is to be kind' (Edel 1972: 316). By discovering commonalities between ourselves and others, there is a greater likelihood that the rightful demand for just punishment does not serve as a rationalisation for sadistic cruelty or revenge.

Compassion without justice is mere sentimentality: justice without compassion is but tyranny

At the basis of compassion lies an empathic identification and a feeling of solidarity with the sufferer as a fellow human being; the recognition that similar misfortunes may also befall oneself, insofar as one is human living in an imperfect world. For Romantic poet William Blake, 'attraction and repulsion, reason and energy, love and hate are necessary to human existence' (1991: 150); and from his 1794 poetical work 'The Human Abstract' in *Songs of Experience*, 'Pity would be no more, If we did not make somebody poor: And mercy no more could be, If all were as happy as we' (Blake 1990: 39). In other words, without oppositions and contradictions there is no progression; so without laws and criminality there would be no prisons, and without religion and sin there would be no brothels. Blake's two faces of human divinity (ideal/innocence) and human corruption (real/experience), although comprising a moral paradox and difficult to reconcile, are read interchangeably and, therefore, indicate the permeability of the boundaries between 'innocence' and 'experience'. Although in 'The Human Abstract' Blake juxtaposes poverty with pity and misery with mercy, unlike mercy, empathy, altruism or pity which is manifest in rhetoric, compassion is personified in action rather than being simply a bystander emotion. The individual is motivated to do something to help a vulnerable person or an oppressed group of people within a particular social field; for example, the victims of human rights abuses whose appalling experiences of horrifying forms of suffering may first evoke empathic concern and thereafter, moved by compassion, spur the onlooker into action.

It could be argued that the basis of society is, therefore, the interdependence between justice and compassion in pursuit of individual human flourishing and the common good. While it is possible to frame compassion as an ethical virtue which relates to justice, it is not formally recognised in modern law. The legal profession exhibits some difficulty with either formally expressing compassion in judgments or accepting compassion as a legitimate defence. For example, in *R (Nicklinson) v Ministry of Justice* [2012] EWHC 2381 (Admin), (2012) MHLO, para 54, s.7.7 the Commission on Assisted Dying stated:

> Under the current law, the compassionate motives of the 'mercy' killer are in themselves never capable of providing a basis for a partial excuse. Some would say that this is unfortunate. On this view, the law affords more recognition to other less, or at least no more, understandable emotions such as anger (provocation) and fear (self-defence). Others would say that recognising a partial excuse of acting out of compassion would be dangerous. Just as a defence of necessity 'can very easily become simply a mask for anarchy', so the concept of 'compassion' – vague in itself – could very easily become a cover for selfish or ignoble reasons for killing, not least because people often act out of mixed motives.

It is interesting to note how, in the above example, the law conflates the positive emotion of compassion with the negative emotions of fear and anger. Also, while compassionate or mercy 'killing' attracts a murder sentence, killing out of provocation, anger or fear (especially if considered to be in self-defence) can lead to the reduced sentence of manslaughter. Noting a similar disparity in *The Ballad of Reading Gaol* (1898), while not excusing criminality or suggesting criminals don't exist, Oscar Wilde questions whether the cruel and excessively harsh punishments that deprive inmates of their humanity exacted by members of the criminal justice system – i.e., from judges to prison officials and governors – are really any less 'criminal' than the original misdemeanours for which the inmates were incarcerated. He describes the appalling unsanitary living conditions, inadequate exposure to fresh air, the poor-quality food, solitary conditions and the silence. In the poem Wilde, who received a prison sentence of two years' hard labour in HM Prison Reading, formerly Reading Gaol, for acts of 'gross indecency', shifts the emphasis from the individual's culpability to the humiliating horrors of life in a Victorian prison: 'every prison that men build is built with bricks of shame' (2003: 897). That is to say, it was not the prisoners who should burn with the shame of imprisonment but the callous and indifferent society that placed them there. The inmates were simply the product of society's ills and a criminalising culture; consequently to find oneself on the wrong side of the law is a misfortune that could happen to anyone, inasmuch as we are all human. The corollary of Wilde's line of reasoning is that what is legal is not always just; and, in the end, everyone is in need of a compassionate response from the justice system, and not simply retribution.

As de Beauvoir points out, humans can find justification of their own existence only in the existence of other humans; and even though rationality is historically presented as a necessary restraining, compelling and legitimating authority, it is the passions that define our relationships with others in the world – just as compassion is one of a constellation of passions that are indispensable to reason (2000: 17). In the spirit of moral humility, the reasonable person freely accepts the possibility of being in error, as well as according respect to another who holds an alternative and maybe unfamiliar viewpoint which is, nevertheless, deemed worthy of consideration. It is suggested, therefore, that the critical development of legal authorities constitutes an evaluative process in which emotion is a major motivational force, especially since formal (legal) and informal (ethical) obligations embrace a broad set of external social relations with consequences for real people; and, more significantly, without compassion there is no shared humanity and no inclusivity, only instrumentality.

Furthermore, a broader conceptualisation of empathy which involves a complex combination of physical, cognitive, emotional, social and ethical capabilities, along with the cultivation of an empathic imagination, is at the basis of human rights and, arguably, forms an integral part of the foundations of justice. This is because empathy encourages individuals to recognise the suffering and share the plight of the Other, thereby stimulating a compassionate response aimed at alleviating their distress. However, as evidenced in the example of the US criminal justice system, too often the moral aims of compassion and legal aims of justice are in conflict. For this reason, literature and aesthetics are important for the law and lawyers in their creation of complex narratives which cultivate and outline responses of identification with the lives, fate and fortunes of others from within a range of historical, political and social contexts in which acts of empathy are embedded.

Moreover lawyers are unable to remove themselves, in either ethical or jurisprudential terms, from the stories of others; which suggests the usefulness of inculcating in legal advocates a narrative empathy, by the sharing of feeling and common perspective stimulated by reading, hearing, seeing or imagining narratives which articulate another individual's position. At the beginning of *Poetic Justice*, Nussbaum asserts that novels can play an important role in public reasoning because they lay the claim of another's story. In support of the emotionally evocative narrative technique she argues, 'I defend the literary imagination precisely because it seems to me an essential ingredient of an ethical stance that asks us to concern ourselves with the good of other people whose lives are distant from our own' (Nussbaum 1995: xvi). William Shakespeare, Charles Dickens and modern authors such as John Grisham are renowned for foregrounding law in the moral and ethically complex stories they tell, and in their sympathetic exploration of the status of the individual as legal subject. Dickens, for instance, was well regarded for his strong social conscience, and used his fiction as a catalyst for debates about moral and social reform in the Victorian era. He articulated the connection between poverty, slums and crime for a large and impressionable audience, and was committed to writing novels which would 'take the roofs off houses' in order to reveal what lay concealed within (Wiener 2004: 152). Robin West observes, in her essay on 'Literature, Culture and Law', that even 'popular narrative fiction, television shows and films – no less than canonical literature – may, on occasion, have something true to teach us about law … its value in our lives, and the harms it can do' (2008: 27, 28).

Compassion can be activated by literature, as it offers significant insights into the nature of law which are not easily found elsewhere. In the form of a film, play, novel or other narrative fiction, literature presents an account of the lives of those who are different from ourselves, with whom we can engage empathically through reading and at the same time acquire a critical perspective on a previously unfamiliar reality. Moreover, for the consciously interdisciplinary law and literature movement, the construction of law and society is essentially a reciprocal process which resides beyond legal doctrine and calls for a return to the humanities, specifically literature, in order to enliven the legal imagination and properly situate the ethical constituent of law. The law and literature relationship is, therefore, a particularly valuable locus for scrutinising the wider impact of narrative on improving the cold abstractions of law in relation to its empathic and compassionate response to suffering.

The application of narrative empathy in nurturing compassionate legal reasoning encourages a sympathetic consideration of those circumstances which impact on socially marginal groups, against the stereotyping and stultifying effects of arbitrary rule formalism; as well as acknowledging the perhaps more pedestrian misfortunes that befall ordinary people in everyday life. In *Poethics and Other*

Strategies of Law and Literature, it is proposed that only literature can reanimate the ethical dimension of law, as aesthetic integrity leads to moral integrity, or 'no bad judicial opinion can be well written' (Weisberg 1992: 251). Since literature is uniquely able to articulate the circumstances and range of possibilities for compassionate judgment, it would appear that the law is in need of a jurisprudence of good poesy rather than bad principles.

6 Law as love

Love is patient, love is kind.
It does not envy, it does not boast,
it is not proud.
It does not dishonour others,
it is not self-seeking,
it is not easily angered,
it keeps no record of wrongs.

Love does not delight in evil
but rejoices with the truth.
It always protects, always trusts,
always hopes, always perseveres.
Love never fails.

(1 Corinthians 13:4–8)

Venerable traditions of thought, within religion and philosophy for example, locate emotions such as respect, compassion and love at the very core of morality. In Canto XXXIII of *The Divine Comedy: Paradiso*, love is accredited with the ability to 'move the sun and the other stars' (Dante 1984: 145). De Sousa presents a similarly lofty claim that emotions, and particularly love, are at the foundation of all moral considerations; they provide 'the starting point of morality' (1987: 307). For Weil, the legal concept of justice cannot exist without moral righteousness which, in turn, depends on love and faith. Love directs our 'creative attention' towards the suffering and ill-treatment of the oppressed, afflicted and reviled, much like 'the Samaritan who stops, looks and gives his attention all the same to this absent humanity' (Weil 1973: 95). Using fragmentary, provocative and poetic language in the search for beauty, truth and goodness in order to expose the paradoxes involved in the experience of compassionate engagement between a sufferer and sympathiser, when Weil refers to justice she clearly also means love. Love as justice creates the intellectual and emotional space from which to see even that which is often rendered invisible within law, namely the perspective of the outcast, and accords them dignity regardless of their 'absent humanity'. In this way, the secular (justice) is bound to the sacred (love) to the extent that the secular is always either transformed by, or seeks to eradicate, the sacred.

The legal community is characterised by a different kind of love, viz. a love of tradition, ceremony and the rituals of law as objects comprising 'a plastic art, of architecture, statuary, dress, heraldry, painting and insignia-gold rings, rods, coifs, seals and rolls – which provide popular consciousness with a Justice which can be seen and remembered' (Goodrich 1996: 96). Beneath the pomp and ritual, and at the core of law's self-love, is a fondness for history and text, from which an auto-generative formulation of precise rules and concepts as pure law seeks to distinguish itself from what it perceives as non-legal entities. In its undifferentiated universalist form, law removes the magic and supernatural from the social world by insisting on predictability and reason unfettered by emotion. Many influential philosophers have focused their attention on reason; for example, Immanuel Kant, who developed concepts of pure and practical reason whilst urging the rejection of the destructive impulse and desire. Similarly, Thomas Aquinas in *Summa Theologica* focused on reason, which enabled natural law to be derived in the first instance from his conception of divine law made known by God. However, it might be argued that the legal realm is not constructed a priori. Like any other language, law has found its voice and authority through the influential articulations of key actors from history, wherein events and behaviours have been evaluated and fixed as paradigm material through which the practices and ideologies of a society are legitimated. Consequently, it might be argued that the value-laden language of law is inevitably underpinned by emotion as a feeling towards the favouring and privileging of certain principles above others – an idea the legal community would most likely find unacceptable.

Although law as reason is set up as a natural enemy of the unbounded and disorganised love, it has been suggested that 'it is this law of love and its recognition as a rule of conduct in all our relations – with friends, enemies and offenders – which must inevitably bring about the complete transformation of the existing order of things' (Tolstoy 1948: 38). Hume situates all our motivations in the passions. The moral distinctions which found the law cannot be derived from reason, which he described as a 'slave of the passions', because they are rooted in feelings of approval and appreciation towards a particular characteristic or value (Hume 1967: 145). Consequently, reason is inert and unable to generate impulses for the intellect. This does not mean that reason is irrelevant; rather, that reason alone is unable to motivate us to act. It only effects our actions in two ways: by directing the passions to focus on appropriate objects; and by discovering connections between experiences and events that can create passions and help to determine which action to perform. The future of law is, therefore, one of overcoming the antagonism between law as immutably rule-bound and emotion, love in this instance, as capricious. The emotional intellect is argued to enable the pre-linguistic, preconscious organisation of raw data which facilitates the operation of formal inductive reasoning, necessary for the formulation of truly moral judgments. It is the possibility for emotional judgment, motivated by a love of the law and its subjects, which is able to realise law's enormous transformative capacity.

Plato insisted that, in many instances, love motivates political association and animates the pursuit of the ideals of justice; similarly, in *Living Lawfully: Love in Law and Law in Love* Bankowski claimed we need 'justice and love' in order to create a lawful world, one which is morally valid (2001: 230). Love is the unique antithesis to the instrumentalisation of the person, a bridge between heteronomy and autonomy; however, autonomy needs love in order to elevate itself from mere self-interest. Not only can love increase the inclination to secure justice for the person with whom one empathises, it can also stimulate the sensibilities to take into account a wider range of mitigating and exculpatory aspects in a complicated social encounter. Clearly, love takes many different forms and applies to a diverse range of frameworks and foundations; however, when understood as a positive constitutive force it is founded on our responsibility to others and the recognition of difference. This chapter will explore the theoretical scope of the important concept of love by analysing not only the cultural contexts that foster the engendering of love in legal judgment, but will also investigate the parameters of pro-social feelings and the mechanisms that lead to their advancement and impediment.

Determining the 'right kind of love': love as a moral emotion

While emotions such as love are referred to in the courts of law, these are commonly contemplated only obliquely in legal texts and commentary. Despite a variety of lofty claims by theologians and philosophers that love fuels the promotion of justice beyond the letter of the law, a socially constructed notion of romantic love led to legal proscriptions against same-sex marriage. Bound up with notions of patriarchy and heterosexuality, the love that dare not speak its name was, and still is across many jurisdictions, fettered by archaic rules and gendered restrictions – unable to deliver its promise of freedom and equality. Only recently in an historic ruling, *Obergefell v Hodges* [2015], the US Supreme Court extended the right to marry to any two people; summarised in Justice Kennedy's closing statement:

> No union is more profound than marriage, for it embodies the highest ideals of love … In forming a marital union, two people become something greater than once they were. As some of the petitioners in these cases demonstrate, marriage embodies a love that may endure even past death … [t]he court now holds that same-sex couples may exercise the fundamental right to marry. No longer may this liberty be denied to them ([2015] 576 US 28).

In this case, a recasting of love within law offered a site of resistance to heteronormativity. It actualised the possibility of transformation and agency, and echoes Danish philosopher Søren Kierkegaard's reference to the consolidation of love as the 'immanent purpose of marriage' and the prime example of an 'ethical life choice' for all; because in marriage 'erotic love is transformed by neighbour love' which is determined by 'love alone' (1987: 73). This continues to be a problematic proposition for many feminists, however: such as Carol Smart, who describes love as 'an aspect of patriarchy's ideological armament through which women [and men] became hooked into dependent relationships … and enter into an unfavourable legal contract' such as marriage; and Simone de Beauvoir, who similarly associates marriage with a 'cursed love' or 'dream of annihilation' in which '[t]he innumerable martyrs to love bear witness against the injustice of a fate that offers a sterile hell as ultimate salvation' (2007: 60; 1953: 669). That is not to say that either love or marriage are of themselves oppressive or liberating; rather, they become so because of the social context in which they are organised.

Love is inevitably a fluid concept, being both simple and complex; yet, in its purest form and, like compassion, love relies on a perception of the significance and value of others. This is illustrated by the New Testament directive to love one's neighbour as oneself, along with a diverse range of proverbs which relate to love – including the classical aphorisms, *amor timere nemenem verus potest* or 'true love can fear no man' and *amor vincit omnia* or 'love conquers all' (Virgil 1984: *Eclogues* 10.69; Seneca 2014: *Medea* 416). Alternatively, love is an emotion which is often rooted in exclusion; it singles out the object of love from everything else and focuses on the relevant facets of the situation. In Seneca's *Medea*, her romantic love for Jason is singular, overwhelming and has tragic consequences, as it overrides all other attachments such as maternal love. Her motivation for extending love toward another was founded in her special relationship with that person, rather than a wider concern for others in consideration of what they are. In this example, love is understood as merely a response to an essentially egocentric value, in that individuals other than her lover had no intrinsic worth for Medea. The moral imperative for impartiality is, therefore, frustrated in this conception of an emotion which the ancient Greeks, for example, recognised as having at least six distinct varieties. These included *agape* – spiritual love; *storge* – familial affection; *philia* – dispassionate virtuous love; *ludus* – playful love; the complex *philautia* – self-love; and *eros* – sensuous passion. *Agapic* love was considered to be the definitive moral emotion, understood as enduring, unwavering and directed toward impersonal humanity, whereas *erotic* or romantic love tended to be viewed as irrational and unreliable. Emotions are both innate and universal, and all societies have evolved their own distinct definitions of love. These range from benevolent intent or concern for the well-being of others, to romantic attachment and intimacy (Konstan 2005: 231).

In the poem 'i carry your heart with me' (1926), e.e. cummings used inventive lyric poetry to infer that the assumption of responsibility for the 'heart' of another expresses an ethical duty – from which, ultimately, all that matters is the simple idea of the beloved as the primary motivation for all thoughts, hopes, dreams and actions:

> i carry your heart with me (i carry it in
> my heart) i am never without it (anywhere
> i go you go, my dear; and whatever is done
> by only me is your doing, my darling)
> i fear
> no fate (for you are my fate, my sweet) i want
> no world (for beautiful you are my world, my true)
> and it's you are whatever a moon has always meant
> and whatever a sun will always sing is you

here is the deepest secret nobody knows
(here is the root of the root and the bud of the bud
and the sky of the sky of a tree called life; which grows
higher than the soul can hope or mind can hide)
and this is the wonder that's keeping the stars apart
i carry your heart (i carry it in my heart)

This conception of love assumes the character of an ongoing activity and never of a final moment. Rather, love is portrayed as immeasurable, inexhaustible and eternally renewable, which is also typical of an overarching structure such as law. This is illustrated in the well-known poem 'Law Like Love' in which W.H. Auden applied the romantic definition most prevalent in modern culture, using a sustained single metaphor to explore the lyrical interchangeability of law with love (1976: 208). He likens law to the sun in the first stanza, rising and setting according to the laws of nature under which the gardener must be alert for all seasonal and climatic variations. This mirrors the certainty and force of legal decrees under which the individual is expected to adapt his behaviour. There is a tension at the heart of the poem which conveys the state of indeterminacy that arises when we attempt to arrive at some universal conception of the purpose and legitimate ends of law. Buried beneath layers of imagistic language and symbolism, Auden implies it is only possible to acknowledge the mystery in law and refer to it analogically, stating that 'law [is] like ...' something. His identification of law with love (as a transcendent yet often capricious state of being) not only suggests the disappointment and fallibility intrinsic to both, it also reveals the way in which the law beloved of legal practitioners is never questioned; its central position in life is taken for granted. Auden further depicts law as something inscrutable, an enigma which customarily and craftily evades any rational explanation.

The 1930s was a period of great social and political upheaval in Europe, and contemporary poetry tended to warn against selfish individualism and the authoritarian state. In 1939 when 'Law Like Love' was composed, the legal structure was understood to be precarious, incapable of guaranteeing safety and well-being in such an unstable social environment. In the present day, the transformative influences of globalisation, expansion of the global corporation, advancement of the consumption-driven society facilitated by sophisticated communication and information technologies, have presented equally difficult challenges for law: not least of all, in the growing disparity between the wealthiest and poorest in society and rapidly expanding regulatory state powers which threaten basic human rights. The consequent reimagining and recalibration of the fundamental concepts of democracy, freedom, fairness and justice have exacerbated the imbalance of power, fostered feelings of alienation and resulted in the destabilisation of society. This current mood of disenchantment and disillusionment with legal strategies resonates with Auden's poetic expression of law as an unfettered, unpredictable and rather dangerous place which can offer no better account of its integrity than that most nebulous of ideas, love:

> Law, says the judge as he looks down his nose,
> Speaking clearly and most severely,
> Law is as I've told you before,
> Law is as you know I suppose,
> Law is but let me explain it once more,
> Law is The Law ...
> ... Like love we don't know where or why,
> Like love we can't compel or fly,
> Like love we often weep,
> Like love we seldom keep.

Much like *eros* or erotic love, for Auden law is often obscure and unreliable. It imposes restrictions which are always compelling but not always observed. Because of the complicated and abstract character of love, many traditional discourses of love are based on the stratification of intimacy and desire, often underpinned by a limited range of well-worn clichés. However, this chapter elucidates a more practical conception of love and one which befits law, rather than pathological love or love as inclination or possession. In *Liquid Love: On the Frailty of Human Bonds* Zygmunt Bauman, for instance, describes an altruistic form of love:

> Love is about adding to the world – each addition being the living trace of the loving self; in love, the self is bit by bit transplanted onto the world. The loving self expands through giving itself away to the loved object. Love is about self's survival-through-self's-alterity. ... Love grows with its acquisitions and is fulfilled in their durability (2003: 9, 10).

For Zenon Bankowski, 'law in its universalist form, takes the magic away from the social world by producing predictability and rationality' (1996: 40). Untempered by love, regulation goes to the root of any relationship and 'questions it, makes it eternal, routine, simplifies it, and cuts out chance'; whereas love, which is characterised by tenderness and spontaneity, lives in the present and 'operates in the now' (1996: 38). This is not a love which is fixated on the lofty traditions, emblems, hierarchies and institutions of law; rather, it identifies with distinct individuals standing together under the law, and seeks to address the imagination of human possibilities within the context of universally valid moral principles. As law seeks the universal, love sees the particular; however, meeting the ideals of justice requires the ability to move from one to the other.

Whilst famous for poetry depicting autumn winds, empty deserts and the arresting beauty of nature, for nineteenth-century English Romantic poet Percy Bysshe Shelley the most exquisite image was the uprising of a citizenry acting in the spirit of moral reason for freedom and justice. He refers to 'the great secret of morals' as love, described as the state of mind produced by imagistic language that works on the imagination and in so doing enlarges our sensitivity. This form of virtuous love is typified as selfless, going against its own nature and interests in order to identify with 'the beautiful which exists in thought, action, or person, not our own'. Shelley urges cultivating a creative imagination, in order that a moral agent is motivated to 'intensely and comprehensively … put himself in the place of another and of many others; [so that] the pains and pleasure of his species must become his own' (1977: 517). Love is, therefore, not without obligations to other individuals: it is characterised as a moral duty which is inextricably linked with responsibilities, and all the more virtuous because of not being motivated by any externally imposed duty. This conception is put forward as the 'right kind' of love, namely a pervasive, compelling and inclusive emotion which motivates one's involvement and engagement. Our emotional defences are tested when we encounter the Other, and Velleman even considers love to be a more worthy motivation to treat others well than respect: 'respecting someone, we take care not to do various things to him or to let various things happen to him; loving someone, we are open to caring about him in all sorts of ways' (2008: 201).

The social world reveals itself to us in emotion, and it is only in emotions that we are able to connect with the Other. Caring for, or extending love to, another person irrespective of the appropriate or proximate worth of that individual is a unique human characteristic; it is a core moral emotion. The capacity for selfless identification with and concern for others, especially the stranger, lends life coherence and promotes moral unity. De Beauvoir refers to these bonds in the scene at the beginning of *Pyrrhus et Cinéas*: 'I knew a child who cried because the concierge's young son had died. His parents let him weep but shortly became irritated: "He wasn't your brother." The child dried his tears' (1944: 207). The parents were indifferent to the death of the working-class child or the suffering of the caretaker's family, because all significant social connections were rendered meaningful only by virtue of their proximity to an immediate familiar circle of individual acquaintances. This is not to say that the stranger is more important than one's own family or close friends; rather, de Beauvoir's ethical essay conceptualises the concrete interdependence between the self and the Other whereby the key principle which resolves any difference, or distance, between oneself and others – namely 'the reason I can call the other mine' – is love. Love is presented as an intersubjective ideal which is uniquely capable of creating an empathic and reciprocal bond with all and any other human beings. She continues:

> The child wiped the tears from his face and replied 'although the caretaker's son is not my younger brother and no family relation, when I cry for him he is no longer a stranger. Therefore who will be my fellowman cannot be determined in advance: my tears decide' (de Beauvoir 1944: 210).

As demonstrated by Heisenberg's Uncertainty Principle, to the extent to which anything exists, everything else in the world has the task of attempting some level of modification in relation to it. The world possesses a moral significance, however, when we apply this principle to our encounters with others; as evidenced by the actions of each individual directing their own free will, 'the world itself becomes the world court of justice' or 'world history is the world's court of judgment' (Schopenhauer 2016: 410; Hegel 1967: 371). In a world lived with others there can be solidarity and unity, but inevitably there is also a possibility of separation and conflict. The condition of being human, however, accords every person the right to be judged worthy of consideration, regardless of externalities such as social class, ethnicity, religion, education or wealth. Moving beyond Rawls' 'original position', Ricoeur suggests that individuals are not only able to surpass their prejudices, but also possess an innate preunderstanding of what is just and unjust. Consequently, he maintains that society can be defined in terms of its distributive function because of 'the capacity of ordinary citizens as regards rationality, that is, their aptitude for putting themselves in the place of another or, better, transcending their place' (2000: 56, 57). It follows that, in reuniting that which is separated, love is the motivating principle of justice as they are both ontologically bonded; and, although not identical, love permeates justice.

Without love, justice tends to be taken over by cold calculations based on the arbitrary application of inflexible legal frameworks. As bare calculative juridicalism, justice could easily be perverted by those who would try to obtain private advantage within the relative security of an accepted rule. The 'logic of equivalence' implied in the golden rule – 'do unto others as you would have them do unto you' – would, according to Ricoeur, 'be constantly drawn in the direction of a utilitarian maxim whose formula is *Do ut des*: I give *in order that* you may give. The rule "Give *because* it has been given you" corrects the "in order that" of the utilitarian maxim and saves the golden rule from an always possible perverse interpretation (1996: 35, 36). When informed by the corrective of love's logic of superabundance, generosity and disproportionality, justice is based on not only moral duty but also a deep awareness of mutual interdependence, consistent with the principles of universal moral respect and reciprocity.

If a particular moral and virtuous form of love is appropriate or even necessary for law to be more than coolly calculative justice or just-*ice*, there remain practical questions relating to nature of obligation, scope of application and the forms it ought or ought not to take. For example, is there a general duty to love others; must all people be loved equally, or should love only be extended to those who are deemed to be worthy, or with whom the agent can have a meaningful relationship? In the Judeo-Christian tradition, the Bible begins by identifying the people who surround us as those with whom we have a necessary and mutually binding obligation of loving consideration: 'love your neighbour as yourself (Leviticus 19:18). The New Testament parable of the Good Samaritan extends the category of 'neighbour' from a particularist definition (people like us, people close to us) to a universalist reading in which, at least in theory, neighbourly love is deserved by all human beings (Luke 10:27–37).

In the later configuration, the idea of the neighbour is neither universal nor specific but is framed by proximity; and includes not only one's enemies but also absent or even unknown others who may be rightfully considered to be within our contemplation. Proximity anticipates danger or harm to another who may be adversely affected by our actions, and therefore imposes a duty of care. This broadened scope of personal responsibility, which for Levinas emerges from love rather than calculation, is described as an 'ethics of the Other' which is immediate, non-reciprocal, fluid, open and infinite, and as such can never be satisfied (1969: 150). Situated at the opposite end of the spectrum to legal practice and adjudication, which frequently displays cruel indifference to the suffering of others, the demand of an alertness to the endless 'call and command of the Other' raises one of the oldest questions of law itself: namely, what is the proper meaning and scope of 'responsibility' for law?

Love enriches and extends the scope of the lawyer's question 'who is my neighbour?'

If humans existed alone in the world, then their actions would have limited significance and make no sense; human actions only have meaning in the context of society as the world of meaning. Individuals as social beings are dependent on the ideal of community which means that if actions are to have any meaning, they must be recognised by others. Since the world is shaped by everybody who lives in it, all undertakings are defined by their relationships with other projects and, therefore, the target of our ethical obligations is our 'neighbour'; in other words, every single individual in the 'neighbourhood'. The recognition of others, especially the stranger, is the opposite of single-minded self-interest and separation; rather, it is to display love as care, concern and consideration. This universal extension of loving concern persists irrespective of whether the person is sick, despised, poor or simply unlovable; rather, the particularity of each individual must be abstracted in order to apply to everyone without distinction. As Kierkegaard explains, 'when you open the door … and go out the very first person you meet is the neighbour whom you *shall* love' (1998: 50, 51).

The legal definition of a neighbour is set out by Lord Atkin in his 'neighbour principle', articulated in *Donoghue v Stevenson* [1932] AC 562 as 'persons who are so closely and directly affected by my act that I ought to reasonably have them in contemplation as being so affected when I am directing my mind to the acts and omissions which are called into question'. The rule which demands 'you are to love your neighbour' becomes in law 'you must not injure your neighbour', which requires a lesser level of commitment or obligation. This narrow formulation imposes a bare negative duty of restraint and abstention from harming one's neighbour, whereas a positive duty arises from the motivational emotion of love which assumes the character of a moral obligation to take an active interest in their well-being. It is not by the application of reason or rational universal principles that we may respond to the call of the Other; rather, the voluntary assumption of responsibility by a person for another in respect of those interests for which they might 'rightfully' assume responsibility is only possible after eliciting the right emotions. For example, suffering can only be recognised emotionally, and only in that recognition is there the possibility of a motive to alleviate the pain of the vulnerable.

Just as love is central to how we recognise and respond to suffering, justice is the essential medium of love because love is a hyper-moral emotion which depends on justice for its expression. Love enters the practical and ethical realm only under the aegis of justice. In the case of assisted dying in the UK, if legitimacy for certain actions were to be based on the application of a selfless and unsentimental love which equated to moral duty, then an individual would be able to lawfully assist another human being to end their suffering with dignity, and without the threat of an 'up to a maximum of fourteen years' prison sentence under the UK Suicide Act 1961. Love acknowledges that whatever an individual's measure of contentment may be, it is not something that can be easily determined by another person or law-making institution and imposed from the outside. For de Beauvoir, the good of others is 'an absolute end ... but we are not authorised to decide upon this end *a priori*' because 'no behaviour is ever authorised to begin with'. She approves the rejection of 'every principle of authority' because the only legitimate precept is 'to treat the other (to the extent that he is the only one concerned) as a freedom so that his end may be freedom' (de Beauvoir 2000: 142). Accordingly, each person is free to acknowledge the moral responsibility they have towards others in an informal and non-codified manner.

In the context of unbearable suffering with no hope of respite, assisting the autonomous and mentally competent subject in exercising their free will to make a death-hastening decision becomes morally appropriate. The action has moral worth because it is not based on the will and desires of the assister. Also, it is not so much a matter of dispassionately assisting their death with dignity; rather, it is enabling the anguished human being to die with loving consideration and respect for their final wishes. The needs and interests of others are the primary concern in de Beauvoir's concept of ethical responsibility:

> Contrary to the formal strictness of Kantianism for whom the more abstract the act is the more virtuous it is, generosity seems to us to be better grounded and therefore more valid the less distinction there is between the Other and ourselves and the more we fulfil ourselves in taking the Other as an end (2000: 143).

By contrast, while having the capacity to make a valuable contribution to the ideals of justice, the language of human rights and human rights legislation is deficient and too often fails to convey or adequately respond to the true nature of suffering, as evidenced in the case of *R (Pretty) v DPP* [2002] 1 AC 800 and the subsequent Strasbourg case of *Pretty v United Kingdom* [2002] 35 EHRR 1; *R (Purdy) v the Director of Public Prosecutions* [2009] UKHL 45; and *R (Nicklinson) v Ministry of Justice* [2014] UKSC 38 and [2015] AC 657. In *R (Conway) v the Secretary of State for Justice* [2017] EWHC 2447 (Admin), Lord Justice Sales, along with Justices Whipple and Garnham, declined to interfere with the prohibition on assisted dying in section 2 of the Suicide Act 1961, as amended by the Coroners and Justice Act 2009 (s.2) on the following grounds:

> As the conscience of the nation, Parliament is entitled to maintain in place a clear bright-line rule which forbids people from providing assistance to an

> individual to commit suicide. Parliament was and is entitled to decide that the clarity of such a moral position could only be achieved by means of such a rule. Although views about this vary in society, we think that the legitimacy of Parliament deciding to maintain such a clear line that people should not seek to intervene to hasten the death of a human is not open to serious doubt. Parliament is entitled to make the assessment that it should protect moral standards in society by issuing clear and unambiguous laws which reflect and embody such standards (s. 112).

In this and all of the above-mentioned cases, section 2 was considered to serve a legitimate aim under Article 8(2) by protecting the weak and vulnerable, and was therefore justified on that basis. Although it could be argued that the weak and vulnerable were precisely that group of terminally ill people, victims of debilitating and dehumanising diseases facing agonising and undignified death. The prohibition on assisted suicide was also claimed to reflect the concern amongst doctors that if the prohibition were to be relaxed, then patients would have less confidence in their physicians, which, while not backed by evidence, is a moot point. Finally, since the treatment of death and dying in English law remains to a large extent grounded in Judeo-Christian axiology, the recent decision by judges in the *Conway* case endorses the long-standing wider moral and theological 'sanctity of life' (SOL) principle.

The courts' reliance on the SOL principle and their application of theistic language is evident throughout various debates which question the inherent value, across a variety of circumstances, of the contested space between life and death. In *Re A (Children) (Conjoined Twins: Surgical Separation)* [2001] Fam 147 at 213, for example, Lord Justice Brooke cited a long-standing opponent of euthanasia in defending the religious basis for his opinion, insisting 'the sanctity of life doctrine holds that human life is created in the image of God and is therefore possessed of an intrinsic dignity which entitle it to protection from unjust attack' (Keown 2007: 481). Lord Mustill in *R v Brown* [1993] 2 WLR 556 asserted the value of 'transcendental arguments' in supporting the maintenance of life as an overriding imperative 'so strong as to outweigh any consent to its termination'. In a similar vein, Lord Bingham in *R (Pretty) v DPP* [2002] 1 FLR 268 based his judgment on *inter alia* the SOL principle and referred to the significance of the religious perspective to any decision which might allow assisted dying for the terminally ill, emphasising the 'intrinsic value of life'. Since Glanville Williams suggested 60 years ago that 'euthanasia can be condemned only according to religious opinion' (1957: 312), assisted dying remains a revolutionary concept in response to which opposition has continued to be characterised as almost exclusively religious (Battin 1998: 21–27).

The rhetorical stratagems employed in maintaining the illusion of an impartial moral community, whilst asserting religious authority in this contentious area of supposedly secular English law, are particularly evident in parliamentary debates, the fullest and most recent of which took place in September 2015 when the House of Commons decisively rejected the Assisted Dying Bill, which would have legalised assisted dying in some cases. In this respect Marinos Diamantides suggests there is little difference between monotheistic and Western legalisms, describing the Abbasid-type Islamic politics as 'no less a secular politics with a religious cloak than Western liberalism is a secular cloak for Christian politics' (2006: 114). The desire of the courts and law-makers is 'above all else not for human flourishing in either secular or spiritual terms, but for a stable and predictable social order guaranteed by the absolute rule of positive law … which both presupposes and facilitates centralised state control' (Diamantides 2006: 114). Neither divine revelation nor scientific invention, the use of evocative theistic imagery in legal pronouncements in end-of-life cases and debates is analogous to the ecclesiastical eye or *speculum pastoralis* (the watchtower that surveyed the soul), and has profound persuasive force (Goodrich 1995: 233). Suggesting as it does the sacred and immutable, the ideologically biased and theologically grounded SOL principle serves to justify the symbolic violence of the legal community in prolonging actual suffering and existential anguish.

During an earlier reading of the Assisted Dying for the Terminally Ill Bill, Lord St John of Fawsley advised:

> the last period of life, is not a wasteland necessarily. It can be a wonderful period of renewal, reconciliation and acceptance … let us say so out loud the Lord's Prayer, the Hail Mary and the Prayer of the Trinity … Our prayer is that, if it is the will of God, [one] will rise through this crisis (Hansard HL 681, col. 1196, 12 May 2006).

This is typical of the kind of rudimentary dogmatic theological determinism which exemplifies how the legal parameters of end-of-life discussions, even in the highest echelons of the law-making machinery, are often delimited by broader discourses and grand narratives which create meaning and structure the legal conception of death. Furthermore, the body of semiotic information insinuated by the tendentious term 'suicide' espouses a particularly negative set of signifiers. It is the only word for the variety of self-harm which results in death, whatever the significance of the act to the victim or others likely to be affected (Shaw 2013a: 106). The paucity of vocabulary available to articulate the nuanced act of 'committing suicide' is 'calculated to poison the unsuspecting mind with its false semantic overtones, for apart from the dangerous practice of committing oneself to an opinion, most other things committed are, as suicide once was, criminal offences' (Barrington 1986: 231). Szasz similarly criticises the limitations of disapprobative language as 'emptying the act or phenomenon of its rich meaning and imposing on it a single signification, typically of badness or madness' (2002: 4). Also, while 'mercy killing' attracts a murder sentence, killing out of provocation, anger or fear (particularly if considered to be in self-defence) more often attracts the reduced sentence of manslaughter.

End-of-life jurisprudence is largely driven and determined, to a large extent, by pernicious emotionalism rooted in fear, and the application of emotional language which is a form of rhetorical rather than rational speech with the aim of strategic manipulation rather than communication. The customary use of sanctimonious and emotionally loaded language underscores the characteristic religiosity embedded in the moral assumptions of law-makers. For example, in relation to physician-assisted dying, Lord Nickson introduced the terrifying spectre of 'mortal sin' and 'objectionable vices', citing eighteenth-century English poet Alexander Pope: 'Vice is a monster of so frightful mien, As to be hated needs but to be seen; Yet seen too oft, familiar with her face, We first endure, then pity, then embrace' (Hansard HL 681, col. 1223, 12 May 2006). The Lord Bishop of Oxford in an earlier reading also quoted from a favourite poem, this time 'One Foot in Eden' by Edwin Muir: 'Blossoms of grief and charity bloom in these darkened fields alone ... Strange blessings never in paradise fall from these beclouded skies.' He continues, 'For me, that poem has always hinted at and pointed to some fundamental truths about what it is to be a human being, particularly when the clouds are dark or beclouded' (Hansard HL 658, col. 1319, 10 March 2004). This ethically dubious paean of praise for a law which compels (religious and non-religious) individuals to continue living with unbearable suffering until an often undignified and painful demise is nothing less than rhetorical brutalism. The whimsical reference to 'in these darkened fields' is redolent of the idealised Christian attitude towards affliction as a meaningful, even welcome, God-given 'trial by fire' (1 Peter 1:7), which serves as a reminder that the temporary human condition of sin and suffering on earth will be superseded by a heavenly reward.

It is evident that the development of English law on physician-assisted dying has been adversely influenced by the dominant Christian heritage which is one of the foremost metanarratives inhibiting the possibility of debating voluntary euthanasia (*euthanatos*, or a 'good death') as an individually determinable and, under the circumstances, perhaps even a positive cultural experience. As the last two decades have witnessed the relativisation of death due to medical and technological advancements and resuscitation innovations also despite the advances in palliative care, the death process is too often protracted, painful, undignified and lonely. Consequently, many academics and legal practitioners have expressed concern that the provisions of the UK Suicide Act 1961, s.2 prohibiting assisted dying are now archaic, unethical and ripe for reform. Yet in spite of frequent private members' bills brought before the UK Parliament in support of physician-assisted dying, and surveys showing widespread public acceptance of mercy killing, 'assisted suicide' still carries a maximum sentence of 14 years' imprisonment. Historically, English courts and juries have also been reluctant to convict, particularly in relation to persons accompanying a terminally ill family member to an overseas clinic such as Dignitas in Switzerland in pursuit of a dignified end to their suffering. Still, there are no plans to translate this new morality into radical statutory reform which would enshrine a positive right to self-determination. Meanwhile, in the absence of legislative reform, the judiciary continue to exercise a diluted variety of moral judgment by adopting a lenient sentencing policy towards those lawbreakers who have acted out of sympathy and love.

In *R (Conway) v the Secretary of State for Justice* [2017] EWHC 2447 (Admin), the courts were asked to consider outlining a set of criteria and safeguards for terminally ill adults allowing them to make their own decisions about ending their lives. The applicant, retired lecturer Noel Conway, suffers from motor neurone disease, is confined to a wheelchair, uses an oxygen mask for 20 hours each day and is not expected to survive beyond 12 months. His primary objective is to be able to spend his final days at home with his family, in the knowledge that he will be legally permitted a relatively easeful death once the pain becomes too much to bear. Before going into court, he told *The Guardian* newspaper:

> If I decided I was going to Switzerland, I would have had to have gone by now. That would have deprived me of much more important and valued time with my family. At the moment, the quality of life and experience is sufficiently positive for me to want to continue (21 March 2017, p. 2).

Having to travel to Dignitas in Switzerland because of this draconian and arguably antiquated law means the choice to end life humanely must be made much earlier than ought to be the case, meaning less precious time with loved ones. As Lord Falconer of Thoroton explained in the second reading of the 2014 Assisted Dying Bill in the House of Lords, 'the compassionate [are] treated like criminals' and 'many people, caring so much for those they leave behind, are dying earlier and alone because they fear implicating their loved ones in a criminal enterprise' (Hansard HL, col. 775, 18 July 2014).

There is an elemental relationship between emotion, justice and time. Einstein argued that space and time are modes by which we think and not conditions in which we live, in common with Kant and Heidegger who understood space and time as the framework of thought rather than mechanisms which structure the universe. Clearly, the occupation of time and space constitutes our being-in-the-world; but, at the same time, we have an innate sense of time and space that is not learned from the purely physical, material world of phenomena. Rather, it can be understood as the context for the interplay of different determinations of human experience, as articulated by Douzinas and Gearey describing the loss of a beloved friend in 'Passages':

> The love for the friend becomes stronger now he is not there. The feeling of loss leads to a sense of injustice; the dead friend was not given his due, he was not given the time he deserved, and this deprivation of time deprives the world. … Mourning is emotion released by injustice. The sense of injustice is heightened by impotence before death. There is nothing the friend can do to bring his dead friend back. Death is irreversible, [it] is destiny both known and strange, and yet the destiny of the friend, his inevitable fate, fires a sense of injustice. The injustice of the friend's death, the sense of loss and lack, stems from the love of another and deprivation of the love-object. Justice is time, and injustice the deprivation of time. … The sense of injustice is a powerful emotion of loss or lack; linked to the deprivation another has suffered and heightened by the unavoidable but untimely character of the deprivation. Time, lack, suffering for the other, and inevitability or fate, are all part of the sense of injustice (2005: 138–139).

Applied to the example of assisted dying, law as justice is the sanctioning of extra time for the sufferer with their loved ones. It means being able to live a while longer with the confidence that it is possible to avoid a prolonged death and spare their relatives extra anguish. Legal codes alone cannot produce ethical behaviour and judgment, because they arise from developmentally pre-social categories and ontological assumptions about right or rational behaviour. Complex moral dilemmas, such as those raised in the cases of *Pretty* [2002], *Purdy* [2009], *Nicklinson* [2014] and *Conway* [2017], demonstrate that the law ought to be more than just reason and a clever compilation of distinct rules; rather, it needs to acknowledge the necessity of an emotional dimension. Even so, only those emotions grounded in love and sympathy for others are capable of engendering a proper commitment to shared goals and interests, by assuming responsibility for the common good of the community and the flourishing of one's neighbours.

The emotional connectivity of humans transcends the limits of the realm of law as exclusively rational or philosophical. It can determine a moral order within which it is possible to recognise and act on a shared understanding of injustice, and conceive the ethical basis for rejecting an inhumane law or outcome. Against the often estranging conditions of human existence, the pursuit of justice gives form to love's reunion of the separated. Accordingly, emotional sense is an invaluable human instrument because it can enable the courts to recognise and give expression to those aspects of fallible human experience which demand a kind, merciful and just response. For this reason, legal principles need a proper emotional basis from which to create a sense of cohesion by encouraging the cultivation of sentiments; for instance, sympathy and mercy which may lead to actions based on moral emotions such as love.

Law and love: against the entitlement of wealth and the obstruction of justice

Love does not simply suffuse and stimulate justice; love presupposes and transcends justice by sometimes doing more than justice requires but never less. Paul Tillich uses the example of inherited wealth to illustrate the ontological relation between love and justice. While justice demands a fortune is to be distributed equally between all those with the same legal claim, love may induce one of the heirs to surrender their right to one of the other heirs; in which case it may be deduced that 'justice is just because of the love which is implicit in it' (Tillich 1954: 13–15). A fixed and inflexible account of justice instantly loses touch with love and, by extension, with justice itself. Alternatively, when love participates in understanding the uniqueness of a particular situation, for example the human suffering of a terminally ill individual as discussed above, there is a better possibility of determining the most appropriate type and level of response. Otherwise, according to the demands of the universal law alone, there is a danger of conflating the rights of the oppressed with legal claims and arguments which are more suitable to the commercial, property or contractual realm – a distinction described by Simone Weil as:

> Whenever a man cries inwardly: 'Why am I being hurt?' harm is being done to him. He is often mistaken when he tries to define the harm, and why and by whom it is being inflicted on him. But the cry itself is infallible. The other cry, which we hear so often: 'Why has somebody else got more than I have?' refers to rights. We must learn to distinguish between the two cries and to do all that is possible, as gently as possible, to hush the second one, with the help of a code of justice, regular tribunals, and the police. Minds capable of solving problems of this kind can be formed in a law school. But the cry 'Why am I being hurt?' raises quite different problems, for which the spirit of truth, justice, and love is indispensable (2005: 93).

Weil's thesis dismisses the concept of 'personalism' which constitutes the basis of most human rights discourses and rights claims. This is because the essentialist reduction of the individual to being endowed with a particular set of properties denies the richness and diversity which characterises human beings. The 'impersonal' is for Weil absolutely prior to any individual aspects of the human. Therefore, it is not only their personhood but, more importantly, their potential which is in need of being safeguarded by a moral language and moral resources which can recognise and respond to those in pain and torment (Weil 2005: 78). She offers, by way of contrast, the example of a labourer who is maligned for his work and a girl who has been defiled by being forced to work in a brothel to illustrate how the intricacy and distinctiveness of an individual's cries of suffering are diminished when equated with a monetary claim.

The 'professionals of speech' learned in law schools, tribunals and police departments can take care of aggrieved employees; however, for Weil the juridification of human rights means it is impossible to adequately interpret the profound and complex cries of injustice of the defiled girl (2005: 80). Also human rights reasoning does not expressly forbid unjust decision-making and objectionable or unconscionable behaviour in relation to, for example, indefensible levels of global poverty or immense disparities of wealth which have a detrimental impact on public health and well-being. It is incapable of serving as a principle of action or motivational force which might cause the influential to empathise with the many forms of human suffering and vulnerability. For this reason we cannot rely on conceptual tools of human rights; only the dialectic of love and justice can hope to articulate the correct response to such types of suffering. This is because love's capacity to respond to the concrete circumstances continually compels justice to adopt new forms to fit new situations.

The emotional remoteness and objective detachment expected of parties and the adjudicator(s) in a human rights dispute is quite possibly one of the biggest obstacles to being able to empathise with, or feel concern for, a person whose rights have been violated. Although formal legal and quasi-legal obligations are part of a wider set of external social relations with consequences attached to real people in the living world, without love there is no warmth, no connection to the reality outside, only instrumentality. When people are used as 'means only' (in the Kantian sense) constituted within the system of narrowly constructed formal rules, as an agglomeration of individuals they effectively disappear from view as if invisible. They comprise the minority interest groups, the world's poor; they are the collectively dispossessed who have disappeared as individuals – which is what happens within legal discourse when it is purely self-referential. The current global financial and economic crisis – which continues to have economic, social and environmental impact on urban life, inflicting severe hardship across a wide range of industries and communities – is an example of the failure of moral responsibility, a failure to extend loving concern to a wider set of stakeholders.

The heart, unlike the mind, desires the object to be achieved, and this can take place at a personal, local, national or international level. Local businesses may, for example, be motivated to visualise and actualise a wider set of object (environmental) and subject (social) responsibilities; for example, to include within their contemplation a broader class of people and places likely to be adversely affected by their actions. At a national or international level, the assumption of moral obligations by corporate actors has potentially even more far-reaching consequences. The senior managers and employees of large enterprises including WorldCom, Enron, Barings, Lehman Brothers, Parmalat and Gowex were aware of their moral responsibilities, and accordingly made promises, composed elaborate mission statements, displayed codes of conduct expressing core values and assumed contractual obligations which imposed, at least, a minimum duty of care. Yet they were emotionally and intellectually disconnected from a wider group of stakeholders, those who were at risk of being negatively impacted by their irresponsible and reckless behaviour; comprising the unloved strangers not worthy of being contemplated in future planning. Their ethical duty was based on a 'preferential love' for 'only those who share one's passions' and so, 'the more alike the lovers the better the love' (Kierkegaard 1998: 45, 56). In short, if preferential love is love for those who look, sound and act like oneself, then the ultimate object for such love is 'me' – a blatant self-interest which marks 'the very peak of self-esteem, the I intoxicated in the other I'.

The power of global corporations to control is simultaneously the power to dissemble, reimagine and exclude (Shaw & Shaw 2016: 38). This triumph of egoism over altruism and negation of a universalist reading of the neighbour principle is offered by Sigmund Freud in *Civilization and Its Discontents* in which, via his quintessentially pessimistic interpretation of human nature, we are reminded that hospitality shares its origin with hostility:

> Not merely is this stranger in general unworthy of my love, I must honestly confess that he has more claim to my hostility and even my hatred. He seems not to have the least trace of love for me and shows me not the slightest consideration. If it will do him any good he has no hesitation in injuring me, nor does he ask himself whether the amount of advantage he gains bears any proportion to the extent of harm he does to me. Indeed, he might not even obtain an advantage; if he can satisfy any sort of desire by it, he thinks nothing of jeering at me, insulting me, slandering me and showing his superior power;

> and the more secure he feels and the more helpless I am, the more certainly I can expect him to behave like this to me (1961: 67).

For Freud, the neighbour relationship was interpreted as destructive and characterised by a fundamental mutual hostility. Reciprocity, based on contract and promise-keeping, was considered to be the only fair way in which to create responsibility with strangers and friends alike, as opposed to what Freud perceived as a grandiose assertion of superiority by Christianity. He preferred the maxim 'do unto others as you would have them (intend to) do unto you' because, even with the best intentions, the law has proved to be incapable of addressing the more cautious and refined manifestations of human malevolence and an elemental inclination towards aggressive and self-centred behaviour.

Undeniably, an absence of 'neighbourly' feeling in the commercial sector has been facilitated by the legal protection accorded to the pursuit of narrowly conceived ruling-class interests, often against the greater good. Also a lack of adequate regulatory provisions has rendered law complicit in furthering the ambitions of a, largely unaccountable, profit-driven global capitalist societal paradigm. The consequences of this have been disastrous for many developed countries in terms of, for example, the merciless deployment of austerity measures, shortage of meaningful employment, wage deflation, unsustainable levels of consumer debt and the concentration of wealth in elites and winner-takes-all cities such as New York and London (Shaw 2018: 315). Whilst both enslavement and empowerment are built into the logic of narratives of economic progress, the focus of corporate culture on the performance principle can be seen as exploitative and comprising nothing less than metaphorical economic slavery. This metaphor applies not only to the poorest of the world, millions of whom are trafficked into slavery and a life of extreme hardship and drudgery, but also to the typical middle-class consumer who shuffles along the workhouse treadmill, living in order to work and working in order to consume (Wolcher 2013: xvi). As elucidated by Costas Douzinas in his essay 'A Humanities of Resistance': 'Judges, like legislatures and administrators, are now involved in complicated issues of governance, in the definition of the public interest for all aspects of social life, and in the implementation of public policy'; and, consequently, cold and dispassionate 'economic efficiency has become the aim of the legal system' just as economics has become 'the dominant jurisprudential tradition' (2010: 57).

Not only has economic efficiency become the main objective of the legal system; many corporations are now powerful enough to influence legislative developments, thereby reversing the normal flow of power in the democratic process. Too often they are only accountable to soft law mechanisms, vague notions of corporate social responsibility or their own codes of conduct, and are, to a large extent, immune to the force of formal regulation. In the twenty-first century landscape of power, corporations are increasingly more likely to be the central players in global affairs than nation states. Also, although commonly referred to as multinational, they are more accurately described as post-national, transnational or even anti-national, because they repudiate the very idea of the nation or any other parochialism that may limit their spheres of activity. Being hypermobile and lacking attachment or loyalty to people or place, the global corporation typically evades responsibility for the consequences of its actions by existing in a trans-locational space, committed to nowhere in particular. For example, Google, Facebook, Amazon, McDonald's, Coca-Cola, Microsoft and Apple are all largely stateless superpowers whose brands transcend their national origin. The loss of meaning inherent in the 'placelessness' of global corporations translates into the placelessness of consumption; and, in turn, the placelessness of individuals as consumers of products, services, leisure and information (Relph 1976: 17). According to situationist Guy Debord, this gradual diminution of human life was produced by the regime of (mis-)representation in the 'society of the spectacle', which commodified 'being' into 'having' and further transformed 'having' into 'appearance' (Shaw 2017: 97). For Debord, under capitalism all relationships are transformed into the purely transactional, with society divided into actors and spectators, producers and consumers, operating under a hierarchical system of masters and slaves in a 'candy-floss world' of sensationalist entertainment.

With the loosening of traditional bonds, this variant *homo economicus* or *homo consumens* – founded on a functional model of social structures and individual identity formation according to consumption habits – constitutes both an artificial construct and something of a fiction. The placeless world created by information and communications technology (ICT) and cyberspace has further transformed real-world spatiality and the relationships between people and place. Accordingly, the multiple technologies that mediate our daily lives and interactions with others in cyberspace hardly determine who we are; similarly the texts, emails and social media messages people transmit to each other are not significant in themselves. Rather, 'we belong to the even flow of words and unfinished sentences (abbreviated, to be sure, truncated to speed up the circulation). We belong to talking, not to what is talked about' (Bauman 2003: 34, 35). To paraphrase Marshall McLuhan, the circulation of messages is the message. The technologically mediated consumer society is, for Bauman, symptomatic of 'liquid modernity' and the emergence of a society of people who have no authentic relationships and meaningful social attachments (Bauman 2003: 69).

In this context the expression of loving concern is more akin to *philautia* or self-love, having a fundamentally narcissistic construction: namely, this is love as a letter which 'always arrives at its destination' because the addressee is 'from the very beginning the sender himself', and the content of the message is nothing more than a reflection of his own being (Žižek 2001: 13). Compounded by the deprivation of a sense of place, humans lack not only a sense of freedom, security and self-identity, but also 'without place one could say that man cannot love; without love he cannot commit, be loyal to people, and things, around him' (Heidegger 1958: 19). Love without place is a mirage without authenticity, significance or meaning. Physical place is argued to be the foundation of all human sensate interactions, comprising experiential and material realities where the fullest range of human impulses, needs and desires are incubated and expressed; yet the 'liquid modern' is forever at work, continually replacing quality of relationship with quantity (Bauman 2003: 102).

This display of dispassion and dislocation is antithetical to the traditional conception of the 'moral economy', which is traditionally based on sharing goods and services, neighbourly help, the cooperation of friends and familial consideration – in other words, the motivations, impulses and sometimes random acts of kindness from which human bonds and lasting commitments are secured. Instead, 'placeless' corporations have often adopted an ersatz language of love based on the artificial corporate family developmental model; for instance, referring to the Asda UK supermarket chain as a member of the 'Wal-Mart family' (Shaw 2008: 8). At the same time, such corporations regularly behave unethically, without loving concern and familial consideration. This is evidenced by the often arbitrary flouting of legislation designed to protect individuals who ought to be within their contemplation; namely, the widest group of stakeholders likely to be affected by their day-to-day business operations and activities. There have been many instances of companies hiding behind laws and regulation in order to evade responsibility and the assumption of blame. Major retailers have also frequently been accused of disregarding planning and environmental laws, indulging in anti-competitive behaviour and poor employment practices (Shaw & Shaw 2019: 70, 74–79).

In a recent landmark US case, *Rainey et al v Mylan Specialty LP, U.S. District Court, Western District of Washington* [2017] No. 17-cv-05244, a pharmaceutical company colluded with pharmacy benefit managers (companies that act as intermediaries between pharmacies, insurers and drug companies) to dominate the market and overcharge consumers for an 'EpiPen', that treats life-threatening allergic reactions by automatically injecting a dose of epinephrine. Mylan increased the cost of a twin pack of the device to $600 from a more affordable $100 in 2008, leading to a lawsuit being filed under the Racketeer Influenced and Corrupt Organizations (RICO) Act, which is historically used against organised crime. Many American families, especially those with high-deductible health insurance, struggled to afford the $600 price label for the life-saving medication. In spite of a $465 million settlement Mylan did not admit wrongdoing, which effectively allowed the company to keep the money it embezzled from an American public in desperate need of life-saving and affordable drugs. This is not an isolated case as company directors making decisions from cocooned boardrooms, across a diverse range of public and private enterprises, have frequently demonstrated an inability or unwillingness to contemplate the hardship their strategies create for their customers, suppliers, local communities and a wide variety of other stakeholders; as if such people and places were entirely disconnected from the corporate world (Stiglitz 2002: 24).

Such examples resonate with Robert Musil's unfinished novel *Der Mann ohne Eigenschaften*, which comprises a series of allegorical investigations into an eclectic assortment of existential themes concerning humanity and the nature of attachments, and reason and emotion (1996). The passivity and indifference of the central character, a man named Ulrich, has led to him failing to develop either family or social ties and becoming 'a man without qualities'. This means he has to bring together whatever bonds he can find, using his own insight and judgment, in order to engage with the rest of human society. However, since the world is often confusing and people are likely to behave in a capricious manner, it is unclear to Ulrich which qualities he should strive to acquire. The bonds he seeks to create may not last, and so they must be only loosely fastened in order to be untied and reconnected again as circumstances require. The novel explores the frailty of human relationships and their characteristic conflicting impulses towards keeping kinship bonds tight, to nurture socio-emotional attachments and avoid feelings of insecurity, yet loose enough to avoid commitment and the threat of unwanted responsibility. As Ulrich discovers, although people are frequently unpredictable and subject to selfish and competitive inclinations – and as the Latin proverb warns, *Homo homini lupus* (man is wolf to other men) – it must be remembered that humans are nevertheless inherently social, and our survival is closely dependent on group life and cooperation (Freud 1961: 68).

Modern life has, of course, been irrevocably transformed by technological advancements and enhancements leading to almost global connectivity, notwithstanding substantial levels of inequality in bandwidth, efficiency and price. Cyberspace renders place inconsequential, identities fluid and reality multiple. The impact of the digital revolution has produced major socio-cultural changes, marked by an increased emphasis on individual progression, a decline in sociality and atomisation. Online social networking for example, most often contrived by myriad complex personalised algorithmic calculations, has replaced the randomness of meetings with strangers of different persuasions which traditionally took place in the public square. The erasure, or restructure, of the ersatz public space comprises primarily an auditory reconfiguration, often resulting in 'mediated urban isolation' (Shaw & Shaw 2015: 242). This is inevitable as web life encourages commitment and consequence-free experimentation because only the self is relevant. Therefore, as a result of multiple mediations of our experience 'we can come to live in places without ever fully integrating into the place-defined community, such as the local government, local community groups or local religious organisations' (Meyrowitz 2005: 27).

By generating new capacities to act at-a-distance, contemporary social life has been reconstituted along the lines of what Scott Lash describes as 'sociality and culture *at-a-distance*' (2001: 107–108). As mouse clicks and routine public acts of auditory separation have supplanted physical human contact we no longer recognise ourselves in the Other; and, importantly, our interest in, respect for and tolerance of the alterity of the Other and their opinions has waned to the point of atomisation (Shaw 2018: 317). These new technologies of power are based on both connection and isolation, and constitute a mix of private sensory enhancement and public sensory deprivation which, for Debord, constantly reinforces 'the conditions of isolation of lonely crowds' (1994: 26). Even so, while society's public and private spaces and places of interaction become more complex, the cyber-consciousness of the self remains physically situated in the lived space of pure subjectivity – of human experiences, imagination and feeling.

It is, therefore, still within the borderlands of lived space that we encounter the past, the present and the future, the historical and the imagined, together with the endless negotiations of power and control (Shaw 2019).

Although territories no longer constrain people and restrict their life choices, the radical reconfiguration of corporations as global actors, the increasing privatisation of what were once public goods and services, and the transformation of private enterprise in finance, industry and trade facilitated by the ability of ICTs to collapse space-time have led to considerable levels of urban-regional restructuring and the retreat of the state. This has resulted in a growing disregard for the rule of law, a diffusion of legal authority over global corporations and, in general, a regulatory retreat. As our familiar institutional landmarks continue to disappear, large privately owned companies frequently fulfil the traditional role of the state in providing public services; while many global corporations are now more powerful than states and their legislatures, to which ultimate political authority over society and economy has customarily belonged. Consequently, and as noted above, reports of unjust, unconscionable or discriminatory business practices and an increasing number of social and environmental scandals, particularly those relating to the financial sector, have proliferated. It is evident that companies have evolved to serve the interests of whoever controls them, at the expense of whoever does not.

Considering the broad configuration of the global capitalist system, voluntary measures such as those which fall under the heading of corporate social responsibility (including mission statements and vision statements) are, in too many instances, perfunctory and empty gestures in which the concept of responsibility is reduced to a half-hearted set of vapid principles. Such initiatives tick a box and serve to justify the deeper extension of market forces into an already imploding social body. It is evident that the assumption of responsibility without love often leads to discord and suffering, as powerful corporate actors may believe they are acting out of altruism when in fact they are constructing their own values with which to oppress others. As corporations aggressively pursue profit above all else, many formerly thriving manufacturing regions no longer provide skilled work, inequalities in wealth and income have increased, and the burden of austerity has fallen largely on the poor, having a detrimental impact on both physical and mental health. In the face of growing corporate self-interest and indifference, there is a necessity for governments to prioritise corporate responsibility for, and accountability to, the widest group of stakeholders in a region or country, above the provision of a business-friendly environment.

Although the free market operates on the basis of self-interest, even a kind of self-love, there is nonetheless a moral imperative to offer adequate and appropriate legal protections towards the facilitation of a just economy – not least of all because:

> To hurt, in any degree, the interest of any one order of citizens, for no other purpose but to promote that of some other, is evidently contrary to that justice and equality of treatment which the sovereign owes to all the different orders of his subjects (Smith 1981: 271).

For Adam Smith, a nation's wealth should be measured by the well-being of its people; which to a large extent depends on the impact of political institutions on law, economy, culture and the effective representation of society as a whole. In determining the ethical creation, enforcement and application of legislation and legal policy, political institutions are uniquely capable of uniting human beings under forms of justice that must be constantly reconsidered and reimagined if they are not to lose touch with the dynamic power of loving concern and crystallise into progressively unjust juridicalism. Only justice can prevent power from becoming oppressive and offer support to the communication of law as love, inasmuch as love is the foundation rather than the negation of power.

To return to the example of 'neighbourliness' and against the underlying particularist foundations of the lawyer's question in relation to identifying the class of persons who constitute one's 'neighbours', this was answered in a public address at the Chautauqua Institution, New York on 14 August 1936, by US President Franklin D. Roosevelt. Using the principle of neighbourliness as a flexible and historically contingent metaphor, he extolled the virtues of his 'good neighbor policy'. This was presented as a necessary provision for economic recovery, stability and security, and to improve relations with Latin America. Roosevelt went on to recommend 'the neighbor who resolutely respects himself and, because he does so, respects the rights of others. He respects his obligations and respects the sanctity of his agreements in and with a world of neighbors', and concluded, 'Let those who wish our friendship look us in the eye and take our hand.' This compelling speech as a commitment to caring and cooperative international foreign policy ensured good relations, even partnerships and friendships, with this wider set of 'distant neighbors' for many years.

Neighbourliness, as well as its emotional corollary love, needs to be redefined and reimagined in contemporary legal, social and political life in order to properly envision a more inclusive society where each citizen exists in a relationship of fraternity with other stakeholders in the world, even without expecting reciprocity (Shaw & Shaw 2019: 55). A key issue would be how to bridge the gap between acting in accordance with justice (institutional) and being impelled by justice (motivational) in all circumstances, holding others in equal regard. The way forward is suggested by Adam Smith in *Wealth of Nations* and lies in humanity's social instincts or sense of primordial oneness, in which we instinctually aspire to a common consciousness that at the same time encourages the flourishing of individuals. Otherwise, inevitably, any institution that loses touch with the form of justice that unites its members faces decay, decline and eventual death.

This view is echoed in the original final line of W.H. Auden's war poem 'September 1, 1939' in which he states, 'we must love one another or die', proposing that love for each other could save us from war and desolation, or even confer a kind of immortality. Similarly, Virgil wrote *amor vincit omnia* (love conquers all) and Philip Larkin finished his poem 'An Arundel Tomb' with the poignant (and perhaps ironic, considering the overall tone of the piece) last line, 'what will survive of us is love'. The corollary of such sentiments seems to be that love is not only the operating principle of humanity, but is also the driving force of justice, with the ability to augment justice particularly when it has reached its limits.

The heart as law's attorney: there can be no justice without love

Comprising members of a historical community of people, region, nation, and so on, individuals have developed a natural aptitude for putting themselves in the place of others, or, better, transcending their place. From an ethical perspective, self-knowledge and self-worth are only achievable through our interpersonal relations and meaningful relationships with fellow members of society, thereby connecting the inner self with the outer world. Whilst conflict and antagonisms are an inevitable part of being human, according to Ricoeur – who produced what might be referred to as a non-conclusive dialectic of hope – such intersections are constitutive because they contain the possibility of creating new meaning. Even within these oppositional contexts identities can be negotiated along with the formation of dialogic and collaborative relationships, as heterogeneous ideas and conversations have the capacity to meld into composite discourses whilst retaining both specificity and distinction. By reaching out and responding to the other-than-self thoughtfully and selflessly, the considerate and loving self is capable of bringing about a better life for others and, in turn, themselves. This essentially emotional response as loving concern is based on mutuality (recognition of the 'other self') and arises unprompted; it also acknowledges the dual significance of the Other, as they appear and as they are fully encountered in their own right (Ricoeur 2000).

As well as increasing an understanding of self in relation to others, a commitment to respond humanely comprises the foundation for evaluating the ethical and moral determinations of action. Before choosing to act, therefore, our actions ought first to be envisaged from an outside perspective; and in this way our intentions take the form of imagined actions in which the external is first internalised. This is a mimetic characteristic of human behaviour which directs all human relationships and civil life, signalling a primordial ontic openness, a lacuna across which it is possible to 'feel' a moral duty or respect for the Other. For example, it is not enough to simply recognise that discrimination is unlawful; rather, to feel the wrongness of discrimination, its capacity for reductionism and dehumanisation, is a sensate impulse that can reinforce any motivation to right action.

The ancient Greek idea of promoting ethical judgment by a process of enculturation into a virtuous mindset so as to better realise the consistent application of just and morally consistent laws has particular significance for common law jurisdictions, because the common law originates from the tradition of a collective community morality rather than from the abstract generalisations which characterise Continental legal systems. Arguably, common law judges have the possibility of pursuing values which accord with Aristotle's conception of practical wisdom in individual cases, yet still tend to prioritise the bare application of negative rights which are often supported by vague technical propositions. An example is the case of *A and others v Secretary of State for the Home Department* [2004] UKHL 56, challenging the legality of Part IV of the 2001 Anti-terrorism, Crime and Security Act (ATCSA) which allowed the indefinite detention of foreign nationals in high-security Belmarsh Prison without trial, on the grounds of a risk to national security. As this provision infringed Article 5(1) of the European Convention on Human

Rights (ECHR), incorporated into English law as the Human Rights Act (HRA) – which guarantees that everyone has the right to liberty and security of person – a derogation was notified under Article 15 of the ECHR and the 'designated derogation order' under s.14 of the HRA.

The majority judgment in the House of Lords held that, given the circumstances, there was sufficient evidence of 'an emergency which threatened the life of the nation'; however, the measures implemented under Part IV of ATCSA were 'not strictly required by the exigencies of the situation'. They further conceded that s.23 of ATCSA discriminated against non-nationals, in this case on the basis of the appellants' nationality and immigration status, in violation of Article 14 of the ECHR. Although several Law Lords agreed that such forms of 'executive detention' were antithetical to 'the right to liberty and security of person', and 'unwarranted declarations of emergency are the familiar tool of tyranny' or 'the stuff of nightmares', only Lord Hoffmann (dissenting) of the nine panellists was prepared to move boldly beyond a technical debate about statutory interpretation. Laying the groundwork for possible cultural change, he alone argued the wider ethical implications of the case by engaging in a deeper moral analysis of the extra-legal context, as to what exactly might realistically constitute a 'threat to the *life of the nation*':

> Your Lordships who are also in favour of allowing the appeal would do so, not because there is no emergency threatening the life of the nation, but on the ground that a power of detention confined to foreigners is irrational and discriminatory. I would prefer not to express a view on this point. I said that the power of detention is at present confined to foreigners and I would not like to give the impression that all that was necessary was to extend the power to United Kingdom citizens as well. In my opinion, such a power in any form is not compatible with our constitution. ... The technical issue in this appeal is whether such a power can be justified on the ground that there exists a 'war or other public emergency threatening the life of the nation'. ... What is meant by 'threatening the life of the nation'? The 'nation' is a social organism, living in its territory under its own form of government and subject to a system of laws which expresses its own political and moral values. When one speaks of a threat to the 'life' of the nation, the word life is being used in a metaphorical sense. The life of the nation is not coterminous with the lives of its people. The nation, its institutions and values, endure through generations. ... The real threat to the life of the nation, in the sense of a people living in accordance with its traditional laws and political values, comes not from terrorism but from laws such as these (paras. 86–97).

Whilst intellectual rigour and a deep knowledge of the law are the basis of most legal principles, as illustrated above members of the judiciary are often subtly and unconsciously influenced by their interactions with people in their immediate circle and the prevailing attitudes of those people. Until the late eighteenth century, judges were even more likely to share the same mindset; for example, in routinely exercising leniency towards unscrupulous landlords and employers in the protection of business interests while showing little or no compassion for women and children toiling long hours in factories, and by refuting the claims of employees and tenants irrespective of the circumstances. Also most writers on the function of government in relation to the poorest in society maintained that governments should keep the poor in poverty, so that they would behave with appropriate deference to their superiors and not squander money on drink and women.

Adam Smith had more influence than his contemporaries in changing this discriminatory attitude, and was one of the foremost impassioned defenders of the rights of the poor, arguing against wage controls and other restraints that kept the underprivileged from becoming socially and economically mobile. In *The Theory of Moral Sentiments* (1759), he argued that justice must act as a constraint on the prioritising of, for instance, economic activity over an inclusive conception of the rule of law, maintaining that only 'kindness or beneficence' cannot 'among equals be extorted by force' (Smith 2002: 81). It was further recommended that all judgment be preceded by self-reflection or moral-mirroring, which obliged an examination of 'our own conduct as we imagine any other fair and impartial spectator would imagine it. ... It is only by consulting this judge within that we can ever make any proper comparison between our own interests and those of other people' (2002: 128–129). Smith placed aesthetic perceptions and emotional reactions at the heart of moral judgment, and took the view that legal judgment is as much a property of feeling as of intellectual understanding or reason. To situate institutions such as slavery and destitution within a discourse of compassion and love, for example, comprises a form of sentimental jurisprudence which prioritises the synthesis of morality and compassion with social reality. More importantly, this requires the ability to visualise, without self-interest, the real-life circumstances in which the oppressed find themselves. Smith also believed the common law to have an informational advantage in that, relying on decisions from the past, it draws on the accumulated wisdom and rich experience of many actors – although he also acknowledged, as illustrated above, the homogenous nature of the judiciary, and the tendency to confirm each other's prejudices and enflame each other's passions.

Nevertheless judicial compassion, loving concern and responsiveness to the wider interests and concerns of an idealised, well-informed and impartial community are necessary elements of moral decision-making. This would ensure the modern judge is rightfully attuned to the predicament of those most affected by legal judgment, particularly where such cases concern the justification of unequal treatment. On the other hand, judicial activism has met with criticism in relation to understating the threat of legitimate terrorist activities or overstating the remit of executive duty. In para. 97 of *A and others v S.S.H.D.* [2004] UKHL 56, Lord Hoffmann referred to the duty that the government has to protect lives and property 'which it owes all the time and must discharge without destroying our constitutional freedoms'; yet no constitution provides for absolute protection by the state against the actions of, for example, private actors, or even the state itself, if sanctioned by law. Rather, the law imposes typically arbitrary limits on what governments may and may not do in relation to their citizens, comprising a set of negative liberties. Although negative duties are important, most public law institutions would be reluctant to prescribe right and just actions which impose positive duties on others (particularly non-state actors), such as a right to work, free housing or education, being inimical to economic freedom; preferring to consolidate ethical values in typically negative terms such as non-interference.

The ECHR offers another example in that, whilst purporting to support positive obligations, the provisions are negative in their application or, at best, ambiguous. Although Article 8 imposes a positive obligation to respect family and private life, the right to life outlined in Article 2 is open to both a positive and negative interpretation. Combined with the Suicide Act 1961, s.2, a moral claim to the right to life does not create a corresponding negative right to self-determination in deciding how to end one's life; nor does it confer an entitlement to choose assisted dying for medical or existential reasons. Such an extension of Article 2 is unsupported by law in the UK and is, therefore, not recognised as a legal right, as evidenced in *R (on application of Pretty) v Director of Public Prosecutions* [2002] 1 AC 800; *Pretty v United Kingdom* (2002) 35 EHRR 1; *R (Nicklinson) v Ministry of Justice* [2014] UKSC 38 and [2015] AC 657 or *R (Conway) v the Secretary of State for Justice* [2017] EWHC 2447 (Admin).

Emmanuel Levinas suggested that because the law seeks to have the last word, we need rights because we cannot have justice. In *Otherwise than Being, or Beyond Essence* he states that the failure to recognise that responsibility arises primarily from the vulnerability with which the Other approaches us and pleads for our assistance (Levinas 1981: 157). However in too many recent human rights cases and parliamentary debates, the decision-making process illustrates a lack of sympathetic imagination, and an inability or unwillingness to 'put oneself into the shoes of another'. The relapse into juridicalism and rigid legalism in the case of assisted dying, for instance, is a reminder of the deficiency of contemporary legal thinking on the nature and purpose of justice. Specifically, it is not yet fully recognised or understood that justice motivated by love is not only virtuous but also innovative and dynamic; it is grounded in the very texture of being human and pervades everything in nature.

For Aristotle, all human actions seek to achieve some specific good or a component of the 'good life', often with and on behalf of others. It is the intersubjective social context within which such interactions take place, with the corollary that it is 'only as citizens that we become human. The wish to live within just institutions signifies nothing else' (Ricoeur 2000: xvi). From this perspective, citizenship, justice and love are correlative, which implies that the privileges and opportunities granted by our political and legal institutions must also conform to a common and 'universalisable' sense of justice. This ethical aim requires acknowledging the mutual vulnerabilities and capabilities of individuals in relation to institutions, traditions and discourses as these determine how new laws and categories of meaning are created and shared. In *Nicomachean Ethics* Aristotle distinguished legal, or procedural, justice as the application of general laws (universalism) from moral 'equity' (altruism), arguing that the misshapen manner in which general or universal legal rules are made to fit particular contexts to which they are unsuited can only be overcome by the exercise of 'practical judgment' or discretion (1998: 141). The development of virtuous practical judgment, he argued, is only possible due to the human capacity for learning to feel the right ennobling emotions, such as love, at the right time in the right circumstances. Moral education and evolution requires, therefore, a conscious habituation in learning, knowing, understanding and choosing to perform right or just actions in order to become just.

The imperative of a sentimental education: in recognition of law as an activity of the heart, soul and intellect

Just as law is founded on an assumption of responsibility for the Other, justice is grounded in the moral turn to the Other who as an equal must be treated according to the equal application of norms. Although unaligned with any particular modern ideology, the writings of Aristotle on the place of morality in law, as necessary for justice, still have relevance. He considered moral education to be a necessary prerequisite of leadership in law, politics, and other branches of civil society, and extolled the benefits of having a morally educated citizenry by proposing a scheme of public education for everyone. On the basis that not all emotions can claim moral authority, he proposed that 'educating the emotions' was a priority: advising that 'to feel at the right times, with reference to the right objects, towards the right people, with the right motive, and in the right way, is what is both intermediate and best, and this is characteristic of virtue' (1998: 38, 43–45). The education of our emotional responses was argued to be crucial for the development of a virtuous character, associated with being good human beings who take pleasure in the right objects and live well. Since virtue is associated with the idea of actions and passions, emotions were held to acquire moral significance only when aligned with the ethical imperatives of the 'right objects' and the 'right motive'. The moral pedigree of an emotion was also not to be determined solely on the basis of its intrinsic properties (what it is directed at, what it motivates us to do), but on its timely application to the immediate circumstances of the life of an individual or community.

In *Waiting for God*, Simone Weil claims that 'love sees what is invisible; it sees [and seeks] what does not exist' (1973: 92). The idea that the poor and oppressed, the neglected and forgotten are invisible to most of us until 'seen', as they rarely are, with the eyes of love confirms that ethics and morality are products of the will. Accordingly, justice is something that we feel; it engages the emotions, passions and experience. It respects the 'ethics of alterity' and 'forgets the difference of the different and the otherness of the other' (Douzinas 2004: 214). As Rousseau advised in *Émile: Or on Education*, to 'see suffering without feeling it is not to know it'; rather, a person has to 'sense' oneself in others and 'be touched by the laments of others [and] suffer their pains' (1979: 222). In

Venus and Adonis Shakespeare refers to the tongue, or eloquent and impassioned speech, as the 'heart's attorney' as the tongue pleads on behalf of the heart, from the emotions: 'but when the heart's attorney once is mute, the client breaks, as desperate in his suit' (1988: 331). The cultivation of an empathic imagination is fundamental to understanding what is most basic to human nature, namely, that which best embodies humanity. It enables a mutual connectivity between individuals of free and equal status which not only forms the basis for morality, but also serves as the foundation for how we want to be treated and how we ought to treat others.

The impetus towards justice, and theories of justice and morality, is predicated on our natural ability to attune our emotional senses to mutually shared feelings of injustice, hurt and suffering, which in turn has the capability of inspiring the creation of a just system of law. Although lawyers, as aggressive litigators, are commonly unconcerned with wider appeals to truth and justice, at the same time, being influential citizens, it is suggested they should be trained in, for example, normative ethical reasoning which promotes impartiality and enables the examination of alternative accounts of decision-making, social justice and related topics. To this end, Martha Nussbaum identifies three capacities necessary for the fostering of humanity in the modern world: (1) a critical examination of self, and one's traditions and values; (2) the appreciation of a world beyond the local, regional, national – i.e., the notion of international citizenship; and finally (3) the cultivation of a 'narrative imagination' which is essential in order to be able to put oneself in another's shoes (1997: 9–11). Through the stories of others we can perceive people and situations that were once invisible and, by a process of critical reflection and expansion of our interpretive horizons, begin to understand a wider world of new and important alternative meanings and possibilities. Becoming a good lawyer, therefore, involves more than learning the rudiments of legal reasoning and argument; rather, it requires an enlargement of our empathic understanding by training oneself to become a human being capable of love and imagination.

There have been a variety of initiatives from law schools and faculties in the UK, the US and Australia to support the development of empathic ethical and social skills, acknowledging that at the heart of lawyering is a concern for people and their difficulties (Sullivan *et al* 2007). Recent decisions relating to, for example, assisted dying, same-sex adoption, and transgender and intersex rights in relation to sex-free passports (following the Australian M/F/X provision, which is currently under judicial review in the UK), all indicate the important connection between loving consideration, empathic imagination and legal judgment. In each case, presumptions, pre-judgments and legal proscriptions have been overcome in order to allow the space within which to consider an empathic response. For Goodrich, this constitutes an 'irruptive requirement of justice' which requires 'a momentary suspension of law' – thus enabling justice to act as 'an empty space' which is prior and undetermined (1999: 114). Justice is not determined in advance, and it is from within this blank space that members of the legal community are able to offer an authentic response to the Other in their singularity and on their own terms. It is further suggested that justice as a place of 'becoming' represents the significant and enduring intersection between law and feeling – in this case, love.

The development and deployment of emotions such as compassion, sympathy and benevolence (which are virtuous when prompted by love as the 'benevolent concern for the welfare of others') were prized by Hume because of their ability to motivate individuals to treat each other well (1987: 162). Considering morality to be grounded in the passions relating to 'character, virtue and vice, rather than rules, duty and obligation', Hume believed emotions can only achieve the status of 'moral' when properly articulated as stable and universalisable principles, which become integrated into the moral code of an institution or community, replacing the more capricious impulses of fleeting sentiment (1987: 230). Although the phrase 'moral emotions' is polysemous and therefore somewhat imprecise, many philosophers concur that it refers to those emotions that are associated with the best interests or flourishing of society as a whole rather than a set of narrow or privileged interests. In agreement with Hume and as noted earlier, De Sousa even claims that emotions, and particularly love, are at the foundation of all moral considerations because they provide the 'starting point of morality'; however, for emotions to be taken seriously in an ethical context their power to motivate right actions and conduct 'must be grounded in reality' (1987: 307). The reality to which emotions offer access is the relatively objective world of human values in the wider realm of social relations, because of the social nature of human life. Each individual creates social reality by attaching meaning to their actions and intentions – occupying the realm of thought, of rational consciousness – which enables meaningful interaction with both the world and each other.

Since there is no external world of law independent of the social world of individuals and groups, it follows that all law-making bodies are situated and determined in the embodied pre-theoretical, yet already transcendentally constituted *lifeworld*, experienced by all human subjects together (Husserl 1970: 65). This means our being in society is not only contingent upon our co-existence with others and necessitates their freely given acknowledgement of our independent subjectivity, but our quest for self-justification must include a desire to further their freedom. Clearly, the assumption of responsibility for, and accountability to, other members of society, law, justice and love are correlative and complementary. When love is understood as a constructive constitutive force – which not only recognises and respects difference but also seeks to maintain and accommodate the distinctiveness of human nature rather than assimilate or negate such differences – it enhances law and begins to fulfil the requirements of justice. Accordingly, in *Politics VII–VIII*, Aristotle recommended that, as well as literacy and numeracy, future judges and decision-makers must gain an insight into the working of the universe, learn to appreciate the beauty of the world surrounding them, and acquire an understanding of those who inhabit it. The purpose of such a sentimental education was to encourage members of the judiciary, lawyers and legal scholars to understand their own being as that which is ultimately summoned by, and according to, the will and interests of others. Ideally, this would mean every individual must be considered worthy of being lovingly presenced, properly recognised and reconstituted as a primary consideration of the law-making mind-set; not least of all because humans can find justification of their own existence only in the existence of other human beings (de Beauvoir 2000: 17).

Bibliography

Abrams, K. and H. Keren (2010) 'Who's Afraid of Law and the Emotions?', *Minnesota Law Review* 94: 1997–2074

Adorno, T.W. (1973) *Negative Dialectics*, London: Routledge & Kegan Paul

Adorno, T.W. (1983) 'Cultural Criticism and Society', in *Prisms*, trans. S. Weber and S. Weber, Cambridge, Massachusetts: MIT Press

Agamben, G. (1998) *Homo Sacer: Sovereign Power and Bare Life*, Stanford, CA: Stanford University Press

Agamben, G. (2005) *State of Exception*, Chicago: University of Chicago Press

Aladjem, T.K. (2008) *The Culture of Vengeance and the Fate of American Justice*, New York: Cambridge University Press

Andreas, P. (2011) 'Illicit Globalization: Myths, Misconceptions and Historical Lessons', *Political Science Quarterly* 126(3): 406–425

Aquinas, T. (1947) *The Summa Theologica* 1, q. 61, part. 4, trans. Fathers of the English Dominican Province, New York: Benziger Brothers Inc.

Arendt, H. (1977a) 'Crisis in Culture', in *Between Past and Future: Six Exercises in Political Thought*, New York: Meridian

Arendt, H. (1977b) 'Truth and Politics', in *Between Past and Future: Six Exercises in Political Thought*, New York: Meridian

Arendt, H. (1992) *Lectures on Kant's Political Philosophy*, Chicago: University of Chicago Press

Arendt, H. (2006) *On Revolution*, London: Penguin Classics

Aristotle (1991) *On Rhetoric: A Theory of Civic Discourse*, trans. G.A. Kennedy, New York: Oxford University Press

Aristotle (1995) *Poetics*, trans. S. Halliwell, Cambridge, Massachusetts: Harvard University Press

Aristotle (1996) *The Politics and the Constitution of Athens*, trans. S. Everson, Cambridge: Cambridge University Press

Aristotle (1998) *Nicomachean Ethics*, trans. D. Ross, Oxford: Oxford University Press

Auden, W.H. (1976) *W.H. Auden Collected Poems*, London: Random House

Austen, J. (1994) *Northanger Abbey*, London: Penguin Classics

Avebury, Lord P.C. (1908) *The Pleasures of Life*, London: Macmillan

Aviv, R. (2015) 'The Death Treatment: When should people with a non-terminal illness be helped to die?', *The New Yorker* (22 June) 25–28

Bacon, F. (1999) 'Of Revenge', in *The Essays or Counsels Civil and Moral*, B. Vickers (ed.), Oxford: Oxford University Press

Bacon, F. (2001) *The Advancement of Learning*, Modern Library Edition, New York: Random House

Bakhtin, M.M. (1981) *The Dialogic Imagination*, Austin: University of Texas Press

Bandes, B. (1996) 'Empathy, Narrative, and Victim Impact Statements', *University of Chicago Law Review* 63: 361–412

Bankowski, Z. (1996) 'Law, Love and Computers', *Edinburgh Law Review* 1(1): 25–42

Bankowski, Z. (2001) *Living Lawfully: Love in Law and Law in Love*, Dordrecht: Kluwer

Barrie, J.M. (2011) *Peter Pan*, A. Hiebert Alton (ed.), Ontario, Canada: Broadview Press

Barrington, M.R. (1986) 'The Case for Rational Suicide', in *Voluntary Euthanasia: Experts Debate the Right to Die*, A.B. Downing and B. Smoker (eds), London: Peter Owen

Barthes, R. (1972) 'The World of Wrestling', in *Mythologies*, A. Lavers (trans.), London: Jonathan Cape, 13–23

Baudelaire, C. (1964) 'Une Mort Héroïque', in *Oeuvres Complètes*, Paris: Pléiade

Battin, M.P. (1998) 'Is a Physician Ever Obligated to Help a Patient Die?', in *Regulating How We Die: The Ethical, Medical and Legal Issues Surrounding Physician-Assisted Suicide*, L.L. Emanuel (ed.), Cambridge, Massachusetts: Harvard University Press

Baudrillard, J. (1993) *Symbolic Exchange and Death*, London: Sage

Baudrillard, J. (1995) *The Gulf War Did Not Take Place*, Bloomington: University of Indiana Press

Baudrillard, J. (1998) *The Consumer Society: Myths and Structures*, London: Sage

Bauman, Z. (1993) *Postmodern Ethics*, Oxford: Blackwell

Bauman, Z. (1989) *Modernity and the Holocaust*, Cambridge: Polity Press

Bauman, Z. (2003) *Liquid Love: On the Frailty of Human Bonds*, Cambridge: Polity Press

Bauman, Z. (2006) *Liquid Fear*, Cambridge: Polity Press

Beckett, J.A. (2011) 'The Violence of Wording: Robert Cover on Legal Interpretation', *No Foundations* 8: 3–39

Ben-Dor, O. (2011) 'Introduction: Standing Before the Gates of Law', in *Law and Art: Justice, Ethics and Aesthetics*, O. Ben-Dor (ed.), London: Routledge

Benjamin, W. (1999) 'Critique of Violence', in *Selected Writings: Volume 1*, trans. E. Jephcott, M. Bullock and M.W. Jennings (eds), Cambridge, Massachusetts: Harvard University Press, 236–252

Bennett, A. (1932) *The Journals of Arnold Bennett: Entry for 18 March 1897*, Harmondsworth: Penguin

Bentham, J. (1789) 'Publicity in the Courts of Justice', in *The Works of Jeremy Bentham with an Outline of his Opinions on the Principal Subjects Discussed in his Works*, vol. IV, J. Bowring (ed.), Edinburgh: William Tait

Bentham, J. (1977) *A Comment on the Commentaries and A Fragment on Government*, J.H. Burns and H.L.A. Hart (eds), Oxford: Oxford University Press

Berry, W. (2002) 'Economy and Pleasure', in *The Art of the Common Place: The Agrarian Essays of Wendell Berry*, N. Wirzba (ed.), Berkeley: Counterpoint

Bierce, A. (1911) *The Devil's Dictionary*, London: Bloomsbury

Blake, W. (1794/1990) *Songs of Innocence and Experience*, Oxford: Oxford University Press

Blake, W. (1991) *Blake: Complete Writings with Variant Readings*, G. Keynes (ed.), Oxford: Oxford University Press

Bourdieu, P. (1987) 'The Force of Law: Toward a Sociology of the Juridical Field', *Hastings Law Journal* 38(5): 805–853

Bourdieu, P. (1990) *The Logic of Practice*, Stanford, CA: Stanford University Press

Bourdieu, P. (1991) *Language and Symbolic Power*, Cambridge: Polity Press

Bourdieu, P. (2001) *Masculine Domination*, Stanford, CA: Stanford University Press

Bourdieu, P. (2014) *On the State: Lectures at the College de France 1989–1992*, D. Fembach (trans.), P. Champagne, R. Lenoir, F. Poupeau and M. Riviere (eds), Cambridge: Polity Press

Bourdieu, P. and J.-C. Passeron (1990) *Reproduction in Education, Society and Culture*, London: Sage

Braidotti, R. (2013) *The Posthuman*, Cambridge: Polity Press

Bridgeman, J. (2015) 'Misunderstandings, Threats, and Fear of the Law in Conflicts over Children's Healthcare: In the Matter of Ashya King [2014] EWHC 2964', *Medical Law Review* 23(1): 477–489

Brzezinski, Z. (2007) 'Terrorized by the War on Terror: How a Three-Word Mantra Has Undermined America', *Washington Post* (25 March) 3

Burke, E. (2001) *Reflections on the Revolution in France*, J.C.D. Clark (ed.), Stanford, CA: Stanford University Press

Butler, J. (1997) *The Psychic Life of Power*, Stanford, CA: Stanford University Press

Butler, J. (2000) 'Competing Universalities', in E. Laclau and C. Mouffe (eds), *Contingency, Hegemony, Universality: Contemporary Dialogues on the Left*, London: Verso

Butler, J. (2004) *Undoing Gender*, New York: Routledge

Butler, J. (2006) *Precarious Life: The Powers of Mourning and Violence*, London: Verso

Butler, J. (2007) *Gender Trouble*, London: Routledge

Cafcass (2018) 'Private Law Data', in *Report of the Children and Family Court Advisory and Support Service*. Available at: https://www.cafcass.gov.uk/about-cafcass/research-and-data/private-law-data/; accessed on 1 July 2018

Cahill, A. (2001) *Rethinking Rape*, New York: Cornell University Press

Camus, A. (1986) *Neither Victims Nor Executioners*, Philadelphia: New Society

Cardozo, B.N. (1921) *The Nature of the Judicial Process*, New Haven: Yale University Press

Carroll, L. (1871) 'Jabberwocky', in *Through the Looking-Glass and What Alice Found There*, London: Macmillan

Carroll, L. (2003) *Alice's Adventures in Wonderland and Through the Looking-Glass*, London: Penguin Classics

Chen, A. (2018) 'Cambridge Analytica and our lives inside the surveillance machine', *The New Yorker* (21 March) 8–10

Cixous, H. (1976) 'The Laugh of the Medusa', trans. K. Cohen and P. Cohen, *Signs*, 1(4): 875–893

Cooke, B.J. and D.P. Farrington (2016) 'The Effectiveness of Dog Training Programs in Prison: A Systematic Review and Meta-Analysis of the Literature', *The Prison Journal* 96(6): 854–876

Cooley, C. (1922) *Human Nature and the Social Order*, New York: Charles Scribner's Sons

Cooper, L. (1913) *Aristotle on the Art of Poetry*, New York: Harcourt Brace & Company

Cover, R.M. (1983) 'The Supreme Court 1982 Term – Foreword: Nomos and Narrative', *Harvard Law Review* 97(4): 4–68

Cover, R.M. (1986) 'Violence and the Word', *Yale Law Journal* 95(8): 1601–1629

Crichton, M. (2004) *State of Fear*, New York: HarperCollins

Cummings, E.E. (1926) *Is 5*, New York: Liveright Publishing Co.

Dalberg, J.E.E. (1877) 'The History of Freedom in Antiquity', in *Selected Writings of Lord Acton, Vol. 1*, J. Rufus Fears (ed.), Indianapolis: Liberty Classics

Damasio, A.R. (1996) *Descartes' Error, Emotion, Reason and the Human Brain*, London: Macmillan

Damasio, A.R. (2003) *Looking for Spinoza: Joy, Sorrow, and the Feeling Brain*, New York: Harcourt
Damasio, A.R. (2010) *Self Comes to Mind: Constructing the Conscious Brain*, New York: Pantheon
Dante, A. (1984) *The Divine Comedy: Paradiso*, trans. A. Mandelbaum, Berkeley and Los Angeles: University of California Press
Danziger, S., J. Levav and L. Avnaim-Pesso (2011) 'Extraneous Factors in Judicial Decisions', *Proceedings of the National Academy of Sciences* 108(17): 6889–6892
Davies, M. (2018) *Law Unlimited: Materialism, Pluralism and Legal Theory*, London: Routledge
Day Lewis, C. (1936) *A Hope for Poetry*, Oxford: Blackwell
Day Lewis, C. (1969) *The Poetic Image*, London: Jonathan Cape
De Beauvoir, S. (1944) *Pyrrhus et Cinéas*, Paris: Gallimard
De Beauvoir, S. (1953) *The Second Sex*, trans. H.M. Parshley, New York: Alfred A. Knopf
De Beauvoir, S. (2000) *The Ethics of Ambiguity*, trans. B. Frechtman, New York: Citadel Press
De Sousa, R. (1987) *The Rationality of Emotion*, Cambridge, Massachusetts: MIT Press
Debord, G. (1994) *The Society of the Spectacle*, trans. D. Nicholson-Smith, New York: Zone Books
Denning, Lord A.T. (1960) 'The Way of an Iconoclast', *Sydney Law Review* 3(2): 209–220
Derrida, J. (1992) 'Force of Law: the Mystical Foundation of Authority', in *Deconstruction and the Possibility of Justice*, D. Cornell, M. Rosenfeld and D. Carlson (eds), New York: Routledge, 3–67
Derrida, J. (1997) *Deconstruction in a Nutshell: A Conversation with Jacques Derrida*, J. Caputo (ed.), New York: Fordham University Press
Descartes, R. (1989) *Passions of the Soul*, trans. S. Voss, Indianapolis: Hackett Publishing Company
Descartes, R. (1986) *Meditations on First Philosophy*, trans. J. Cottingham, Cambridge: Cambridge University Press
Devlin, P. (1965) *The Enforcement of Morals*, Oxford: Oxford University Press
Diamantides, M. (2006) 'Toward a Western-Islamic Conception of Legalism', in *Law, Text, Terror: Essays for Pierre Legendre*, P. Goodrich, L. Barshack and A. Schütz (eds), London: Routledge
Dickens, C. (2003) *Hard Times*, London: Penguin Classics
Dorf, M. (2003) 'Legal Indeterminacy and Institutional Design', *New York University Law Review* 78(3): 875–930
Dostoevsky, F. (1960) *Notes from Underground*, trans. R.E. Matlaw, New York: Dutton
Dostoevsky, F. (2004) *The House of the Dead*, trans. C. Garnett, New York: Dover Publications, Inc.
Doughty, S. and A. Dolan (2013) 'Jailed in secret – for trying to rescue her father from care home where she believed he would die', *Daily Mail* (London 23 April) 4, 5
Douglas, M. (1988) *Purity and Danger: An Analysis of the Concepts of Pollution and Taboo*, Oxford: Routledge
Douzinas, C. (2004) 'Law and Justice in Postmodernity', in *The Cambridge Companion to Postmodernism*, S. Connor (ed.), Cambridge: Cambridge University Press, 196–223
Douzinas, C. (2007) *Human Rights and Empire: The Political Philosophy of Cosmopolitanism*, London: Routledge
Douzinas, C. (2010) 'A Humanities of Resistance: Fragments for a legal history of humanity', in *Law and the Humanities: An Introduction*, A. Sarat, M. Anderson and C. Frank (eds), Cambridge: Cambridge University Press

Douzinas, C. and A. Gearey (2005) *Critical Jurisprudence: The Political Philosophy of Justice*, Oxford: Hart Publishing

Douzinas, C. and R. Warrington (1991) 'A Well-founded Fear of Justice: Law and Ethics in Postmodernity', *Law and Critique* 2(2): 115–147

Douzinas, C. and R. Warrington (1994) *Justice Miscarried: Ethics, Aesthetics and the Law*, London: Harvester Wheatsheaf

Durkheim, E. (1964) *The Division of Labor in Society*, trans. G. Simpson, New York: Free Press

Durkheim, E. (1982) *The Elementary Forms of the Religious Life*, London: George Allen & Unwin

Dworkin, R. (1978) *Taking Rights Seriously*, Cambridge, Massachusetts: Harvard University Press

Dworkin, R. (1993) *Life's Dominion: An Argument about Abortion and Euthanasia*, London: HarperCollins

Dylan, B. (1963) *The Freewheelin' Bob Dylan*, Columbia Records

Dylan, B. (1975) *Blood on the Tracks*, Columbia Records

Eagleton, T. (1990) *The Ideology of the Aesthetic*, Oxford: Blackwell

Edel, L. (1972) *Henry James: A Life, vol. V: The Master 1901–1916*, Philadelphia and New York: J.P. Lippincott Co.

Edwards, L.H. (2010) 'Once Upon a Time in Law: Myth, Metaphor, and Authority', *Tennessee Law Review* 77: 883–916

Elias, N. (2000) *The Civilising Process: Sociogenetic and Psychogenetic Investigations*, Oxford: Blackwell

Europa (2017) 'EU-wide Protection Needed for Whistle-blowers'. Available at: http://www.europarl.europa.eu/news/en/press-room/20171020IPR86550/eu-wide-protection-needed-for-whistle-blowers; accessed on 1 December 2017

Fenichel, O. (1953) *The Collected Papers of Otto Fenichel*, H. Fenichel and D. Rappaport (eds), New York: W.W. Norton & Company

Fineman, M.A. (2011) 'The Vulnerable Subject: Anchoring Equality in the Human Condition', in *Transcending the Boundaries of Law: Generations of Feminism and Legal Theory*, M.A. Fineman (ed.), London: Routledge

Forster, E.M. (2005) *Maurice*, S.D. Levitt (ed.), London: Penguin Classics

Foucault, M. (1980) *Power/Knowledge: Selected Interviews and Other Writings 1972–1977*, C. Gordon (ed.), Brighton: Harvester Press

Foucault, M. (1991) *Discipline and Punish: The Birth of the Prison*, trans. A. Sheridan, Harmondsworth: Penguin

Foucault, M. (1998) *The History of Sexuality: Vol.1*, trans. R. Hurley, Harmondsworth: Penguin

Foucault, M. (2002) *The Order of Things: An Archaeology of the Human Sciences*, London: Routledge Classics

Fox, L. (2007) *Conceptualising Home: Theories, Laws and Policies*, Oxford: Hart Publishing

Freud, S. (1961) *Civilization and its Discontents*, trans. J. Strachey, New York: W.W. Norton & Company

Freud, S. (1964) 'An Outline of Psychoanalysis', in *The Complete Works of Sigmund Freud*, Vol. 23, trans. J. Strachey, London: Hogarth Press

Freud, S. (1979) 'Resistance and Repression', in *Introductory Lectures on Psychoanalysis: Sigmund Freud*, J. Strachey and A. Richards (eds), New York: Penguin

Friedman, M. (2009) *Capitalism and Freedom: Fortieth Anniversary Edition*, Chicago: University of Chicago Press

Frith, S. (1996) 'Music and Identity', in *Questions of Cultural Studies*, S. Hall and P. du Gay (eds), London: Sage

Fuchs, C. (2008) *Internet and Society: Social Theory in the Information Age*, New York: Routledge

Gallup (2017) 'Iraq', in *In Depth: Topics A to Z*. Available at http://www.gallup.com/poll/1633/iraq.aspx; accessed on 27 November 2017

Garland, D. (2001) *The Culture of Control: Crime and Social Order in Contemporary Society*, Oxford: Oxford University Press

Gatrell, V.A.C. (1994) *The Hanging Tree: Execution and the English People, 1770–1868*, Oxford: Oxford University Press

Gearey, A. (2012) 'I Wish you Well: Notes towards an Aesthetics of Welfare', in *Law and Art: Justice, Ethics and Aesthetics*, O. Ben-Dor (ed.), London: Routledge

Gellman, B. (2013) 'Code name "Verax": Snowden, in exchanges with Post reporter, made clear he knew risks', *The Washington Post*, June 9. Available at https://www.washingtonpost.com/world/national-security/code-name-verax-snowden-in-exchanges-with-post-reporter-made-clear-he-knew-risks/2013/06/09/c9a25b54-d14c-11e2-9f1a-1a7cdee20287_story.html?utm_term=.6e34e70ca85e; accessed on 1 January 2018

Geoghegan, R. (2018) 'The Future Prison Population 2022: Justice Select Committee Submission', The Centre for Social Justice: Criminal Justice Unit. Available at https://www.centreforsocialjustice.org.uk/core/wp-content/uploads/2017/12/Justice-Inquiry-Prison-Population-FINAL.pdf; accessed on 22 May 2018

Gerbner, G. (1970) 'Cultural Indicators: The Case of Violence in Television Drama', *Annals of the American Academy of Political and Social Violence* 388: 69–81

Gerlach, W. (2000) *And the Witnesses were Silent: The Confessing Church and the Jews*, Lincoln: University of Nebraska Press

Gibb, F. and D. Brown (2018) 'Rape trials under threat: Former Lord Chief Justice warns blunders by CPS and police will help attackers walk free', *The Times* (London, 20 January) 5

Goodrich, P. (1987) *Legal Discourse: Studies in Linguistics, Rhetoric and Legal Analysis*, London: Macmillan

Goodrich, P. (1990) *Languages of the Law: From Logics of Memory to Nomadic Masks*, London: Weidenfeld & Nicolson

Goodrich, P. (1993) 'Gynaetopia: Feminine Genealogies of Common Law', *Journal of Law and Society* 20(3): 276–308

Goodrich, P. (1995) *Oedipus Lex: Psychoanalysis, History, Law*, Berkeley: University of California Press

Goodrich, P. (1996) *Law in the Courts of Love: Literature and Other Minor Jurisprudences*, London: Routledge

Goodrich, P. (1999) 'The Iconography of Nothing: Blank Spaces and the Representation of Law in Edward VI and the Pope', in *Law and the Image: The Authority of Law and the Aesthetics of Law*, C. Douzinas and L. Nead (eds), Chicago: University of Chicago Press

Goodrich, P. (2004) 'Grammatology in America: A Sketch of the Return of Philology in Legal Studies', in *Recht Verstehen: Verständlichkeit, Missverständlichkeit und Unverständlichkeit von Recht*, K. Lerch (ed.), Berlin: de Gruyter

Goodrich, P. (2006) 'A Theory of the Nomogram', in *Law, Text, Terror*, P. Goodrich, L. Barshack and A. Schütz (eds), London: Routledge

Goodrich, P. (2011) 'Flores quae faciunt coronam or the Flowers of Common Law', in *Law and Art: Justice, Ethics and Aesthetics*, O. Ben-Dor (ed.), London: Routledge

Goodrich, P. (2015) *Legal Emblems and the Art of Law: Obiter Depicta as the Vision of Governance*, Cambridge: Cambridge University Press

Granick, J. (2017) *American Spies: Modern Surveillance, Why You Should Care, and What to Do About It*, Cambridge: Cambridge University Press

Greenfield, S., G. Osborn and P. Robson (2001) *Film and the Law*, London: Routledge Cavendish Publishing Limited

Gurnham, D. (2016) *Memory, Imagination, Justice: Intersections of Law and Literature*, Aldershot, UK: Ashgate Publishing

Hanson, J. (1996) 'The Architecture of Justice: Iconography and Space in the English Law Court', *Architectural Research Quarterly* 1(4): 50–59

Haraway, D. (1991) *Simians, Cyborgs and Women: The Reinvention of Nature*, New York: Routledge

Hawking, S.W. (1995) *A Brief History of Time: From Big Bang To Black Holes*, London: Bantam Press

Hawthorne, N. (2007) *The Scarlet Letter*, London: Penguin Classics

Hegel, G.W.F. (1967) *Philosophy of Right*, trans. T. Knox, Oxford: Oxford University Press

Heidegger, M. (1958) 'Introduction: An Ontological Consideration of Place', in *The Question of Being*, W. Kluback and J.T. Wilde (eds), New York: Twayne Publishers, 18–26

Heidegger, M. (1990) *Being and Time*, London: Blackwell

Heidegger, M. (2002) 'The Origin of the Work of Art', in *Off the Beaten Track*, trans. K. Haynes, J. Young (ed.), Cambridge: Cambridge University Press

Herman, B. (1993) *The Practice of Moral Judgment*, Cambridge, Massachusetts: Harvard University Press

Hobbes, T. (2005) *Leviathan Parts 1 and II*, A.P. Martinich (ed.), Ontario, Canada: Broadview Press

Holmes, Jr., O.W. (1897) 'The Path of the Law', *Harvard Law Review* 10(8): 457–478

Holmes, Jr., O.W. (1923) *The Common Law*, Boston, Mass: Little, Brown & Co.

Hugo, V. (1982) *Les Misérables*, London: Penguin Classics

Hume, D. (1967) *A Treatise of Human Nature*, Oxford: Oxford University Press

Hume, D. (1975) *Enquiries Concerning Human Understanding and Concerning the Principles of Morals*, L.A. Selby-Bigge (ed.), Oxford: Oxford University Press

Hume, D. (1987) *Essays Moral, Political, and Literary*, 2nd revised edition, E.F. Miller (ed.), Indianapolis: Liberty Fund Inc.

Hume, D. (2007) *A Treatise of Human Nature: A Critical Edition*, D.F. Norton and M.J. Norton (eds), Oxford: Clarendon Press

Huntington, C. (2008) 'Repairing Family Law', *Duke Law Journal* 57(5): 1245–1319

Husserl, E. (1970) *Crisis of European Science and Transcendental Phenomenology*, Evanston: Northwestern University Press

Husserl, E. (1980) *Ideas Pertaining to a Pure Phenomenology and to a Phenomenological Philosophy: Third Book – Phenomenology and the Foundation of the Sciences*, trans. T.E. Klein and W.E. Pohl, The Hague: Martinus Nijhoff

Husserl, E. (1988) *Lectures on Ethics and Value Theory (1908–1914)*, U. Melle (ed.), London: Kluwer Academic

Hutcheson, F. (2003) *Essay on the Nature and Conduct of the Passions and Affections with Illustrations on the Moral Sense*, A. Garrett (ed.), Indianapolis: Liberty Fund Inc.

Immordino-Yang, M.H. (2016) 'Emotion, Sociality, and the Brain's Default Mode Network', *Policy Insights from the Behavioural and Brain Sciences* 3(2): 211–219

Irigaray, L. (1999) 'When Our Lips Speak Together', in *Feminist Theory and the Body: A Reader*, J. Price and M. Shildrick (eds), Edinburgh: Edinburgh University Press
James, H. (2009) *The Ambassadors*, New York: Oxford World Classics
James, W. (1884) 'What is an Emotion?', *Mind* 9(34): 188–205
James, W. (1950) *The Principles of Psychology, Volume II*, New York: Dover Publications Inc.
Jones, P. (2006) 'Toleration, Recognition, and Identity', *Journal of Political Philosophy* 14(2): 123–143
Jonson, B. (1906) *Discoveries: A Critical Edition*, M. Castelain (ed.), Paris: Librairie Hachette et Cie
Justinian (1955) *Institutes of Justinian*, trans. J. Moyle, 5th edition, Oxford: Oxford University Press
Kafka, F. (1961) 'Before the Law', in *Parables and Paradoxes*, New York: Schocken Books
Kafka, F. (2009) *The Trial*, trans. M. Mitchell, R. Robertson (ed.), Oxford: Oxford University Press
Kant, I. (1956) *Critique of Practical Reason*, trans. L.W. Beck, New York: Library of Liberal Arts
Kant, I. (1987) *Critique of Judgement*, trans. W.S. Pluhar, Indianapolis: Hackett Publishing Company
Kant, I. (1991) *The Metaphysics of Morals*, trans. M.J. Gregor, Cambridge: Cambridge University Press
Kantorowicz, E.H. (1957) *The King's Two Bodies: A Study in Mediaeval Political Theology*, Princeton, New Jersey: Princeton University Press
Karstedt, S., I. Loader and H. Strang (2011) *Emotions, Crime and Justice*, Oxford: Hart Publishing
Keating, F. (2017) 'Scores of prison sentences declared "unduly lenient" after victims complain', *The Independent* (London 30 July) 3
Kelsen, H. (1970) *The Pure Theory of Law*, trans. M. Knight, Berkeley: University of California Press
Keown, J. (2007) 'Restoring Moral and Intellectual Shape to the Law after Bland', *The Law Quarterly Review* 113: 481–503
Kermode, F. (2000) *The Sense of an Ending*, Oxford: Oxford University Press
Kierkegaard, S. (1962) *The Present Age*, W. Kaufmann (intro), trans. A. Dru, New York: Harper & Row
Kierkegaard, S. (1978) *Two Ages: The Age of Revolution and the Present Age. A Literary Review*, H.V. Hong and E.H. Hong (eds and trans.), Princeton, New Jersey: Princeton University Press
Kierkegaard, S. (1987) 'The Aesthetic Validity of Marriage', in *Either/Or*, Vol. II, H.V. Hong and E.H. Hong (eds and trans.), Princeton, New Jersey: Princeton University Press
Kierkegaard, S. (1998) *Works of Love*, H.V. Hong and E.H. Hong (eds and trans.), Princeton, New Jersey: Princeton University Press
Konstan, D. (2005) 'The Emotions of the Ancient Greeks: A Cross-Cultural Perspective', *Psychologia* 48: 225–240
Kristeva, J. (1980) *Desire in Language: A Semiotic Approach to Literature and Art*, T. Gora, A. Jardine and L.S. Roudiez (eds), trans. L.S. Roudiez, New York: Columbia University Press
Kristeva, J. (1982) *Powers of Horror: An Essay on Abjection*, trans. L.S. Roudiez, New York: Columbia University Press

Kristeva, J. (1984) *Revolution in Poetic Language*, trans. M. Waller, New York: Columbia University Press

Lacan, J. (1992) *The Seminar of Jacques Lacan, Book VII: The Ethics of Psychoanalysis: 1959–1960*, J. Miller (ed.), trans. D. Porter, New York: W.W. Norton & Company

Lacan, J. (1998) *The Seminar of Jacques Lacan, Book XI: The Four Fundamental Concepts of Psychoanalysis*, J. Miller (ed.), trans. A. Sheridan, New York: W.W. Norton & Company

Lacan, J. (2004) *Écrits: A Selection*, trans. B. Fink, New York: W.W. Norton & Company

Lakoff, G. (2004) 'George Lakoff Manifesto', *Change This* 5(1): 1–25

Lakoff, G. and M. Johnson (1980) *Metaphors We Live By*, Chicago: University of Chicago Press

Lash, S. (2001) 'Technological Forms of Life', *Theory, Culture and Society* 18(1): 105–120

Latour, B. (1993) *We Have Never Been Modern*, trans. C. Porter, Cambridge, Massachusetts: Harvard University Press

Lecercle, J.-J. (1990) *The Violence of Language*, London: Routledge

Lee, H. (2010) *To Kill a Mockingbird*, London: Arrow Books

Leibovitch, A. (2016) 'Relative Judgments', *The Journal of Legal Studies* 45(2): 281–330

Leonard, T. (1995) 'Situations Theoretical and Contemporary', in *Reports from the Present*, London: Jonathan Cape

Levinas, E. (1969) *Totality and Infinity*, trans. A. Lingis, The Hague: Martinus Nijhoff

Levinas, E. (1981) *Otherwise than Being, or Beyond Essence*, trans. A. Lingis, The Hague: Martinus Nijhoff

Levinas, E. (1985) *Ethics and Infinity: Conversations with Philippe Nemo*, trans. R.A. Cohen, Pittsburgh, Pennsylvania: Duquesne University Press

Levinas, E. (1989) 'The Pact', in *The Levinas Reader*, S. Hand (ed.), Oxford: Blackwell

Levinas, E. (1993) 'The Meaning of Meaning', in *Outside the Subject*, trans. M.B. Smith, Stanford, CA: Stanford University Press

Levinas, E. (1998) *Entre Nous: On Thinking-of-the-Other*, trans. M.B. Smith and B. Harshav, New York: Columbia University Press

Liss, S. (2012) 'The Caging of America: Why do we lock up so many people?', *The New Yorker* (30 January) 16–18

Lister, R. (2011) 'Reading Law and Literature: Three Cases for Conversation', in *Law and Art: Justice, Ethics and Aesthetics*, O. Ben-Dor (ed.), London: Routledge

Lodge, R.C. (1953) *Plato's Theory of Art*, New York: Russell & Russell

Lord Hope of Craighead (2014) 'Writing Judgments', *Conference Proceedings on Judicial Independence: The Challenges of the Modern Era*, 7–11 September. Available at: https://cmja.org/downloads/confreports/Conference%20Report%20Zambia.pdf; accessed on 14 February 2019

Lynch, M.P. (2014) *In Praise of Reason: Why Rationality Matters for Democracy*, Cambridge, Massachusetts: MIT Press

Lyotard, J.-F. (1984a) *The Postmodern Condition: A Report on Knowledge*, trans. G. Bennington and B. Massumi, Minneapolis: University of Minnesota Press

Lyotard, J.-F. (1984b) *Driftworks*, R. McKeon (ed.), New York: Semiotext(e)

Lyotard, J.-F. (1988) *The Differend: Phrases in Dispute*, trans. G. Van den Abbeele, Minneapolis: University of Minnesota Press

Lyotard, J.-F. (1993) 'A Svelte Appendix to the Postmodern Question', in *Political Writings*, trans. B. Readings and K.P. Geiman, Minneapolis: University of Minnesota Press

Machiavelli, N. (1950) *The Prince and the Discourses*, Modern Library Edition, New York: Random House

MacIntyre, A. (1984) *After Virtue: A Study in Moral Theory*, 2nd edition, Notre Dame, Indiana: University of Notre Dame Press

Manderson, D. (2000) *Songs Without Music: Aesthetic Dimensions of Law and Justice*, Berkeley and Los Angeles: University of California Press

Manderson, D. (2003) 'From Hunger to Love: Myths of the Source, Interpretation, and Constitution of Law in Children's Literature', *Law and Literature* 15(1): 87–141

Marcuse, H. (1966) *Eros and Civilization: A Philosophical Enquiry into Freud*. Boston: Beacon Press

Markesinis, B. (2007) *Good and Evil in Art and Law: An Extended Essay*, Vienna: Springer-Verlag

Maroney, T.A. (2011) 'The Persistent Cultural Script of Judicial Dispassion', *California Law Review* 99: 629–682

Maroney, T.A. (2012) 'Angry Judges', *Vanderbilt Law Review* 65(5): 1207–1286

McDonald, I. (2011) 'When Hate is Not Enough: Tackling Homophobic Violence', in *Gender, Sexualities and Law*, J. Jones, A. Grear, R.A. Fenton and K. Stevenson (eds), Oxford: Routledge, 147–160

McGregor, L. (2015) 'Alternative Dispute Resolution and Human Rights: Developing a Rights-Based Approach through the ECHR', *European Journal of International Law* 26(3): 607–634

McLuhan, M. (1996) *Forward Through the Rearview Mirror: Reflections On and By Marshall McLuhan*, P. Benedetti and N. DeHart (eds), Cambridge, Massachusetts: MIT Press

McLuhan, M. (1999) 'Electric Consciousness and the Church', in *The Medium and the Light: Reflections on Religion*, E. McLuhan and J. Szklarek (eds), Toronto: Stoddart Publishing

McLuhan, M. (2001) *Understanding Media*, Oxford: Routledge Classics

Mead, G.H. (1918) 'The Psychology of Punitive Justice', *American Journal of Sociology* 23(5): 577–602

Merleau-Ponty, M. (1962) *Phenomenology of Perception*, trans. C. Smith, London: Routledge

Meyrowitz, J. (2005) 'The Rise of Glocality: New Senses of Place and Identity in the Global Village', in *A Sense of Place: The Global and the Local in Mobile Communication*, K. Nyiri (ed.), Vienna: Passagen Verlag

Montaigne, M. de (1991) *The Complete Essays*, trans. M.A. Screech, London: Penguin

Montesquieu, C. (1977) *The Spirit of Laws: A Compendium of the First English Edition*, ed. D.W. Carrithers, Berkeley: University of California Press

Moran, L.J. (1996) *The Homosexual(ity) of Law*, London: Routledge

Moran, L.J. (2001) 'Affairs of the Heart: Hate Crime and the Politics of Crime Control', *Law and Critique* 12(3): 331–344

Morse, S.J. (2004) 'Rationality and Responsibility', *Southern California Law Review* 74: 251–268

Muggar, R. (2016) 'Terrorism is on the Rise – But There's a Bigger Threat We're Not Talking About', *World Economic Forum Report*. Available at: https://www.weforum.org/agenda/2016/04/terrorism-is-on-the-rise-but-there-s-a-bigger-threat-we-re-not-talking-about/; accessed on 4 January 2017

Murphy, J.G. (2012) *Punishment and the Moral Emotions: Essays in Law, Morality, and Religion*, New York: Oxford University Press

Musil, R. (1996) *The Man Without Qualities Vol. 1: A Sort of Introduction and Pseudo Reality Prevails*, New York: Vintage Books

Nietzsche, F. (1954) *Twilight of the Idols*, trans. and ed. W. Kaufmann, Harmondsworth: Penguin

Nietzsche, F. (1966) *Beyond Good and Evil*, trans. W. Kaufmann, New York: Random House

Nietzsche, F. (1967) *The Birth of Tragedy and the Case of Wagner*, trans. W. Kaufmann, New York: Random House

Nietzsche, F. (1968) *The Will to Power*, trans. W. Kaufmann and R.J. Hollingdale, ed. W. Kaufmann, New York: Vintage Books

Nietzsche, F. (1974) 'On Truth and Falsity in Their Ultramoral Sense', in *The Complete Works of Friedrich Nietzsche*, trans. M.A. Magge, ed. O. Levy, New York: Gordon Press

Nietzsche, F. (1978) *Thus Spoke Zarathustra*, trans. W. Kaufmann, New York: Penguin

Nietzsche, F. (1979) *Philosophy and Truth: Selections from Nietzsche's Notebooks of the Early 1870's*, ed. and trans. D. Breazeale, Atlantic Highlands, New Jersey: Humanities Press

Nietzsche, F. (1980) *Sämtliche Werke: Kritische Studienausgabe*, ed. G. Colli and M. Montinari, Berlin: de Gruyter

Nietzsche, F. (1982) 'The Antichrist', in *The Portable Nietzsche*, W. Kaufmann (ed.), New York: Penguin

Nietzsche, F. (1996) *Human, All Too Human: A Book for Free Spirits*, trans. R.J. Hollingdale, Cambridge: Cambridge University Press

Nozick, R. (1990) 'Emotions', in *The Examined Life: Philosophical Meditations*, New York: Simon & Schuster

Nussbaum, M.C. (1995) *Poetic Justice: The Literary Imagination and Public Life*, Boston: Beacon Press

Nussbaum, M.C. (1996) 'Compassion: The Basic Social Emotion', *Social Philosophy and Policy*, 13(1): 27–58

Nussbaum, M.C. (1997) *Cultivating Humanity: A Classical Defense of Reform in Liberal Education*, Cambridge, Massachusetts: Harvard University Press

Nussbaum, M.C. (2001) *Upheavals of Thought: The Intelligence of Emotions*, Cambridge: Cambridge University Press

Nussbaum, M.C. (2004) *Hiding from Humanity: Disgust, Shame, and the Law*, Princeton, New Jersey: Princeton University Press

Nussbaum, M.C. (2010) *Not for Profit: Why Democracy Needs the Humanities*, Princeton, New Jersey: Princeton University Press

Nussbaum, M.C. (2013) *Political Emotions: Why Love Matters for Justice*, Cambridge, Massachusetts: Harvard University Press

Nussbaum, M.C. (2018) *The Monarchy of Fear: A Philosopher Looks at Our Political Crisis*, New York: Simon & Schuster

O'Sullivan, N., P. Davis, J. Billington, V. Gonzalez-Diaz and R. Corcoran (2015) 'Shall I Compare Thee: The Neural Basis of Literary Awareness, and its Benefits to Cognition', *Cortex* 73(12): 144–157

Office for National Statistics (2017) *Public Perceptions of Crime in England and Wales: Year Ending March 2016*. Available at: https://www.ons.gov.uk/peoplepopulationandcommunity/crimeandjustice; accessed on 27 November 2017

Olson, G. (2016) 'The Turn to Passion: Has Law and Literature become Law and Affect', *Law and Literature* 28(3): 335–353

Oppenheimer, H. (1913) *The Rationale of Punishment*, London: University of London Press

Orme, N. (2006) *Medieval Schools: From Roman Britain to Renaissance England*, New Haven: Yale University Press

Orwell, G. (1949) *Nineteen Eighty-Four*, London: Secker & Warburg

Orwell, G. (1996) *Animal Farm: A Fairy Story*, London: Penguin

Pascal, B. (1995) *Pensées*, trans. A.J. Krailsheimer, New York: Penguin

Pettit, H. (2017) 'A zombie outbreak could come close to wiping out humanity in 100 days: Scientists reveal their tips to survive', *Daily Mail* (London 5 January) 6

Pew Research Center (2017) 'Public Perception of Crime Rate at Odds with Reality'. Available at: http://www.pewresearch.org/fact-tank/2016/11/16/voters-perceptions-of-crime-continue-to-conflict-with-reality/ft_16-11-16_crime_trend-2/; accessed on 27 November 2017

Plato (1972) 'Ion', in *Ancient Literary Criticism: The Principal Texts in New Translations*, D. A. Russell and M. Winterbottom (eds), trans. D.A. Russell, Oxford: Oxford University Press

Plato (1991) *The Republic*, trans. B. Jowett, New York: Vintage Classics

Plato (1997) *Plato: Complete Works*, J.M. Cooper (ed.), Indianapolis: Hackett Publishing Company

Posner, R.A. (2010) *How Judges Think*, Cambridge, Massachusetts: Harvard University Press

Poulantzas, N. (2000) *State, Power and Socialism*, trans. P. Camiller, London: Verso

Povoledo, E. (2017) 'Italy to Allow Living Wills and the Refusal of End-of-Life Care', *The New York Times* (14 December) 1

Preston, M.J. (2004) 'Off the Record: An Anthology of Poetry by Lawyers', in J.R. Elkins (ed.), *The Legal Studies Forum* 28(1): 1–19

Puig, M. (1984) *Kiss of the Spiderwoman*, New York: Vintage Books

Purkey, A.L. (2013) 'A Dignified Approach: Legal Empowerment and Justice for Human Rights Violations in Protracted Refugee Situations', *Journal of Refugee Studies* 27(2): 260–281

Quintilian (1976) *Institutio oratoria* (reprint), trans. H.E. Butler, Cambridge, Massachusetts: Harvard University Press

Rawls, J. (1990) 'Justice as Fairness: Political not Metaphysical', in *Collected Papers*, S. Freeman (ed.), Cambridge, Massachusetts: Harvard University Press

Rawls, J. (1996) *Political Liberalism*, New York: Columbia University Press

Rawls, J. (1999) *A Theory of Justice* (revised edition), Oxford: Oxford University Press

Relph, M. (1961) 'Letter', *Films and Filming* (May issue)

Relph, E. (1976) *Place and Placelessness*, London: Pion Limited

Reynolds, J.R. (1997) *Seven Discourses on Art: Discourse III*, R.R. Wark (ed.), New Haven: Yale University Press

Rich, A. (2007) *Poetry and Commitment*, New York: W.W. Norton & Company

Ricoeur, P. (1984) *Time and Narrative Vol. 1*, trans. K. McLaughlin and D. Pellauer, Chicago: University of Chicago Press

Ricoeur, P. (1996) 'Love and Justice', in *Paul Ricoeur: The Hermeneutics of Action*, R. Kearney (ed.), London: Sage

Ricoeur, P. (2000) *The Just*, trans. D. Pellauer, Chicago: University of Chicago Press

Ritzenhoff, K.A. and A. Krewani (2015) *The Apocalypse in Film: Dystopias, Disasters, and Other Visions About the End of the World*, Lanham, Maryland: Rowman & Littlefield

Rousseau, J.-J. (1966) 'Essay on the Origin of Languages', in *On the Origin of Language*, trans. J.H. Moran and A. Gode, Chicago: University of Chicago Press

Rousseau, J.-J. (1979) *Émile: Or on Education, Book VI*, trans. A. Bloom, New York: Basic Books

Rousseau, J.-J. (1997) *The Social Contract and Other Later Political Writings*, V. Gourevitch (ed.), Cambridge: Cambridge University Press

Sagan, C. (1980) *Cosmos*, New York: Random House

Sander, D. and K. Scherer, eds. (2009) *Oxford Companion to Emotion and the Affective Sciences*, Oxford: Oxford University Press

Sarat, A. (2001) *When the State Kills: Capital Punishment and the American Condition*, Princeton, New Jersey: Princeton University Press

Sartre, J.-P. (1956) *Being and Nothingness*, trans. H.E. Barnes, New York: Philosophical Library

Sartre, J.-P. (1964) *The Words*, trans. B. Frechtman, New York: George Brazillier

Sartre, J.-P. (1989) *The Emotions: Outline of a Theory*, trans. B. Frechtman, New York: Citadel Press

Sartre, J.-P. (2007) *Nausea*, London: Penguin

Sartre, J.-P. (2012) 'The Metamorphosis', in *Saint Genet: Actor and Martyr*, trans. B. Frechtman, Minneapolis: University of Minnesota Press

Scheler, M. (1979) *Formalism in Ethics and Non-formal Ethics of Values: A New Attempt toward a Foundation of an Ethical Personalism*, Evanston: Northwestern University Press

Schelling, F.W.J. (1978) 'The Organ of Transcendental Philosophy', in *System of Transcendental Idealism*, trans. P. Heath, Charlottesville: University Press of Virginia

Schlag, P. (2002) 'The Aesthetics of American Law', *Harvard Law Review* 115: 1047–1119

Schopenhauer, A. (2016) *The World as Will and Presentation: Volume I*, trans. R.E. Aquila, London: Routledge

Scott, W. (1954) *Guy Mannering*, London and New York: Dent and Dutton

Sellers, M.N.S., ed. (2017) *Law, Reason and Emotion*, Cambridge: Cambridge University Press

Seneca, L.A. (2014) *Medea*, trans. A.J. Boyle, Oxford: Oxford University Press

Seneca, L.A. (2016) *Seneca's Letters from a Stoic*, trans. R.M. Gummere, Mineola, New York: Dover Publications Inc.

Sentencing Council (2017) 'New Sentencing Guidelines for Magistrates' Courts', press release, 24 January. Available at: https://www.sentencingcouncil.org.uk/news/item/new-sentencing-guidelines-for-magistrates-courts/; accessed on 25 May 2018

Series, L., P. Fennell, J. Doughty and A. Mercer (2017) *Welfare Cases in the Court of Protection: A Statistical Overview*, Cardiff: Cardiff University. Available at: http://sites.cardiff.ac.uk/wccop/files/2017/09/Series-Fennell-Doughty-2017-Statistical-overview-of-CoP.pdf

Shaftesbury, Third Earl of, A.A.C. (1999) *Characteristics of Men, Manners, Opinions, Times*, L.E. Klein (ed.), Cambridge: Cambridge University Press

Shakespeare, W. (1988) *The Sonnets and Narrative Poems: The Complete Non- Dramatic Poetry*, S. Barnet (ed.), New York: Signet

Shakespeare, W. (2017) *Titus Andronicus*, R. McDonald (ed.), New York: Penguin Random House

Shaw, H.J. (2008) 'Resisting the Hallucination of the Hypermarket', *International Journal of Baudrillard Studies* 5(1): 1–30

Shaw, H.J. (2014) *The Consuming Geographies of Food: Diet, Food Deserts and Obesity*, London: Routledge

Shaw, H.J. and J.J.A. Shaw (2019) *Corporate Social Responsibility, Social Justice and the Global Food Supply Chain: Towards an Ethical Food Policy for Sustainable Supermarkets*, London: Routledge

Shaw, J.J.A. (2009) 'Relocating Law and Literature: From the Margins to the Middle', *Contemporary Issues in Law* 9(4): 209–232

Shaw, J.J.A. (2012) 'The Continuing Relevance of Ars Poetica to Legal Scholarship and the Modern Lawyer', *International Journal for the Semiotics of Law / Revue Internationale de Sémiotique Juridique* 25(1): 71–93

Shaw, J.J.A. (2013) 'Reimagining the Humanities within Socio-Legal Studies in an Age of Disenchantment', in *Exploring the Socio of Socio-Legal Studies*, D. Feenan (ed.), London: Palgrave Macmillan

Shaw, J.J.A. (2013a) 'A Study of the Semiotic and Narrative Forms of Divine Influence in Secular Legal Systems', in special issue: 'The Authoriality of Religious Law', *International Journal for the Semiotics of Law/Revue Internationale de Sémiotique Juridique* 26(1): 95–113

Shaw, J.J.A. (2014) 'From Fact to Feeling: An Explication of the Mimetic Relation between Law and Emotion', *Liverpool Law Review: A Journal of Contemporary Legal and Social Policy Issues*, 35(1): 42–64

Shaw, J.J.A. (2015) 'From homo economicus to homo roboticus: An Exploration of the Transformative Impact of the Technological Imaginary', *International Journal of Law in Context*, 11(3): 245–264

Shaw, J.J.A. (2015a) 'Compassion and the Criminal Justice System: Stumbling along towards a Jurisprudence of Love and Forgiveness', *International Journal of Law in Context* 11(1): 92–107

Shaw, J.J.A. (2017) 'Aesthetics of Law and Literary License: An Anatomy of the Legal Imagination', *Liverpool Law Review: A Journal of Contemporary Legal and Social Policy Issues* 38(2): 83–105

Shaw, J.J.A. (2018) 'From Beethoven to Bowie: Identity Framing, Social Justice and the Sound of Law', *International Journal for the Semiotics of Law/Revue Internationale de Sémiotique Juridique* 31(2): 301–324

Shaw, J.J.A. (2018a) *Jurisprudence*, 3rd edition, Harlow: Pearson Education

Shaw, J.J.A. (2018b) 'Law and the Literary Imagination: The Contribution of Literature to Modern Legal Scholarship', in *The Palgrave Handbook of Philosophy and Literature*, M. Mack and B. Stocker (eds), London: Palgrave Macmillan

Shaw, J.J.A. (2019) 'Lefebvre and the Law: Social Justice, the Spatial Imaginary and New Technologies', in *The Routledge Handbook of Henri Lefebvre, the City and Urban Society*, M.E. Leary-Owhin and J.P. McCarthy (eds), London: Routledge

Shaw, J.J.A. and H.J. Shaw (2015) 'The Politics and Poetics of Spaces and Places: Mapping the Multiple Geographies of Identity in a Cultural Posthuman Era', *Journal of Organisational Transformation & Social Change* 12(3): 234–256

Shaw, J.J.A. and H.J. Shaw (2016) 'Mapping the Technologies of Spatial (In)justice in the Anthropocene', *Information and Communications Technology Law* 25(1): 32–49

Shelley, P.B. (1977) 'A Defence of Poetry', in *Shelley's Poetry and Prose*, D.H. Reiman and S.B. Powers (eds), New York: W.W. Norton & Company

Sherwin, R.K. (1992) 'Lawyering Theory – An Overview: What We Talk About When We Talk About Law', *New York Law School Law Review* 37: 9–71

Sherwin, R.K. (1995) 'Picturing Justice: Images of Law and Lawyers in the Visual Media', *University of San Francisco Law Review* 30: 891–901

Sherwin, R.K. (1996) 'Framed', in *Reelism: Movies as Legal Texts*, J. Denvir (ed.), Urbana: University of Illinois Press

Sherwin, R.K. (2012) 'Visual Jurisprudence', *New York Law School Law Review* 57(1): 11–39

Shklar, J. (1986) *Legalism: Law, Morals, and Political Trials*, Cambridge, Massachusetts: Harvard University Press

Shklar, J. (1998) 'The Liberalism of Fear', in *Political Thought and Political Thinkers*, S. Hoffmann (ed.), Chicago: University of Chicago Press, 3–20

Silbey, S.S. (1992) 'Making a Place for Cultural Analyses of Law', *Law & Social Inquiry* 17(1): 39–48

Simon, J. (2015) 'Prison is punishment enough. But in the US, inmates also face violence and humiliation', *The Guardian* (London 9 April) 21

Smart, C. (1989) *Feminism and the Power of Law*, London: Routledge

Smart, C. (2007) *Personal Life*, Cambridge: Polity Press

Smith, A. (1981) *An Inquiry into the Nature and Causes of the Wealth of Nations, Vol. II*, R.H. Campbell and A.S. Skinner (eds), Indianapolis, Indiana: Liberty Classics

Smith, A. (2002) *The Theory of Moral Sentiments*, K. Haakonssen (ed.), Cambridge: Cambridge University Press

Smith, J.A. (1977) 'Symposium on Law and Literature: A Case History with a Happy Ending', *ALSA Forum* 2(2): 21–42

Sobieski, E. (2011) 'Tom Otterness Makes Cents!', *The Art Economist* 1(3): 58–63

Solomon, R.C. (1990) *A Passion for Justice: Emotions and the Origins of the Social Contract*, Reading, Massachusetts: Addison-Wesley

Spinoza, B. (2001) *Ethics*, trans. W.H. White and A.H. Stirling, Ware: Wordsworth Editions

Spinoza, B. (2002) *Spinoza: Complete Works*, trans. S. Shirley, M.L. Morgan (ed.), Indianapolis: Hackett Publishing Company

Stake, J.E. (2001) 'The Uneasy Case for Adverse Possession', *Georgetown Law Journal*, 89: 2419–2473

Stiglitz, J. (2002) *Globalisation and its Discontents*, London: Penguin

Sullivan, W., A. Colby, J. Welch Wegner, L. Bond and L. Shulman (2007) *Educating Lawyers: Preparation for the Profession of Law*, Oxford: Wiley-Blackwell

Sunstein, C.R. (2009) *On Rumors: How Falsehoods Spread, Why We Believe Them, What Can Be Done*, New York: Farrar, Straus and Giroux

Supiot, A. (2007) *Homo Juridicus: On the Anthropological Function of Law*, London: Verso

Swartz, D.L. (2013) *Symbolic Power, Politics, and Intellectuals: The Political Sociology of Pierre Bourdieu*, Chicago: University of Chicago Press

Szasz, T. (2002) *Fatal Freedom: The Ethics and Politics of Suicide*, Syracuse: Syracuse University Press

Tennyson, A.F. (1999) *The Lady of Shalott*, Oxford: Oxford University Press

Tierney, K., C. Bevc and E. Kuligowski (2006) 'Metaphors Matter: Disaster Myths, Media Frames, and Their Consequences in Hurricane Katrina', *Annals of the American Academy of Political and Social Science* 604(1): 57–81

Tillich, P. (1954) *Love, Power, and Justice: Ontological Analyses and Ethical Applications*, Oxford: Oxford University Press

Tobler, W. (1970) 'A Computer Movie Simulating Urban Growth in the Detroit Region', *Economic Geography* 46(2): 234–240

Tolstoy, L. (1948) *Essays from Tula*, Liverpool: Sheppard Press

Van Gelder, C. (1996) 'Mission in the Emerging Postmodern Condition', in *The Church between Gospel and Culture: The Emerging Mission in North America*, G.R. Hunsberger and C. Van Gelder (eds), Grand Rapids, Michigan: William B. Eerdmans Publishing Co.

Van Munster, R. (2011) 'The War on Terrorism: When the Exception Becomes the Rule', *International Journal for the Semiotics of Law* 17(2): 141–153

Vandekerckhove, M., C. von Scheve, S. Ismer, S. Jung, and S. Kronast (2008) *Regulating Emotions: Culture, Social Necessity, and Biological Inheritance*, Oxford: Wiley-Blackwell

Velleman, J.D. (2008) 'Beyond Price', *Ethics* 118(1): 191–212

Virgil (1984) *The Eclogues*, trans. G. Lee, London: Penguin Classics

Von Schiller, F. (1967) *Naive and Sentimental Poetry*, New York: Ungar

Wacquant, L. (2002) 'The Curious Eclipse of Prison Ethnography in the Age of Mass Incarceration', *Ethnography* 3(4): 371–397

Wagner, P. and B. Rabuy (2017) *Mass Incarceration: The Whole Pie 2017*, Northampton, Massachusetts: Prison Policy Initiative. Available at https://www.prisonpolicy.org/reports/pie2017.html; accessed 26 September 2017

Ward, I. (2002) 'The Echo of a Sentimental Jurisprudence', *Law and Critique* 13(2): 107–125

Ward, I. (2009) *Law, Text, Terror*, Cambridge: Cambridge University Press

Weil, S. (1973) *Waiting for God*, trans. E. Craufurd, New York: Harper Collins

Weil, S. (2005) 'Human Personality', in *Simone Weil: An Anthology*, S. Miles (ed.), London: Penguin

Weisberg, R.H. (1992) *Poethics and Other Strategies of Law and Literature*, New York: Columbia University Press

West, R. (1985) 'Jurisprudence as Narrative: As Aesthetic Analysis of Modern Legal Theory', *New York University Law Review* 60: 145–211

West, R. (2008) 'Literature, Culture and Law', Georgetown Law Faculty Working Papers, No. 75

West, R. (2016) 'Law's Emotions', *Richmond Public Interest Law Review* 19(4): 339–361

White, J.B. (1999) 'Writing and Reading in Philosophy, Law and Poetry', in *Law and Literature: Current Legal Issues Volume II*, M. Freeman and A. Lewis (eds), Oxford: Oxford University Press

Whitman, W. (1881) 'You Felons on Trial in Courts', in *Leaves of Grass*, Boston, Massachusetts: James R. Osgood & Company

Wiener, M.J. (2004) *Men of Blood: Violence, Manliness, and Criminal Justice in Victorian England*, Cambridge: Cambridge University Press

Wilde, O. (1997) *The Picture of Dorian Gray*, London: Wordsworth Editions Limited

Wilde, O. (2001) *The Soul of Man Under Socialism and Selected Critical Prose*, London: Penguin Classics

Wilde, O. (2003) 'The Ballad of Reading Gaol', in *The Complete Works of Oscar Wilde*, 5th edition, London: Collins

Wilde, O. (2007) *Epigrams*, London: Wordsworth Editions Limited

Wilde, O. (2010) *The Decay of Lying and Other Essays*, London: Penguin Classics

Williams, B. (1973) 'Problems of the Self', in *Morality and the Emotions*, Cambridge: Cambridge University Press

Williams, B. (2008) *Shame and Necessity*, Berkeley: University of California Press

Williams, G. (1957) *The Sanctity of Life and the Criminal Law*, New York: Alfred A. Knopf

Williams, M.C. (2011) 'Securitization and the Liberalism of Fear', *Security Dialogue* 42(4–5) 453–463

Williams, R. (1977) *Marxism and Literature*, Oxford: Oxford University Press

Winterson, J. (1995) *Oranges Are Not the Only Fruit*, London: Vintage Books

Wistrich, A.J., J.J. Rachlinski and C. Guthrie (2015) 'Heart versus Head: Do Judges Follow the Law or Follow their Feelings?', *Texas Law Review* 93: 854–923

Wittgenstein, L. (2009) *Philosophical Investigations*, Oxford: Wiley-Blackwell

Wolcher, L.E. (2013) *Law's Task: The Tragic Circle of Law, Justice and Human Suffering*, Aldershot, UK: Ashgate Publishing

Wolfenden, J. (1957) *Report of the Departmental Committee on Homosexual Offences and Prostitution: Cmnd 247*, London: HMSO

Zartaloudis, T. (2010) *Giorgio Agamben: Power, Law and the Uses of Criticism*, London: Routledge Glasshouse

Žižek, S. (1995) Ideology between Fiction and Fantasy, *Cardozo Law Review* 16(5): 1511–1532

Žižek, S. (1999) *The Žižek Reader*, E. Wright and E. Wright (eds), Oxford: Wiley-Blackwell

Žižek, S. (2001) *Enjoy Your Symptom! Jacques Lacan in Hollywood and Out*, London: Routledge

Žižek, S. (2002) *Welcome to the Desert of the Real*, London: Verso

Žižek, S. (2008) 'The Tyrant's Bloody Robe' in *Violence: Six Sideways Reflections*, New York: Picador

Zola, E. (1903) *Truth*, trans. E.A. Vizetelly, New York: John Lane, The Bodley Head

Index

A and others v Secretary of State for the Home Department [2004] 80, 167–169
Adorno, T.W. 41
aesthetics 2, 15, 26, 28–29, 36–38, 41, 49–50, 69, 75, 101, 107, 109, 135
affective states 3, 6, 10, 14, 28, 31, 50, 93, 128
Agamben, G. 79, 110, 112
Airedale NHS Trust v Bland [1993] 64
Alice in Wonderland 46, 47
alienation 48, 136, 139, 148
allegory 17, 26, 36, 38, 40, 47, 111, 137, 163
alterity 41, 53, 101, 149, 164, 171
altruism 71, 123, 140, 160, 165, 171
Ancient Greeks 9, 49, 81, 147, 167
Andersen, Hans Christian 41
Aquinas, T. 9, 54, 118,145
Arendt, H. 63, 130–132, 138
Aristotle 5, 13–14, 42–44, 54–60, 76, 109, 118–119, 130, 167–173
Assange, Julian *see* Snowden, Edward
assisted dying 65–67, 95, 140, 153–158, 170, 172
Auden, W.H. 41, 49, 148, 149, 166
austerity *ix*, 66, 108, 161, 165

Bacon, F. 39, 110
Bakhtin, M.M. 96
Bandes, S. 25
Bankowski, Z. 2, 145, 149
Battin, M.P. 154
Baudelaire, C. 41
Baudrillard, J. 47, 48, 57, 82
Bauman, Z. 48, 83, 104, 149, 162–163
Beauvoir, S. de 6, 141, 146–147, 150, 153, 174
Belhaj and another v Director of Public Prosecutions and another [2018] 98
Benjamin, W. 54, 92, 111
Bennett, A. 23
Bentham, J. 29, 98
Best v The Chief Land Registrar & Anor [2014] 129
Bible 88, 118, 144, 147, 151–152, 156
Bierce, A. 46
Blake, W. 86, 111, 140
Bourdieu, P. 89–91, 95, 97, 103, 113
Braidotti, R. 124
Butler, J. 18, 124, 127, 131

Camus, A. 33
canon law 6, 34, 95, 103, 142
capital punishment *see* death penalty
carceral culture *see* prisons
Cardozo, B. 25, 128
Carroll, L. 46, 47, 52
Cartesian dualism 2, 7, 8, 10, 15
censorship 16, 18, 59, 71, 80
children 71, 84, 87, 99, 100–101, 104, 114, 124, 134, 154, 169
Christian 43, 151, 154, 155–156, 161
Cicero 33, 44
Cixous, H. 124
cogito ergo sum 7, 38, 58, 70
conscience 6, 19, 90, 113, 117, 120, 142, 153
corporate culture 59, 62, 71, 123, 160–165, 168
corporate social responsibility 160–161, 165
Court of Conscience 6
Cover, R.M. 50, 86, 87, 97, 101, 103–104
creativity 15, 17, 29, 32, 39, 66, 76
Crichton, M. 81
criminal justice 58, 106, 108, 133–134, 138–141
criminology 6, 133

cummings, e.e. 4, 147
cyberspace 78, 162, 164

Damasio, A.R. 2, 10–13, 25
Dante, A. 144
Dark Web 71, 72
Day Lewis, C. 40, 41, 49
De Sousa, R. 4, 144, 173
death penalty 11, 88, 104–105
Debord, G. 79, 162, 164
Denning, Lord A.T. 20, 68, 84
Derrida, J. 16, 17, 54, 87, 90, 96, 118, 124
Descartes, R. 7, 8, 10, 13, 22, 58, 70
Diamantides, M. 155
dignity 65, 125, 128, 144, 153, 154
dikaiosis 117
discrimination: homosexuality 11, 107–108, 125; the poor 110, 125–126, 139–140, 148, 152, 160–165, 169–171; women 8, 30–31, 53, 123–125, 146, 169
disenchantment *ix*, 146
disgust 11, 15, 29, 70, 106, 109, 130
Donoghue v Stevenson [1932] 152
Dostoevsky, F. 23, 125, 139
Douzinas, C. 50, 90, 92, 101, 161
Duchy of Lancaster [1561] 8
Dürer, A. 132–133
Durkheim, E. 4, 88
Dworkin, R. 19, 65, 68
dystopian 74, 82, 83, 84

Eagleton, T. 107
ecclesiastical law 6, 88, 155
economics 17, 116, 124, 161
education 18, 31, 81, 91, 93, 124, 170: legal education 46, 89; moral education 5, 151, 171–173
Elias, N. 106
English law 9, 75, 78, 84, 154, 156, 168
Enlightenment 8, 69, 121
epistemology 16, 26
ethical behaviour 11, 102, 158
ethical responsibility 23, 153
evil 55, 76, 78, 109, 133, 136, 137, 144

fake news *ix*, 58, 72, 136
family law and family courts 1, 64, 99–101
fantasy 12–13, 69–70, 135
feminist theory 8, 53, 124, 146
Fineman, M.A.126
Foucault, M. 74, 83, 96, 103, 106, 116–117
framing strategies 30, 69, 71, 73, 76, 78, 109
Frank, J. 23
free market model 69, 165
Freud, S. 12–13, 122, 160–161, 164
Fuchs, C. 82, 136

Gearey, A. 50, 101, 157
globalisation 83, 148
Goodrich, P. *ix*, 2, 16–18, 37–40, 46, 50, 75, 88–90, 93, 96, 113, 144, 155, 172
governance 21, 84, 85, 161
Great Ormond Street Hospital v Yates and Charlie Gard [2017] 100
Gurnham, D. 104

Hall & Another v Bull & Another [2011] 108
Haraway, D. 53
Harman v Secretary of State for the Home Department [1983] 100
hate crimes *ix*, 6, 108
Hawking, S. 15, 16
health 62, 66, 70, 99, 100–101, 108, 126, 159, 163–165
Hegel, G.W.F. 34, 150
Heidegger, M. 31, 47, 157, 162
hermeneutic 16, 18, 87
Hinz v Berry [1970] 84
Hoffman, Lord 80, 168, 169
Holmes, Jr., O.W. 5, 23, 128, 129
Holocaust 19, 41
homo homini lupus 164
homo juridicus 35
homo sacer 79, 110
human condition 38, 70, 84, 126, 136
human flourishing 10, 14, 17, 115, 127, 131, 140, 155
humanities *ix*, 3, 26, 82, 161
Hume, D. 18, 22–23, 26, 120–123, 145, 173
Husserl, E. 35, 121, 173
Hutcheson, F. 121, 122

imagination 17, 23, 26, 30–33, 35, 39, 42, 44, 49, 69, 72, 84, 149: empathic imagination 2, 20–21, 26, 28, 50, 76, 84, 114, 130–131, 141, 170, 172; legal imagination 5, 27, 67, 97, 106, 142, 172; literary imagination 38, 42, 45, 48, 113–114, 142, 150, 172; moral imagination 119–122, 164
information and communications technology *see* technology

instrumentality 4, 8, 69, 117, 125, 141, 145, 159
interdisciplinary 3, 6, 9, 26, 142
Internet 39, 54, 71, 78, 80
intersubjectivity 18–22, 132, 150, 170
intuitions 1, 9, 10–13, 15, 23, 29, 36, 49, 122
Irigaray, L. 124
Islamic 70, 155

Jacobellis v Ohio [1964] 197
James, H. 35, 139
James, W. 32, 55, 57, 122
Janvier v Sweeney [1919] 63
Jehovah's Witnesses 19
Jews 19, 121, 135, 151, 154
Jonson, B. 28
judicial decision-making 7, 24, 68, 88, 99, 128, 130, 132, 159, 169
judicial dispassion 6
jurisprudence: literary jurisprudence 49, 143; outsider jurisprudence 19; sentimental jurisprudence 24, 169
justice as fairness 78, 116, 122

Kafka, F. 77, 104, 111–112
Kant, I. 5, 11, 22, 125, 132, 153, 159
Kantorowicz, E.H. 8, 16, 75
Karstedt, S. 1, 6
Kaye v Andrew Robertson & Sport Newspapers Ltd [1991] 62–63
Kelsen, H. 86
Kermode, F. 34
Kierkegaard, S. 58–59, 146, 152, 160
Kristeva, J. 41, 44, 56

LGBTQ 108
Lacan, J. 12, 17, 70
Lakoff, G. 73, 107
Lao Tzu 131
Larkin, P. 42, 166
Lash, S. 164
Latour, B. 52
law and literature 2, 31, 32, 142–143
law schools 159, 172
legal culture 3, 6, 26, 29, 47, 74,88–89, 93, 113
legal discourse 26, 36, 74, 92, 96, 105, 107, 160
legal dogma 29, 74, 75, 89, 112, 114
legal fictions 29, 46, 74, 79, 87, 98
legal formalism 129, 142
legal imagination *ix*, 5, 27, 33, 49, 97, 106, 142
legal institution: an ethical institution 1, 101, 103, 149, 166, 173; a social institution *xi*, 2, 18, 26, 62, 80–81; a meaning-making institution 73–75, 86, 96–97, 116–117; an unethical institution 31, 69, 88, 99, 105, 136
legitimacy 3, 16, 40, 54, 87–89, 92–96, 109, 112, 119, 133, 153–154
Levinas, E. 20–21, 101–103, 118, 151, 170
lex talionis 88, 119
Lister, R. 19
literary imagination 2, 30, 38, 45, 142
Liversidge v Anderson (1942) 46
Lyotard, F. 93, 94

MacFarlane v Relate Avon Limited [2010] 108
Machiavelli, N. 81
machina mundi 15
Manderson D. 42, 49, 72, 113
Marcuse, H. 12, 13
Maroney, T.A. 1, 3, 6
McLuhan, M. 24, 57, 58, 162
memory 12, 17, 25, 34–35, 39–40, 88
metaphors 17, 28, 39–40, 42, 75–76, 78–79, 106–107
metaphysics 8, 20, 35, 118, 120, 137
Meyrowitz, J. 164
Minersville School District v Gobitis [1940] 18–19
minority interest groups, 21 132, 160
monsters 52, 83, 114, 134, 136, 137, 156
Montaigne, M. de 66, 67
Montesquieu, C. 17
moral education 5, 171
moral emotions 107, 133, 137, 158, 173
moral judgments 2, 5, 9, 14, 24, 112, 120–122, 137, 139, 145
moral motivation 23, 90, 121
moral reasoning 1, 149
moral responsibility 14, 104, 124, 127, 137, 153, 160
moral sense 22, 75, 121, 122, 125
Moran, L.J. 97, 107
Murphy, J.G. *ix*, 1, 6, 107, 137
music 36–37, 48–50, 76, 113, 124
Musil, R. 14, 163–164
myths 15, 29, 52, 70–74, 83

narrative imagination 28, 45, 113, 114, 172
neighbour principle 146, 151–152, 158, 160–161, 163, 166

neuroscience 2, 9–10, 24–26, 31
Niemöller, M. 19
Nietzsche, F. 14–16, 38, 39, 49, 75–76, 94, 106, 136
Nussbaum, M. 25, 30–31, 45, 55, 81, 110, 114, 123, 142, 172

Obergefell v Hodges [2015] 146
oppression 19, 21, 33, 82, 90, 96
oratorical skill 32–34, 43, 49
Orwell, G. 54, 74–75, 77, 80, 136–137
outsider jurisprudence 19, 21, 32, 110, 125, 135
Owl of Minerva 34

participatory democracy 21, 115
Pascal, B. 22–23
passiones animae 9
Pawel Bachanek v Regional Court in Warsaw [2013] 39
perspectivism 16
persuasive 72–73: persuasive force of law 28, 84, 155; persuasive imagery 29, 37; persuasive narrative 34, 128; persuasive rhetoric 32, 60–61
philosophy 7, 14, 26, 39, 46, 50, 66, 144: aesthetic philosophy 93; ethical philosophy 13, 102; moral philosophy 29, 54, 120–122
Plato 7, 9, 23, 26, 37, 43–49, 120, 145
Plato's Chariot Allegory 7, 22, 26
Plaut v Spendthrift Farm Inc (1995) 42
poetry 3, 28, 30–32, 36–45, 49, 147–14
politics 3, 50, 62–63, 68, 82, 93, 106, 113, 116, 124, 127, 132, 155, 173: identity politics 69; politics of fear 54–55, 62, 68–69, 81, 135; politics of truth 117
Posner, R.A. 63
Poulantzas, N. 54, 96
poverty 21, 36, 39, 66, 83, 104, 110, 126, 139–142, 159, 169
prejudice 21, 23, 34, 36, 61, 73, 88, 97, 114, 148, 151, 169
prisons 88, 133–135, 138–141, 167
privacy 59–60, 62, 71, 77, 79, 99–100, 131
professionals of speech 159
psychology 3, 26, 55
punishment 14, 19, 40, 53–54, 64–68, 78, 88, 104–110, 117, 127, 129, 133–139, 141

Quintilian 32, 33

R v Brown [1993] 154
R v Metropolitan Police Commissioner, ex parte Blackburn (No. 2) [1968] 20
R (A Child) [2009] 42
R (Conway) v the Secretary of State for Justice [2017] 64–65, 153, 156, 170
R (Khadir) v Secretary of State for the Home Department [2006] 20
R (Nicklinson) v Ministry of Justice [2012]; [2015] 140, 153, 170
R (Nicklinson and Lamb) v Ministry of Justice [2014] 95
R (Pretty) v Director of Public Prosecutions [2002]; *Pretty v United Kingdom* [2002] 153–154, 170
R (Purdy) v the Director of Public Prosecutions [2009] 153
Rainey et al v Mylan Specialty LP, U.S. District Court, Western District of Washington [2017] 163
Rapanos v United States [2006] 16
Re Ashya King [2014] 100
rationality 5, 6, 9–10, 16, 24, 26, 66, 69, 89, 124, 128, 141, 149–151
Rawls, J. 89, 118, 122, 125, 137, 151
reason and emotion 1, 5, 7, 17, 26, 163
reciprocity 21, 48, 74, 88, 119, 151, 161, 166
regimes of truth 74, 84, 89, 96–97, 117, 126
religion 17, 37, 88, 91, 106, 116, 140, 144, 151
Relph, E. 162
responsible and empathic institutions 125–127, 166, 170–171
ressentiment 14, 136
Ricoeur, P. 34, 131, 151, 167, 170
Rousseau, J.-J. 37, 110, 119–123, 171
rule-based rationality 9

Sarat, A. 104–105
Sartre, J. P. 9, 32, 34, 67
Scheler, M. 25
Schelling, F.W.J. 17
Schopenhauer, A. 14, 150
science 17, 18, 23, 26, 33, 37–38, 49, 68, 76, 91–93, 111, 113, 116, 121: cognitive science 75; computer science 60
secret courts 77, 97–101
Seneca, L.A. 66, 147
senses 7, 13, 18, 23, 28, 39, 44–45, 50, 76, 92, 107, 110, 172
sensus communis 125

sentimental jurisprudence 4, 12, 22–26, 30, 36–37, 45, 107, 119–123, 158, 166, 169, 171, 173
Shakespeare, W. 97–98, 142, 172
Shaw, J.J.A. 24, 29, 37, 57, 75–78, 90, 95, 97, 103, 106, 136, 155, 160–166
Shaw, H.J. 45, 75, 77, 136, 160, 163, 164, 166
Shelley, P.B. 31, 42–45, 149, 150
Sherwin, R.K. 29, 30
Shklar, J. 52, 68, 113
shoes 26, 111, 113, 114, 170, 172
signification 17, 39, 44, 73, 89, 95, 101, 105, 113, 117, 135
slavery 24, 135, 138, 161, 169
Smart, C. 124, 146
Smith, A. 24, 26, 27, 74, 121–123, 165–166, 169
Snowden, Edward 54, 70, 71
social justice 122, 172
social media *ix*, 58–61, 68, 74, 162
social reality 6, 12, 24, 38, 169, 173
social relations 4, 6, 17, 20, 29, 33, 47, 82, 103, 109, 121, 141, 159, 173
socio-legal 6, 49
spatial metaphor 12, 16, 39, 112, 162
spectacle 17, 57, 72, 79, 93, 103, 136, 162
Spinoza, B. 21, 65
Stoke City Council v Maddocks [2012] 99
storytelling, law as 30, 32, 34–35, 50, 93, 135, 142, 172
suffering: emotional suffering 1, 2, 6, 97, 159; existential suffering 66–68, 153, 155–58; human suffering 21, 23; 41, 90; suffering and empathy 26, 30, 84, 120–28, 140–42, 171; suffering and injustice 104, 108, 136–38, 152, 165; suffering, love and justice 144, 150, 172
Supiot, A. 35
surveillance 54, 59, 62, 71–72, 77–80, 98
Swift, J. 49
symbolic 33, 35, 40, 44, 47–49, 72–73, 87–92, 94, 97–101, 107, 113, 116, 155
symbols 17, 27, 40, 42, 58, 59, 123
Szasz, T. 155

technology 53, 57, 68, 82, 93, 138, 162, 164–165
Tennyson, A.F. 45, 46
terror 16, 41, 52, 76, 77
terrorism 53–54, 64, 76–83, 98, 109, 167–169
Tillich, P. 158
Tinkerbell Effect 92, 97
Tolstoy, L. 145
tort law 1, 6, 40, 63
tragedy 32, 42–43, 61, 64
truth: art as truth 37–39, 41, 45, 156; language as truth 12, 50, 131; law's truth 33–34, 38, 40, 42, 46, 50, 75–76, 89, 92–98, 106; moral truth 23, 109, 121, 125, 159, 172; truth and 'reality' 15–16, 22, 36, 82, 107, 136; truth and meaning 29, 31–32, 57, 71–75, 103, 117

Van Munster, R. 77
violence: criminal violence 1, 16, 21, 23, 71–72, 119, 135, 139; narrative violence 97–98, 101, 105–106, 112–113; law's symbolic violence 16, 20, 54, 69, 79–80, 87–92, 103–104, 110, 155
Virgil 49, 147, 166
virtue 5, 9, 13, 117, 120, 122 124–125, 127, 138, 140, 166
vulnerability 21, 23, 98, 123, 126–127, 159, 170

Wacquant, L. 139
Ward, I. 2, 76, 79–80
Weil, S. 23, 144, 158–159, 171
Weisberg, R. 143
West, R. 1, 28, 142
West Virginia State Board of Education v Barnette [1943] 18–19
whistleblowers 71, 72
White, J.B. 30
Whitman, W. 116
Wilde, O. 37, 38, 50, 141
Williams, G. 154
Willion v. Berkley [1561] 8
Wittgenstein, L. 55, 56
Wolcher, LE. 161
Wolfenden Report 11, 108

Zartaloudis, T. 110
Žižek, S. 3, 70, 82, 98, 106, 113, 135, 162
Zola, E. 109–110